Islamic Interpretations of Christianity

Islamic Interpretations of Christianity

Edited by
Lloyd Ridgeon

St. Martin's Press
New York

Islamic Interpretations of Christianity

St. Martin's Press Scholarly and Reference Division, 175 Fifth Avenue, New York, N.Y. 10010

First published in the United States of America in 2000

Printed in Great Britain

ISBN 0–312–23854–1

Library of Congress Cataloguing-in-Publication Data

Islamic interpretations of Christianity / Lloyd Ridgeon (ed.).
p. cm.
Includes bibliographical references and index.
ISBN 0–312–23854–1
1. Christianity in the Koran. 2. Koran–Relations to the Bible. 3. Islam–Relations–Christianity. 4. Christianity and other religions–Islam. I. Ridgean, Lloyd V.J.

BP134.C45 I85 2000
297.2′83–dc21 00-034496

Contents

Part II The Modern Period

Acknowledgements

This book emerged from a one day conference held at the University of Glasgow in May 1997. Many people supported this event, but in particular I would like to thank Alastair Hunter who at the time was the Dean of the Faculty of Theology. My colleague Dr. Mona Siddiqui was also an unlimited source of assistance. The conference managed to cover its costs, largely due to the generosity of the Spalding Trust (and I appreciate the encouragement offered by Dr. Michael Loewe and Sir Nicholas Barrington in my fund-raising activities). Several of the papers given at this conference do not appear in this volume for various reasons. Nevertheless, my gratitude is extended to the following who all contributed excellent papers: Dr. Husayn Ghumsha'ī, Mr. Richard Gauvain, Dr. Colin Imber, Prof. Robert Hillenbrand, Prof. Sachiko Murata and Prof. William Chittick. Thanks are also extended to various scholars who suggested various ways in which this volume could be improved.

Needless to say, it is impossible to cover all major Islamic interpretations of Christianity. The aim has been to provide a rough guide from the beginning of Islam, commencing with the Qur'ān, through the *ḥadīth* literature, classical exegesis and esoteric Sufi views. The second section is an attempt to render this book relevant to those who seek to understand the attitude of modern Muslims to Christianity. The chapters in this second section do not make for happy reading, yet I am aware that there are Muslims who do not hold negative views of Christianity and the West. Perhaps one of the most important tasks for this millenium is for Christians and the West to re-assess their understanding of Islam, an understanding which contributes to the contemporary negative Islamic conception of

Christianity. In addition, Muslims themselves must follow the intellectual endeavours of scholars such as Mohamed Talbi, Mohammed Arkoun and Abdul-Karim Soroush who all advocate the possibility and necessity of pluralism and tolerance.[1]

NOTES

1 For the views of these modern Islamic intellectuals, see *Liberal Islam*, ed. C. Kurzman (Oxford: Oxford University Press, 1998).

Contributors

Hugh Goddard has taught Islamic Studies at the University of Nottingham since 1984, where he is now a reader. He is the author of *Christians and Muslims: From Double Standards to Mutual Understanding* (Curzon Press, 1995), and *Muslim Perceptions of Christianity* (Grey Seal, 1996).

Philip Lewis is inter-faith adviser to the Anglican Bishop of Bradford, and lectures in the Department of Theology and Religious Studies at the University of Leeds. He was a commissioner for the Runnymede Trust's inquiry which produced the report "Islamophobia, a Challenge for Us All." He represents the Archbishop of Canterbury on the Advisory council for the Centre for the Study of Islam and Christian-Muslim Relations in Birmingham. He is the author of *Islamic Britain* (I. B. Tauris, 1994).

Leonard Lewisohn is a specialist on Sufism, Persian literature and Islamic studies. His publications include *Beyond Faith and Infidelity: the Sufi Poetry and Teachings of Maḥmūd Shabistarī* (Curzon Press, 1995), and he has editor of *Dīvān-i Muḥammad Shīrīn Maghribī* (Tehran: Tehran University Press, 1993). He is currently the Outreach Co-ordinator at the Department of Academic Research and Publication at the Institute of Ismaili Studies, London, where he also teaches Persian.

David Marshall has taught Islamic Studies at Oxford University and St. Pauls's College, Limuru, Kenya. He is the author of God, *Muhammad and the Unbelievers: a Qur'anic Study* (Curzon Press, 1999).

Jane Dammen McAuliffe is Professor of Islamic Studies and Dean of the College at Georgetown University, Washington D.C. She is the author of *Qur'ānic Christians* (Cambridge University Press, 1991), and is currently editing the *Encyclopaedia of the Qur'ān* (Brill, forthcoming).

Lloyd Ridgeon lectures in Islamic and Persian Studies in the Centre for the Study of Islam at the University of Glasgow. He is the author of *'Azīz Nasafī* (Curzon Press, 1998) and *Crescents on the Cross* (Trinity St. Mungo Press, 1999).

Neal Robinson is Professor of Islamic Studies at the University of Wales, Lampeter. His books include *Christ in Islam and Christianity* (Macmillan, 1991), *Sayings of Muhammad* (Duckworth, 1991), *Discovering the Qur'ān* (SCM, 1996) and *Islam: A Concise Introduction* (Curzon, 1999).

Malise Ruthven has taught Islamic studies and comparative religion at the University Aberdeen and Dartmouth College, New Hampshire, and the University of California, San Diego (UCSD). He is the author, among other works, of *Islam in the World* (Penguin 1984, revised edition 2000); *The Divine Supermarket: Shopping for God in America* (Chatto 1989); *A Satanic Affair: Salman Rushdie and the Wrath of Islam* (Chatto 1990) and *Islam: A Very Short Introduction* (OUP, 1997).

Marston Speight served the church for twenty-eight years in three countries of North Africa. Then for thirteen years he directed the Office on Christian-Muslim Relations of the National Council of the Churches of Christ in the USA, and taught Islamic studies on the adjunct faculty at Hartford (Connecticut) Seminary before retiring in 1992. He is the co-author (with Kenneth Cragg) of *Islam from Within* (Wadsworth, 1980).

David Thomas is Senior Lecturer at the Centre for the Study of Islam and Christian-Muslim Relations, Selly Oak, Birmingham, and a member of the Department of Theology at the University of Birmingham. He is a specialist in the history of Islamic religious thought and Christian-Muslim relations. He is currently collaborating on an annotated edition and translation of a reply to Christian criticisms of Islam by a fourteenth century Syrian Muslim.

Kate Zebiri is Senior Lecturer in Arabic and Islamic Studies at the School of Oriental and African Studies, University of London. She is the author of *Muslims and Christians Face to Face* (Oneworld, 1997) and *Mahmud Shaltut and Islamic Modernism* (OUP, 1993).

Introduction

Malise Ruthven

Islamic attitudes towards Christianity, like Western attitudes towards Islam, occupy a broad spectrum of positions, ranging from outright rejection to inclusivist accommodation. At the exclusivist end of this spectrum lies the Christianophobia of the Hanbalī scholar and exegete Ibn Taymiyya (d. 1328) whose attacks on Christian religious practices are enjoying a revival among Islamists opposed to Muslim governments they regard as too pro-Western. Admirers of Ibn Taymiyya include, paradoxically, some Muslims living in the West who, like the Orthodox Jews belonging to the various Haredi sects, try to disassociate themselves as much as possible from the surrounding society. According to Ibn Taymiyya not even the most trifling resemblance must be allowed to exist between Muslims and non-Muslims, the starting point for all Muslim life being the point at which "a perfect dissimilarity with the non-Muslims has been achieved."[1] In the detailed critique of popular religious practices mounted in his *Kitāb Iqtiḍa' al-sirāṭ al-mustaqīm*, Ibn Taymiyya argues that practices such as the celebration of the Prophet Muḥammad's birthday (*mawlīd al-nabī*) and the construction of mosques around the tombs of Sufi shaykhs are unacceptable borrowings from the Christians: "Many of them [i.e. the Muslims] do not even know of the Christian origin of these practices. Accursed be Christianity and its adherents."[2]

At the opposite, inclusivist end of this spectrum lies the universalist outlook of the poet, philosopher and Isma'ili *da'ī* (missionary) Nāṣir Khusraw (1004–c1075), still a highly venerated figure in the highlands of the Western Pamirs in the former Soviet republic of Tajikistan. Nāṣir not only argues that the messages of the Torah, Injīl (Gospel) and Qur'ān are essentially identical, but that even Hindus whose religious beliefs and practices lie outside the Abrahamic traditions of Judaism, Christianity and Islam are possessors of a Holy Book which they claim to be of divine origin. Nāṣir goes to the point of endorsing this claim: "I have heard many divine words from their learned men."[3]

Between the exclusivist and inclusivist ends of this spectrum lie a variety of religious and political attitudes, some of which are illustrated in these essays. Before addressing them individually, however, it might be worth raising a broader theological dimension that has sometimes been obscured in discussion about Muslim-Christian relations. At a conference in London entitled "Mutualities: Britain and Islam" held under the auspices of the British Council in April 1999 Dr. Tim Winter of Cambridge University suggested that the current popularity enjoyed by Ibn Taymiyya in Islamist circles was part of a broader reformation or "stripping of the altars", comparable to the Reformation in the Latin West, which aimed to "re-establish the supremacy of the transcendent over the immanent sacred." For the younger generation the more inclusivist and spiritual theology of the Imam al-Ghazālī (d. 1111) was being replaced by that of Ibn Taymiyya. Rising Muslim-Christian tension in such widely dispersed places as Indonesia, Nazareth and the Sudan could not be explained by the sociological reductionism current in academic and media discourse, which saw the situation crudely in terms of a fundamentalist or Islamist revolt against national secular élites. Much of what was happening in Muslim communities today could only be understood in terms of the unfolding and implementing of theology.[4]

Even if we reject Winter's implication that the movement towards Ibn Taymiyya's uncompromising transcendentalism can be considered separately from the wider political and cultural context (including attacks on westernised élites and the stranglehold of western-dominated versions of capitalism over the world economy) there is an abundance of material in these essays to support the central thrust of his argument. Islamic exclusivism is associated, historically and currently, with divine transcendence; Islamic universalism with the immanent "God within" and particularly with "higher" states of being or consciousness achieved by Sufi mystics and organised into the emanationist hierarchies of Ithna'ashari and Isma'ili theosophies. The esoteric interpretations of scripture and spiritual states cultivated by the Sufis and theosophists recognise the validity of religious experiences that transcend the limitations of human language, even when that language is understood to proceed directly from God as in the Qur'ān. Implicitly and sometimes explicitly such approaches opened the way towards the acceptance of religious experience framed in non-Islamic terms. The more exoteric interpretations of Islam, however, which are understood as proceeding from God's commands, in which the emphasis is placed on correct religious and legal practice, reinforces boundaries between Muslims and others, in such areas as ritual, physical appearance, dress, diet and details of this-worldly quotidian living. Such boundaries (which are strongly emphasised, for example, in the writings of the influential contemporary Sunni *faqih*, Dr Yousuf al-Qaradawi) may have the positive effect of sustaining Muslim identities in an increasingly pluralistic world, but they may also reinforce the sense of alienation and cultural loss. In the past differences between the Muslims and others (classically, the *ahl al-dhimma* or "protected" communities of Jews and Christians) were predicated on Muslim supremacy – the political corollary of a "supersessionist" theology that regards Islam as the completion or fulfilment of earlier prophetic traditions. The trauma of colonialism followed by the disappointment of national independence and the incorporation of Muslim societies into a pluralistic global order renders such "supersessionist" attitudes increasingly problematic. Muslims who once ruled the world, at least in the broad belt of territories lying between Morocco and Indonesia that became known as Dār al-Islām, have mostly become consumers of goods, services and cultural products created by infidels in the non-Islamic parts of the world, including Europe and North America, the formerly Christian "West". The "best community" ordained by God for "enjoining the good and prohibiting the evil" (*al-amr bi'l-ma'rūf wa nahy an al-munkar*) has been forced onto the defensive. Ironically, it is oil, lifeblood of the global economy and symbol of the dependence of modern technical societies on un-elected Arab dynasties that helps fuel the transcendentalist theology promoting separation between Muslims and infidels. Saudi Arabia, bastion of Ibn Taymiyya's theology of separation, is one of the worlds largest exporters, not just of oil, but of petrodollars. Some of these funds, as argued in chapter 9, are used to sustain religious positions that militate against mutual understanding. Yet the surpluses that allow "Islamic funds" to de-territorialise themselves, contributing to the increasingly dense mesh of interactions around the globe, also serve to render concepts such as "Islam" and the "West" increasingly meaningless as descriptions of distinctive territorial or cultural entities.

As modern communications and technology diminish cultural distances, so the task of inter-cultural exposition becomes ever more important and necessary. The essays in this collection bear witness to this process.

In chaper 1, "Christianity in the Qur'ān" David Marshall addresses ambiguities he perceives in Qur'ānic teachings about Christianity. While Christ is an honoured figure Christians are criticised for deifying Jesus and for practices associated with idolatry and paganism. Christian monasticism is also subject to ambiguous comments, alternatively criticised and commended. While the Muslims are warned against taking Christians as friends, faithful Christians are promised their reward at the Day of Judgement. Marshall suggests that these apparent ambiguities may partly reflect Muḥammad's unfolding relationship with actual Christian communities who failed to accept his mission. A distinction should be made between the ideal Christianity he conceived of and the actual practices of the Christians he encountered. In chapter 2 Marston Speight analyses some 500 *ḥadīth* relating to Christianity and Christians which he regards as broadly representative of the entire corpus of Sunni *ḥadīth*. While there are *ḥadīths* affirming the common spiritual kinship of the *Ahl al-Kitāb* (People of Scriptures), both Jews and Christians are criticised for altering their religious texts. Generally this literature which functioned as part of the Muslim expression of identity in the pluralist world of the 8th and 9th centuries, is more concerned with the Christians as people than matters of theology or faith. In the emerging Muslim empire, the Muslims found a place for Christians by assigning them *dhimmi* status – one that clearly emphasised their social and religious inferiority. In considering the legal status of Christians Jane McAuliffe in chapter 3 argues for the continuing relevance of classical theology in contemporary discussions. The legal commentaries she focuses on are still sources of guidance on the conduct of relations with Christians. Contrasting the comments of the eighth-century legal exegete Muqātil b. Sulaymān (d. 767) who includes Jewish and Christian prayer spaces within the prescriptive scope of Qur'ānic injunctions concerning clothing, with those of other authorities such as Aḥmad b. 'Alī al-Jaṣṣāṣ (d. 981) and Ilkiyā al-Harrāsī (d. 1110) and the fifteenth-century Shi'ī commentary of al-Miqdād al-Ḥillī, she suggests that while no comprehensive conclusion need be drawn from such individual case studies, the direction of legal exegesis in the formation of categories "pushes away from plurality towards binary opposition", with such status distinctions as Christians, Jews, *ahl al-kitāb* and *ahl al-dhimmah* dissolving into the undifferentiated classification of *kuffār* or *mushrikūn* (unbelievers and polytheists).

The actual position of Christians under classical Islam is also considered by David Thomas in chapter 4 where the high social standing they enjoyed in early Abbasid times stands in marked contrast to the legal requirements of their subordinate *dhimmi* status. Turning to the thorniest of theological issues dividing Christians and Muslims, the doctrine of the Trinity, Thomas addresses the problem facing Christians under Muslim rule of explaining a doctrine originally formulated in Greek in the Arabic tongue. For example, the term *hypostasis* was consistently glossed as referring to separate entities rather than as attributes of God subsisting in his essence, confirming Muslim accusations of "tritheism". To Muslim minds the mention of three Persons meant three separate deities, as clearly stated in the Qur'ān. Christian attempts, using concepts borrowed from Islamic theology, to explain that the doctrine did not entail plurality, failed completely – a failure, Thomas suggests, both symptomatic of relations between Christian and Muslims during the early classical period and indicative of how one community would gradually be absorbed into the "thought world" of the other.

In chapter 5 Lloyd Ridgeon explores the figure of Jesus in the work of Jalāl al-Dīn Rūmī, considered to be one of the greatest of Islamic and Persian poets, whose work in translation has reputedly made him the best-selling poet in the United States. Some extra-Qur'ānic references to Jesus suggest a familiarity with the gospel accounts of Jesus. The focus of Ridgeon's chapter, however, is not the provenance of Rūmī's references to Jesus but rather their significance in Rūmī's "unceasing search for the realities behind forms", where Jesus comes to symbolise the Spirit of God with life giving powers applicable to each and every individual. The Jesus of Rūmī belongs to the religious imagination as distinct from the phenomena of the material world. It is consistent with the docetic or gnostic Christology of the Qur'ān where Jesus appears as a divine messenger or illuminator, as distinct from the Redeemer of Pauline Christianity: to speak of Jesus in terms of salvation is meaningless for orthodox Muslims because of the absence of the doctrine of the Fall. In arguing for the need to re-assess Rūmī's inclusivist interpretation of Islam, Ridgeon shares the perspective of Henry Corbin, who suggested that Docetism, unequivocally rejected at the Council of Nicea in 325, points to a more universal way of spiritual knowledge than Pauline Christology. The incarnation of St. Paul and the early Church Councils materialised the divine, in a manner of speaking, by endowing it with flesh and blood and putting it on the plane of human history, instead of perceiving

Christ's image as purely spiritual and timeless. "Without theophany God is only a pure indetermination which cannot be worshipped at all. But if theophany is necessary, it must be accomplished as an anthropomorphosis perceived by mental vision ... not on the plane of material incarnation."[5] The dominant intuition of gnosticism "*is that the soul is not the witness of an external event but the medium in which the event takes place.*"[6] Corbin likened this approach to that of modern phenomenology, the philosophical outlook that many people would argue offers the most fruitful approach for the study of comparative religion. "In our days phenomenology declares that knowledge does not bear upon Being, but it is Being, aware of itself. In this sense the Docetists may be regarded as the first phenomenologists."[7] A similar perspective, formulated somewhat differently, appears in Leonard Lewisohn's essay on the Esoteric Christianity of Islam: chapter 6. While the use of Christian imagery by medieval Persian Sufi poets clearly allowed for the possibility of religious dialogue Lewisohn explains that the subjectivity (or "subject-centrism") of this language is "a world apart from the categories of theologians and philosophers and the abstract moral hypotheses of priests and mullahs." Mystics in both religions share virtually the same esoteric hermeneutic, interpreting their respective scriptures to reveal a world of multiple dimensions; but the transcendent Truth thought to be underlying (or "overflowing") the mystic experience transcends, by definition as it were, its expression in words. The possibilities of dialogue on the basis of mutually consistent esoteric understandings of the scriptures of the two faith traditions are limited by the spiritual élitism according to which the interior meanings or allusions are only accessible to those whose hearts have been purified by the cultivation of mystical disciplines. Lewisohn finds parallels between the "religious promiscuity" of thirteenth-century Persian society following the Mongol invasions and the multi-religious culture of today's post-modern world. The vogue for Ibn Taymiyya's theology of transcendence (which finds its counterpart in parts of the evangelical protestant spectrum, particularly in the United States) should not be allowed to obscure much more encouraging signals suggested by the popularity of Rūmī in the West. Following Corbin's suggestion that the presence of Sufism could radically change the dialogue between Islam and Christianity provided the interlocutors were "Spirituals", it may be the immanentist theologies in all traditions, with their nuanced commitment to the subtleties of language, that point the way towards mutual accommodation and respect.

Sayyid Quṭb's attitude towards Christianity as demonstrated by his extended commentary of the six verses of *sūra* al-Tawba (9:29–35) in *Fī Ẓilal al-Qur'ān*, the subject of chapter 7, is firmly rooted in transcendental theology similar to that of Ibn Taymiyya, though as Neal Robinson reveals, there is unacknowledged input of a distinctly political character. Quṭb follows the classical commentators in stating that co-existence must be based on Muslim supremacy: the Muslims must fight the People of Scripture until they pay the *jizya* tax, or convert to Islam. The majority of Jews and Christians have always been unbelievers, and uncompromising in their hostility to Islam. On the doctrine of the incarnation, Quṭb states, in line with classical polemicists, that it originated with St. Paul, who falsified Christ's message – Christ himself having taught the unity of God. Quṭb's political radicalism reveals itself in his comments on 9: 31 when he "exposes" the label Islam attached by its enemies to man-made statues and human institutions, a position which Robinson points out runs counter to the teachings of the four Sunni law-schools, which recognised *'urf* or existing customary law as a valid source of law. The same goes for his innovative use of the term *jāhiliyya* (the "time of ignorance" or paganism) as applied to contemporary society, and the term *minhaj* ("open path") repeatedly used by Quṭb to mean procedure, method or programme. As Robinson sees it, Quṭb imposes a "highly questionable interpretive grid on the text" of the Qur'ān in line with the radical or even extremist political views he adopted as a leading Muslim Brotherhood intellectual. The international political context, Robinson suggests, helps to account for the continuing influence and popularity enjoyed by his writings more than thirty years after his execution by the Egyptian regime of President Nasser in 1966. Given the consistent support for Israel by the USA – the world's most powerful "Christian" nation – as well as the retaliatory attacks launched by the United States (in defiance of international law) against targets in the Sudan and Afghanistan following the bombing of the US embassies in Kenya and Tanzania in 1998, it is hardly surprising that Quṭb's polemical, an a-historical attack on Christians and Jews still finds a ready audience in Muslim lands.

In her essay on Muslim Perceptions of Christianity and the West (chapter 8), Kate Zebiri draws on several contemporary Muslim writers. Some of these exhibit what the American historian Richard Hofstader calls (in a different context) a "paranoid style" of discourse, seeing in the writings of such distinguished Christian writers on Islam as Kenneth Cragg or William Montgomery Watt attempts at "subversion" of Islam or tactical pauses in an ongoing war aimed ultimately at taking it over. Zebiri locates such literature in the context of past activities of Christian missionaries in Muslim lands, and anxieties about conversion away from Islam, which need to be "understood in the light of the fact that religious identity is differently constructed and perceived in Muslim societies than in the more secular West, where individual choice is now strongly emphasised." While the ascription to Christian missionaries of such infamous techniques as conversion by medical trickery belongs to a long-established tradition of religious polemics, anxieties about the political effects of Christian evangelism are not necessarily out of place or overdrawn. As Zebiri points out, several writers including Safar al-Hawali point to the phenomenon of Christian Zionism (widely neglected by political commentators on the Middle East) as an example of Christian activity explicitly aimed against Islam and Muslims. Christian Zionism is used to describe the doctrine (technically known as pre-millennial dispensationalism) widely held in American evangelical circles and promoted by popular preachers including Jerry Falwell, Pat Robertson and Hal Lindsay (author of *The Late Great Planet Earth*, which has sold more than 30 million copies to date) according to which the state of Israel is entitled to unconditional political support on theological grounds. Premillennialists believe that the foundation of Israel in 1948 and its occupation of the Old City of Jerusalem in 1967 are a necessary part of the Divine Plan preceding the return of Christ and the establishment of His Kingdom on earth.[8] In general, however, Zebiri concludes that the "Occidentalist" attitude exhibited in this literature are the mirror-image of Orientalist attitudes still prevalent in the West. "The view of Christianity which is reflected in some of this discourse, as aggressive, power-mongering, intolerant and fanatical, incompatible with democracy, backward, irrational and primitive is very similar to an image of Islam which has been and still is promoted in some Western sources." As Philip Lewis demonstrates in his account of depictions of Christianity within British Islamic Institutions (chapter 9), much of the discourse about Christianity reflects the same paranoid style noted by Zebiri. Lewis focuses on the figure of Ahmad Deedat, a feisty polemicist and prolific pamphleteer whose booklets are "crude but clever compilations of allegedly damning evidence to prove that the bible is incoherent, full of mistakes and contains sexually reprehensible material, unworthy of any serious publication." Deedat was the recipient of the 1986 King Feisal Award, a prestigious and lucrative prize given by Saudi Arabia for his services to Islam. Lewis is disturbed to find Saudi Arabia lending "lustre and economic support" to a polemicist who contributes nothing to serious Islamic engagement with non-Islamic religious traditions." Turning to the more "significant and informed" voice of the late Dr. Syed Darsh, an Azhar-trained scholar who prior to his death wrote a regular column in the Muslim magazine Q-News, Lewis documents a much more sophisticated and better-informed view of life in Britain and the potential benefits it offers for Muslims. Nevertheless he detects in Darsh's *fatwas* a lack of understanding of the role of Christianity in western society and its political influence. Lewis concludes by demonstrating that while it is radical groups such as Hizb-at-Tahrir (HUT) whose "coinage is political diatribes against the West and whose simplistic appeals to return to the sources of the Qur'ān and the sunnah often discount fifteen hundred years of history and disciplined reflection", serious work of engagement is being undertaken by such institutions as the Centre for the Study of Islam and Christian Muslim Relations in Birmingham and the Islamic Foundation in Leicester. The Presence of Muslim academics capable of addressing the wider issues of dialogue and engagement in a reasoned and practical way is also a cause for optimism. Finally in his chapter on Christian-Muslim relations in Nigeria and Malaysia (chapter 10), Hugh Goddard provides a broader context in which future interaction between the two faith communities are discussed. He concludes that for the foreseeable future in matters religious one of the most important questions on a global level is going to be the relationship between Christianity and Islam, raising fundamental ethical questions for members of both communities. As this Introduction was being written the Serbian nationalist regime of Slobodan Milosovitch withdrew its troops from Kosovo following weeks of NATO bombardment backed by the threat of invasion from the ground. It is not entirely disheartening that the largest military engagement undertaken by nominally Christian powers in Europe since the Second World War was justified as being necessary in order to restore to their homes the Muslim victims of a nationalist regime that draws heavily on the symbols of a Christian Orthodox past. In this instance, at least, the NATO action, for all its destructiveness and waste of innocent lives, gave the lie to predictions about the forthcoming "Clash of Civilizations" between "Islam" and the "West".

NOTES

1 Muhammad Umar Memon, *Ibn Taymiyya's Struggle against Popular Religion* with an annotated translation of *Kitāb Iqtida al-sirat al-mustaqim mukhalafat aṣḥāb al-jahim* (The Hague: Mouton, 1976), p. 78.
2 *Ibid*, p. 210.
3 Nāṣir-i Khusraw, *Wajh-i Din* (Berlin, 1924), p. 54.
4 See the report by M. Ruthven, *Mutualities: Britain and Islam* (British Council, 1999).
5 H. Corbin, *Cyclical Time and Ismaili Gnosis* (London: 1983), p. 172.
6 *Ibid*, p. 62. The italics do not appear in the text.
7 *Ibid loc cit.*
8 See Paul Boyer, *When Time Shall Be No More: Prophesy Belief in Modern American Culture* (Cambridge Ma: 1992).

Part I

The Classical Period

1

Christianity in the Qur'ān

David Marshall

"Christianity in the Qur'ān" is so broad a subject that for the purposes of this study the relevant Qur'ānic material needs to be broken down into more manageable categories. The approach adopted here is therefore to subdivide "Christianity" into three themes suggested by the Qur'ān itself: "Jesus and Mary"; "scripture"; and "Christians." Other categories than these could have been used to subdivide the Qur'ānic material further, such as "Christian practices" (e.g. monasticism), or "Christian doctrines" (e.g. the Trinity). Lines must be drawn somewhere, however, and I hope that the three thematic categories which I have chosen provide a reasonable framework for making sense of the Qur'ānic material. As well as grouping the material thematically in this way, this study also adopts a chronological approach. The basic structure of the study is thus as follows. I begin with an examination of relevant Qur'ānic passages from the Meccan period of Muḥammad's preaching (roughly 609–22 CE), dealing with passages firstly on Jesus and Mary, secondly on scripture, and thirdly on Christians. Then I turn to the Medinan period (622–32 CE) and work through the same three categories again. The intention is to give some sense of how the Qur'ānic treatment of these themes evolves alongside developments in the experience of Muḥammad and his followers.[1]

I. THE MECCAN PERIOD

What the Qur'ān says about Christianity in this period needs to be understood against the backdrop of Muḥammad's experience in Mecca. During the Meccan period, the main challenge facing Muḥammad was to preach to the polytheists of Mecca. The essence of his message was that they should turn from idolatry to the worship of the one true God, and should submit to the moral reformation which God demanded of them. If they rejected the message they faced the prospect of divine punishment, both in this life and in the hereafter. During this period Muḥammad gained some followers, but by and large he encountered rejection and ridicule.

Muḥammad's preaching to the Meccans involved two crucial claims which related his activity to Christianity. These two interdependent claims are that Muḥammad is a messenger sent by God and that he is the bearer of a divine revelation. These claims are set within the wider Qur'ānic vision of the history of God's activity in the world. At the heart of this vision is the belief that God has repeatedly sent messengers entrusted with divine revelations to provide guidance for human beings. The Qur'ān mentions many such messengers, one of whom is Jesus. So Jesus and the revelation brought by him constitute one episode in the great history of divine activity, of which now, in Mecca, Muḥammad and the message revealed through him are the latest manifestation.

Jesus and Mary[2]

As we turn now to Meccan passages dealing with Jesus and Mary, it should first be acknowledged that there are a number of other religious figures about whom the Qur'ān has considerably more to say. At least part of the explanation for this can be grasped if we keep in mind the question of *the immediate relevance to Muḥammad's situation in Mecca* of the different Qur'ānic stories about the messengers sent before him. These stories are not recited by Muḥammad in a spirit of detached interest in religious history; rather, they bear on what is happening around him in the present. For example, there seems to have been a particular relevance to Muḥammad at Mecca in a group of stories which are essentially variants on one basic story-line. These stories depict a messenger sent by God who preaches to his people, is rejected by them, but is finally vindicated when God intervenes to punish the unbelievers (e.g. with the flood in the case of Noah, the destruction of Sodom and Gomorrah in the case of Lot, and so on). These stories are so often repeated in the Meccan period (e.g. notably in *sūras* 7, 11 and 26) that it is natural to assume that they are particularly relevant to Muḥammad at Mecca: they reflect his situation as an embattled preacher of monotheism and his hopes of vindication through God's intervention.[3] The messengers depicted in these stories thus serve as models of Muḥammad in Mecca; their stories are an encouragement to him and his followers in their difficult situation (see 11: 120). For our present purposes the important point is that although a number of other messengers feature in these stories, Jesus does not.

Indeed, the fact that Jesus features in only one extended narrative from the whole Meccan period (19: 16–33) is a strong indication that (unlike Noah, Abraham, Lot, Moses and others) he did not, at this stage, represent an especially relevant model to Muḥammad. This point gathers strength as we look more closely at that narrative and notice that it in fact focuses rather more attention on Mary than on Jesus. An angel sent by God (literally "our spirit" (19: 17)) tells Mary that she is to give birth to a "pure boy" (19: 19). She asks how this can be when she is a virgin; she is assured that it is easy for God and that the child will be "a sign to humankind and a mercy from [God]" (19: 21).[4] Mary then withdraws to a distant place where she gives birth to Jesus and is miraculously provided with food and drink. On her return to her people, however, she is accused of sexual immorality. This evokes a further miracle: the infant Jesus speaks from the cradle, thereby implicitly vindicating his righteous mother and shaming her detractors.[5]

Despite the great significance of this speech by the infant Jesus, it is at least arguable that the main interest of the narrative, and certainly its main relevance to Muḥammad in Mecca, is in Mary's drama. Like Muḥammad, Mary receives a divine message brought to her personally by an angelic being; Muḥammad might therefore naturally have seen in Mary somebody whose experience was similar to his own. Furthermore, like Muḥammad, Mary experiences rejection and vilification by her own people because of this divine initiative singling her out for a special task. Then she is miraculously vindicated by God in the face of those who scoff at her – the dénouement for which the rejected Muḥammad waited and hoped. Thus at least part of the significance of this narrative is that it contains the pervasive Meccan motif of the rejection and vindication of God's chosen servant, a theme which was highly relevant to Muḥammad's experience and his expectations. It may seem strange to think of Mary functioning as a type of Muḥammad in this way, and indeed it may well be that the obvious dissimilarities between Mary and Muḥammad account for the fact that, unlike a number of Meccan narratives, this Mary-narrative is not repeated.[6]

This analysis of the story of Mary indicates that despite the fact that there is comparatively little Meccan material on Jesus and Mary, such material as there is should be interpreted in the light of the basic observation that the Qur'ānic Mary and Jesus have their significance and their coherence in their relatedness to the experience of Muḥammad.[7] They are part of the religious pre-history which culminates in the coming of Muḥammad and the revelation of the Qur'ān. The miraculous speech of the infant Jesus (19: 30–33) further illustrates this point. The self-description of Jesus in vv. 30–31 (as with so much of the speech of the Qur'ānic prophets) could be put into the mouth of Muḥammad without any alteration:

> I am God's servant; God has given me the Book, and made me a Prophet . . . and he has commanded me to pray and to give alms as long as I live.[8]

Of other Meccan references to Jesus and Mary, two brief passages (21: 93–5 and 23: 50) speak of their revelatory significance; together they constitute a "sign" (*āya*). Two other passages merely refer to Jesus in passing in a list of other prophets (6: 85 and 42: 13). One other reference merits some comment:

> And when the son of Mary is cited as an example, behold your people [i.e. the Meccan pagans] turn away from it and say: "What, are our gods better, or he?" They only cite him to provoke an argument; nay, but they are a contentious people! He is only a servant whom we [God] blessed, and we made him an example to the Children of Israel. (43: 57–9, see also vv. 60–65)

The context here is interesting. In reaction to Muḥammad's reference to Jesus, the Meccan polytheists imply that in comparison with their own gods Jesus is only an inferior deity whom they can ignore. The Meccans therefore need to be corrected at two points. Firstly, Jesus is a servant (*'abd*), human, not divine; it is important to grasp that the Qur'ān does not interpret the conception of Jesus without a human father (as mentioned above) as a sign of any kind of incarnation. But secondly, Jesus is more important than the Meccans imagine; he is a significant figure from religious history (a servant blessed by God), who came with miracles and made clear that worship of the one God is the "straight path" to which Muḥammad is pointing the Meccans (vv. 63–4). Furthermore, Jesus is not merely a figure from the past; a mysterious eschatological role seems to be ascribed to him in the enigmatic phrase "he is knowledge of the hour" (v. 61).[9]

The main thrust of this passage is against Meccan paganism; its comments about Jesus primarily have the correction of such paganism in mind. Nevertheless, there is here also an implicit criticism of any tendency to think of Jesus in divine terms; he is indeed a "blessed servant," but no more than that. So even though Christians are not directly addressed in this passage, it may be that we have here an early critical reference to Christian attitudes to Jesus.[10]

Scripture

From the earliest Meccan period there are references to scriptures revealed by God in the past. It is possible that one such reference occurs in the passage traditionally believed to have been the first revelation received by Muḥammad:

> Recite: And your Lord is the most generous,
> who taught by the pen,
> taught man what he did not know. (96: 3–5)

Although the phrase here translated "taught by the pen," (*'allama bi'l-qalam*) could be translated as "taught the art of writing," it is more natural, in both the immediate and the wider Qur'ānic contexts, to see here a reference to the mysterious reality of revelation.[11] What human beings could not otherwise know, God makes known to his chosen servant, and the revealed words, written down "by the pen," are preserved in scripture.

A number of other Meccan passages mention scriptures of the past. For example, the early *sūra* 87 ends:

> Surely this is in the ancient scrolls (*ṣuḥuf*),
> the scrolls of Abraham and Moses. (87: 18–19)

The claim here is that the message which Muḥammad has just recited is in agreement with what is contained in the scriptures of Abraham and Moses. Elsewhere the question is asked in a tone of surprise whether those who doubt Muḥammad's message are not aware of the contents of earlier scriptures, again implying agreement between them and what Muḥammad is reciting (53: 36–7; 20: 133; cf. 21: 7; 16: 43; 10: 94). The point is also made that the Meccans, who previously have received no scripture (68: 37; 43: 21; 34: 44), are now being addressed in a divine revelation in Arabic, their own language (e.g. 43: 3; 12: 2).

So just as Muḥammad claims to be the latest manifestation of the divine activity of sending messengers, he also claims that his message is the latest manifestation (in this case in Arabic) of the divine activity of revealing scripture. In both cases Christianity features in much the same way. Just as Jesus is mentioned among Muḥammad's precursors, so also the scripture revealed through Jesus is understood as a precursor of the scripture revealed through Muḥammad. It is a neat illustration of the Qur'ānic understanding of revelation-history that shortly before the infant Jesus declares that God has given him "the Book" (*al-kitāb*, 19: 30), the term *al-kitāb* has been used of the scripture given to John (the Baptist), the precursor of Jesus (19: 12), and also of the message being received in the present by Muḥammad (19: 16).

The point was made earlier that other messengers are mentioned much more frequently than Jesus in Meccan passages. Not surprisingly, then, there is comparatively little emphasis in this period on the scripture which Jesus brought. There are some general references to earlier scriptures (e.g. 20: 133; 12: 111; 10: 94), which could be taken to include the scripture given to Jesus, but the only specific reference which is clearly Meccan is that at 19: 30.[12] At this stage Moses is a much more significant figure, so there is naturally more interest in the scripture which he brought (e.g. 32: 23; 41: 45; 17: 2; 40: 53; 28: 43).

Christians

In view of what we have seen so far, it is not surprising that in the Meccan period there is very little reference to Christians. "There were ... Christians in Mecca, traders and slaves, but the influence of isolated individuals was probably not so important [as elsewhere in Arabia]."[13] In the absence of any organised Christian community to serve as a substantial subject for Muḥammad's attention, his preaching was naturally directed chiefly towards the polytheists of Mecca.

However, as Bell points out, "during the whole of the Meccan period of his activity Muḥammad's attitude to the People of the Book, which must be taken as including both Jews and Christians ... was consistently friendly."[14] One indication of this attitude can be found in a group of passages, admittedly all somewhat obscure, which might refer to Christians of earlier generations. The earliest such passage (85: 4–8) is often taken as describing the martyrdom of certain sixth century Christians from Najrān (in Southern Arabia) at the hands of "the men of the pit."[15] If so, these Christians are described simply as "believers," and thus serve as models of faithfulness for the persecuted followers of Muḥammad. Another image of Christians being faithful under persecution is present in the story of the "men of the cave" (18: 9–26), the Qur'ānic version of the legend of the "Seven Sleepers" which "was widely known and often referred to in Christian literature."[16] The young men are faithful believers in God and shun idolatry. If the Christian origin of this story was known by those who heard Muḥammad, this again portrays Christians of the past as models for Muḥammad's followers. Again, the unnamed messengers of the narrative at 36: 13–32 have been identified with Christian apostles sent to Antioch.[17] Another relevant passage is 30: 2–5, which has often been interpreted as implying a sympathy for the Christian forces of Byzantium in their wars against the Persians.[18]

In a quite different register, there are Meccan passages in which those who doubt the truth of Muḥammad's message are encouraged to consult those who read a scripture revealed before Muḥammad (21: 7; 16: 43; 10: 94, where it is Muḥammad himself who seems to be attacked by self-doubt). Such passages clearly imply a confidence that the Jews and Christians of his own day will support Muḥammad by vouching for the truth of his claims. Much the same confidence is reflected at 6: 20, which says that those to whom the Book has been given recognise the Qur'ān (or possibly Muḥammad) "as they recognise their sons" (cf. 6: 114).[19] However, it is important to note that these passages speak of Jews and Christians together as the "People of the Book" (*ahl al-kitāb*); they do not refer specifically to Christians. A comparison of these generalised Meccan references with more specific Medinan references, where Jews and Christians are sometimes sharply distinguished (e.g. 2: 113; 5: 82–5), leaves one with a sense that whereas the Medinan passages reflect actual encounters with specific Jews and Christians, the Meccan passages do not give quite the same impression.

So how should we interpret these Meccan references to Jews and Christians as those who vouch for the truth of Muḥammad's message? It is of course possible (as Rahman argues[20]) that Muḥammad did encounter some positive response from Christians at Mecca, although this would be hard to establish conclusively. Alternatively, it might be argued that the Meccan allusions to the People of the Book are based not (or at least not principally) on concrete encounters with specific people, as at Medina, but rather on theoretical assumptions about what Jews and Christians *should be like* and about how they can be *expected* to respond. Just as Jesus and the scripture revealed to him are conceived of as forerunners of Muḥammad and the Qur'ān, so also Christians can only be thought of as people who will acknowledge the truth of Muḥammad's message.

As yet, Muḥammad's confidence in this last assumption has not been dented. But despite the basically positive view of Christians which underlies the Meccan period, there are already one or two slightly discordant notes. In the argument between Muḥammad and the Meccans about the status of Jesus which was discussed earlier (43: 57–65), the Meccans seem to be alluding to some kind of Christian worship of Jesus in their words to Muḥammad ("What, are our gods better, or he?"). So in the response given by Muḥammad (that Jesus is no more than a servant blessed by God) there is clearly an implied criticism of those, Christian or pagan, who regard Jesus as divine. If this indicates that already at Mecca Muḥammad is aware of this aspect of contemporary Christian practice, then this will naturally colour the way we interpret the many Meccan passages which attack the idea of God taking a son (e.g. 23: 91; 21: 26; 25: 2; 18: 4; 10: 68; 112: 3). Although the immediate target of this polemic is presumably polytheistic Arabian ideas of "sons of God," it would be wrong to assume that such passages cannot also be referring to Christian beliefs.[21]

Another recurrent theme in the Meccan period which slightly counterbalances the basically positive view of Christians is that of the divisions among them. It is striking that references to these divisions occur after every significant Meccan passage on Jesus. For example, one brief mention of Mary and Jesus culminates as follows:

> "Surely this community of yours is one community,
> and I am your Lord; so serve me."
> But they split in their affair between them into sects,
> each party rejoicing in what is with them. (23: 52–3; cf. 21: 92–3; 43: 65)

Given the well-known doctrinal and political tensions between the main Christian groupings of the day (Byzantines, Monophysites and Nestorians), it is hardly surprising that these find an echo in the Qur'ān, even at a period when there is little contact between Muḥammad and Christians.

II. THE MEDINAN PERIOD

Muḥammad's move from Mecca to Medina in 622 CE (the *hijra*) was to prove an important transition in several ways. In Medina Muḥammad became the leader of a religio-political community which overcame opposition from many quarters and by the time of his death in 632 CE had grown to be a dynamic new power, poised to conquer an astonishing swathe of territory in the following decades. For our present purposes certain key factors in the Medinan context need to be highlighted.

Firstly, whereas at Mecca it is unclear what, if any, significant contact Muḥammad had with Jews and Christians, at Medina the situation is quite different. Relations with the large Jewish population of Medina are a dominant theme in the early Medinan period (see especially 2: 40–150). There is also significant contact with Christians, although this seems largely to have taken place later in the Medinan period.

Secondly, as a result of these contacts we witness during the Medinan period an increasing sense of definition of Muḥammad and his community over against Jews and Christians. This is reflected in a number of ways. For example, Abraham, a crucial figure from religious history, is claimed as one who prefigured the faith of Muḥammad and his followers, rather than that of Jews and Christians.[22] The most important treatment of Abraham (2: 124–41) leads immediately into a passage (vv. 142–50) discussing the change of the *qibla* (the direction for prayer adopted by Muḥammad and his followers) from Jerusalem to Mecca. This development is generally regarded as the decisive moment in Muḥammad's "break with the Jews" and is therefore a concrete mark of the religious distinctiveness of Muḥammad's community. There also appears to be a gradual process by which *islām*, the Arabic for "submission" (of oneself to God), comes to denote not only an inner spiritual attitude but also adherence to a specific religious way of life, distinct from others, embodied in the community of Muḥammad and his followers (e.g. especially 3: 19–20, 85; 5: 3).

Thirdly, the political and military dimension of Muḥammad's conflict with his opponents in the Medinan period is another key factor determining his attitude to other faith-communities. Towards the end of the Medinan period this factor impinges sharply on relations with Christians.

Jesus and Mary

To understand the Medinan passages on Jesus and Mary it is vital to keep in mind Muḥammad's changing context and the different groups who might be addressed in any particular passage. It is especially important not to assume that passages concerned with Jesus and Mary must originally have been addressed to Christians; as we shall see, some of this material is best explained as having originated in Muḥammad's conflict with the Jews of Medina. The analysis here assumes three broad phases in the portrayal of Jesus and Mary at

Medina: an early phase in which little is said about them; a second phase in which the governing factor is polemic against the Jews of Medina; and a final phase in which polemic against Christians comes to the fore.

The early Medinan period is reflected in *sūra* 2, which dates from between the *hijra* and the battle of Badr (624 CE). It is a further reminder of the comparatively minor place of Jesus and Mary in the Qur'ān that in the whole of *sūra* 2, easily the longest *sūra*, there are only a few passing references to Jesus and none to Mary (other than in the phrase "Jesus son of Mary"). Apart from a mention of Jesus in a list with other prophets (2: 136) and a brief passage which seems to attack Christian beliefs about Jesus (2: 116–17), it is twice said that God gave Jesus "clear signs" (i.e. miracles) and "confirmed him with the holy spirit" (2: 87, 253). Although Christian interest might be aroused by this link between Jesus and "the holy spirit," it should be noted that this theme is not further developed in the Qur'ān and is not central to its portrayal of Jesus. In *sūra* 2 there is much narrative material concerned with various other figures from the past, most notably Adam (vv. 30–9); Moses (vv. 49–74); Abraham and Ishmael (vv. 124–41); and Saul and David (vv. 246–51). Much of this material has no parallels in the Meccan narratives; these are new narratives for a new situation and they have obvious relevance to the challenges facing Muḥammad in Medina, such as his disputes with the Jews and the need to stir up his followers to fight their enemies. Up to this point we can conclude, much as we did when analysing the Meccan material, that Jesus has become neither a particularly significant model for Muḥammad nor a figure around whom important arguments have centred.

This situation begins to change in the second Medinan phase, where we find slightly more attention paid to Jesus and Mary, especially at 3: 33–58. This long narrative section must be understood in the light of Muḥammad's relationship with the Jews of Medina in the period shortly after the battle of Badr. The refusal of the great majority of the Jews to acknowledge Muḥammad as a prophet, along with the political threat to Muḥammad which they posed, made this relationship extremely tense, with the threat of violent conflict in the air; this mood of hostility is reflected at various points in the rest of *sūra* 3 (e.g. vv. 19–25, 65–85, 98–9, 110–12, 187). Just as in *sūra* 2 (vv. 40–150), so here in *sūra* 3 Jewish opposition to the mission of Muḥammad prompts a history-lesson. However, whereas in *sūra* 2 the focus was on the disobedience of the children of Israel in the days of God's messenger Moses, in *sūra* 3 the narrative culminates in the account of Jewish unbelief and hostility towards God's messenger Jesus.

The narrative begins with the birth of Mary and then describes her piety and favoured place in God's sight (vv. 35–7); God also declares that he has purified her and chosen her "above all the women of the world" (v. 42). The great emphasis here on Mary's godliness and purity suggests that this passage is assuming awareness of (and of course rejecting) the accusation of sexual impurity which her Jewish fellow-people made against her. As we saw earlier, this accusation is mentioned in a Meccan Mary-narrative (19: 27–8); it is alluded to again in a later Medinan passage (4: 156). It is natural to assume that this part of the wider Qur'ānic understanding of Mary's story would also be in mind here. If so, the narrative in *sūra* 3 seems to be presenting Mary as a righteous servant of God whom (as was common knowledge) the Jews rejected, but who (unbeknown to them) was greatly honoured by God.

It is possible that the same point is being made by the brief reference to Zachariah and the birth of his son John (the Baptist) which is embedded in the account of Mary (vv. 38–41). John is praised as "a chief, and chaste, a prophet, one of the righteous" (v. 39). Neither here nor in the other references to Zachariah and John (19: 2–15; 21: 89–90) is there any reference to John's death at the hands of ungodly Jews, but as in the account of Mary it may be that a fuller knowledge of John's story is here being assumed. Given the recurrent motif that the Jews had killed prophets sent before Muḥammad (especially frequent in *sūra* 3, e.g. vv. 21, 112, 181, 183), this is not at all implausible. It would certainly make very good sense in the wider context of the Jewish hostility to Muḥammad reflected in *sūra* 3 if these accounts of the births of Mary and John were originally intended to call to mind earlier servants of God whom the Jews rejected but whose honour was upheld by God (and who therefore prefigure Muḥammad at Medina).

Such certainly seems to be the purpose of the passage about Jesus (vv. 45–57). This begins by stressing his high status before God:

> The angels said:
> "Mary, God gives you good news of a word from him
> whose name is Messiah, Jesus, son of Mary;
> high honoured shall he be in this world and the next,
> near stationed to God." (v. 45)

The narrative goes on to emphasise the role of Jesus as "a messenger to the Children of Israel"; he comes with miraculous "signs" from God to validate his mission; he confirms the Torah (their own scripture) and makes lawful "certain things that before were forbidden" (vv. 49–50). The reaction to Jesus is divided. On the one hand his disciples (*al-ḥawāriyyūn*) speak as follows, in language identical to that of the believers at Medina:

> "We will be helpers of God; we believe in God;
> witness that we have submitted ourselves to him.
> Lord, we believe in what you have sent down
> and we follow the messenger." (vv. 52–3)

On the other hand, some respond in unbelief (v. 52) and scheme against Jesus (v. 54). This leads to the mysterious climax of Jesus' earthly life:

> God said: "Jesus, I will take you to myself [or "I will cause you to die"]
> and I will raise you to myself,
> and I will purify you of those who do not believe." (v. 55)

For now, we can leave the question of whether or not this passage speaks of Jesus genuinely dying, an issue to which we shall return. What is important for our present purposes is that Jesus has been presented as one sent by God (like Muḥammad) whom the Jews reject with murderous intent. God, however, frustrates the schemes of the unbelievers (v. 54) and, in some mysterious way, vindicates his servant by raising him to himself.

Here, in this context of Jewish hostility in Medina, the Qur'ānic Jesus functions as a model for Muḥammad to a far greater extent than he has before. The parallels between Jesus and Muḥammad are very clear at many points, perhaps most strikingly in Jesus' appeal: "Who will be my helpers unto God?" (v. 52), where the word for "helpers" (*anṣār*) is the term used of those who became Muḥammad's followers at Medina.[23] The drama of human rejection and divine vindication played out in the life of this earlier messenger to the Jews thus serves to foreshadow Muḥammad's own situation, both encouraging him and warning his Jewish opponents of the futility of their hostility (vv. 55–6).[24]

Other passages from this phase reinforce the same impression. In *sūra* 61 Jesus is again portrayed as a messenger of God addressing the children of Israel, confirming the Torah, summoning helpers (*anṣār*) and provoking a mixed response among the Jews; as at 3: 55–6, the downfall of the unbelievers among them is also guaranteed (61: 6, 14). An important additional detail here is that Jesus announces the coming of a future messenger "whose name shall be *aḥmad*" (61: 6). Whether the word *aḥmad* should be translated as a name (a version of Muḥammad), or as "more highly praised," the reference is clearly to Muḥammad; Jesus is yet more clearly being presented as his forerunner.[25]

4: 153–62 is another passage of polemic against the Jews of Medina. Here the catalogue of sins committed by Jews of the past begins with events in the time of Moses (vv. 153–5). The diatribe continues:

> … and for their unbelief, and their uttering against Mary a mighty calumny,
> and for their saying,
> "We killed the Messiah, Jesus son of Mary, the messenger of God" –
> yet they did not kill him, neither crucified him,
> only a likeness of that was shown to them …
> they certainly did not kill him –
> no indeed: God raised him up to himself … (4: 156–8)

After the brief reference to their accusation against Mary of immorality, the focus here is on the Jews' claim to have killed Jesus, which is rejected. Orthodox Muslim commentators understand this passage to mean that Jesus did not die on the cross; often they suggest that someone else (e.g. Judas) died in his place while God exalted Jesus alive to heaven.[26] Some non-Muslim scholars have argued that the passage does not deny the reality of Jesus' death, but rather denies that it was *the Jews* who were ultimately responsible for this event; a cross-reference to 8: 17 might even suggest that the crucifixion of Jesus should be seen as a divine initiative. Appeal is made to other passages (such as 3: 55) which could be taken to imply that Jesus truly died on the cross.[27]

However, it must be stressed that even if it could be established that the Qur'ān does teach that Jesus genuinely died on the cross and was then raised by God to heaven, this episode would still have to be interpreted within the Qur'ānic frame of reference, which has no place for ideas of atonement. The death and resurrection of the messenger Jesus would in that case be the specific outworking in his story of the wider Qur'ānic theme of God's vindication of his messengers after their rejection by their unbelieving people; the events at the end of Jesus' earthly life would certainly not be seen as the key moment in God's redemptive purposes for humanity.[28]

Although the question of whether or not Jesus truly died on the cross is clearly of some significance for Muslim-Christian dialogue, it need not be pursued further in this context. Here we need simply to note that, however 4: 157 understands what happened on the cross, its essential message, which in context is directed to the Jews, is that their opposition to the messengers of God will ultimately be futile.

Whereas in the second of the Medinan phases defined here the main thrust of passages about Jesus and Mary is polemical against *Jewish* opposition to Muḥammad, in the third phase the main thrust is critical of *Christian* beliefs, reflecting Muḥammad's increased contact with Christians in the last years of the Medinan period. It should, however, be clarified that these phases should not be understood as totally distinct in chronological terms. Rather, there is a certain amount of overlap between them. Some of the passages critical of Christian beliefs (e.g. 4: 171–2) may date from the same time as passages already examined which attack the Jews of Medina. Likewise, in the latest phase the depiction of Jesus can still serve the purpose of polemic against Jewish opponents (e.g. 5: 78). Clearly Muḥammad did not move overnight from a period of conflict with Jews to one of conflict with Christians; passages such as 9: 29–35 reveal that both could be targets of Qur'ānic polemic at the same time. Nevertheless, the phases defined here do represent a useful generalisation which conveys something of the changing audiences and issues addressed by Muḥammad. As we consider this final phase we see how the Qur'ānic portrayal of Jesus and Mary acquires a new facet. They now appear not primarily as models for Muḥammad, but rather as figures at the heart of a theological controversy. As we saw earlier (when discussing 43: 57–65), there may have been intimations of this controversy even in the Meccan period, but it is only in the later Medinan period that it really comes to the fore.

In the final years of the Medinan period it seems that there took place in Muḥammad's attitude to Christians and Christianity something akin to his earlier process of disillusionment with the Jews of Medina. The resulting attitude of hostility was born both of theological controversy and also of political and military conflict, especially with Christian tribes to the north.[29] At the heart of the theological controversy was disagreement over the status of Jesus (and, to a lesser extent, that of Mary).

One passage concerned with the proper status of Jesus begins by warning Christians not to "exceed the bounds" in their religion (4: 171; cf. 5: 77). This idea of "exceeding bounds" (*ghuluw*) is a good summary of what the Qur'ān sees as wrong with Christian attitudes to Jesus. The respect proper to a messenger of God has lost its moorings and drifted into idolatrous worship. This distorted understanding of Jesus needs to be corrected and there is therefore a repeated emphasis on his humanity; he may indeed have been an extraordinary human being, with his birth of a virgin, his miracles and (on the traditional reading) his ascension to heaven without tasting death, but Jesus unambiguously belongs in the category of that which is created. So the passage cited above continues:

> The Messiah, Jesus son of Mary, was only the messenger of God,
> and his word which he committed to Mary, and a spirit from him.
> So believe in God and his messengers, and do not say "Three."
> Refrain: it is better for you.
> God is only one God. Glory be to him – that he should have a son! (4: 171)

The high status of Jesus is affirmed here by a string of honorific titles. Again, however, it is important not to jump to conclusions about the significance in the Qur'ān of titles applied to Jesus which also occur in the New Testament. For example, the reference to Jesus as God's "word" cannot, in the wider Qur'ānic context, be taken to imply anything resembling the pre-existent *Logos* of John's Gospel; Muslim commentators tend to see here an allusion to the divine word of command *by which Jesus was created*. What is certainly clear is that the Qur'ānic affirmations about Jesus, however striking and distinctive, are held within a clear insistence that Jesus was not God's son.[30]

The passage cited above goes on to observe that "the Messiah will not disdain to be a servant of God" (4: 172; cf. 19: 30); in context the implication (again in contrast to the New Testament) seems to be that servanthood and sonship of God are mutually exclusive possibilities. Elsewhere the status of Jesus as a being created out of dust is reaffirmed by a comparison of him with Adam (3: 59). Again, the normal humanity of both Jesus and Mary is emphasised by the reminder that (like other mortals) "they both ate food" (5: 75). In another passage the Qur'ānic Jesus himself speaks out to disown the errors of Christians; when questioned by God as to whether he told people to take him and Mary "as gods, apart from God," he insists: "It is not mine to say what I have no right to" (5: 116). Some kind of Christian doctrine of the Trinity is probably in mind here, as also at 5: 73, where Christians are reported as saying that "God is the third of three." The Qur'ānic rejection of the idea that Jesus could in any sense be divine obviously makes all trinitarian language about God out of the question, as we saw above: "do not say 'Three'" (4: 171).

It has been observed that some of the Qur'ānic attacks on beliefs held by Christians seem to be addressing ideas which are not normally considered orthodox Christianity. For example, the repeated statement "God is the Messiah" (5: 17, 72) is far from being a recognised Christian formulation of the doctrine of the incarnation. Likewise a passage quoted above (5: 116) might suggest that the Qur'ān is responding to a conception of the Trinity which involved the worship of Mary as one of the three persons.[31] Some have therefore argued that the Qur'ān need not be thought hostile to orthodox Christianity *per se*, but only to certain distortions of it.[32] There is not space here for a proper assessment of such arguments, but I am inclined to the view that although we must recognise the heterodox nature of some of the Christianity which Muḥammad encountered, it is somewhat unrealistic to think that representatives of a more "mainstream" Christian theology would have received a significantly more positive response.[33]

Scripture

We saw that in the Meccan period there is an assumption that the message brought by Muḥammad stands in continuity with the scriptures revealed through earlier messengers. This assumption is usually expressed in very general terms, without specifying what scriptures are in mind; we noted that there is only one specific reference to "the Book" which was given to Jesus (19: 30). At Medina this assumption continues, although now, as a result of greater actual contact with Jews and Christians, the claim is made more often, and usually rather more precisely, that the Qur'ān confirms the Torah and/or the Gospel. These earlier scriptures are understood as precursors of the Qur'ān not only in terms of their contents, but also in terms of the manner of their revelation. Thus, on the model of Muḥammad's reception of the Qur'ān, the Gospel (singular, never plural) is seen as having been "sent down" (3: 3) or "taught" (3: 48) to Jesus; again, it is important not to impose New Testament notions of what a Gospel might be, and of how disciples might have been involved in its composition.

A succinct statement of the Qur'ān's relationship to the Torah and Gospel is given at the beginning of *sūra* 3:

> [God] has sent down upon you [Muḥammad] the Book with the truth,
> confirming what was before it,
> and he sent down the Torah and the Gospel before ... (3: 3–4)

The same history of revelation is expounded at greater length at 5: 44–50. This passage begins with the sending down of "the Torah, in which is guidance and light" (v. 44); v. 46 describes God giving Jesus "the Gospel, in which is guidance and light, confirming the Torah before it"; finally, in v. 48, God speaks to Muḥammad of the revelation of the Qur'ān:

> And we have sent down to you the Book with the truth,
> confirming the Book that was before it,
> and a guardian over it (*muhaymin 'alayhi*).

Since the status of the Qur'ān is thus bound up with its relationship to earlier scriptures, it is natural that believers are bidden to believe in the plurality of books which God has revealed (2: 285; 4: 136). However, it is important to note the emphasis placed here on the authority or "guardianship" of the Qur'ān over its scriptural precursors, which are certainly viewed positively, but only within a history of revelation which culminates in the Qur'ān.

Little is said about the actual contents of the Gospel (or of other earlier scriptures). One passage, which compares believers to a seed growing into a plant, adds that this image is present in the Torah and the Gospel (48: 29). Another passage mentions that the promise of Paradise for those who die fighting "in the way of God" is present in the Torah, the Gospel and the Qur'ān (9: 111). Perhaps most significantly 7: 157 claims that Muḥammad is written about in the Torah and the Gospel.[34] Again, the underlying story is of a continuity which culminates in the Qur'ān, Muḥammad and the community of his followers.

The impression given so far in this section is of the Qur'ān's affirmation of earlier scriptures, the Gospel among them. This is not, however, the whole picture. The fact that most of the Jews and Christians encountered by Muḥammad did not accept his claims about himself and his message raises a very important question: if the Qur'ān is the confirmation of the earlier scriptures, why do the Jews and Christians, who read those scriptures, not accept the Qur'ān as revelation and therefore also acknowledge Muḥammad as a prophet? This question, even though it may never be articulated explicitly in quite that form, appears to be the issue which many Medinan passages are addressing. Various answers to the problem are suggested, mainly responding specifically to the rejection of Muḥammad's message by Jews. Despite being addressed to Jews rather than Christians, such passages are nevertheless relevant to this study, both because the Torah is regarded as scripture by Christians as well as Jews and also because later Medinan passages imply that the problem is essentially the same with both Jews and Christians (e.g. 5: 13–15, 68).

The passages in question suggest a range of explanations as to why the People of the Book do not believe in the Qur'ān. Some passages suggest that the actual text of their scriptures has been tampered with. For example, in response to Jewish unbelief in Medina the Qur'ān comments:

> … there is a party of them that hear God's word, and then, after they have understood it, knowingly distort it (*yuḥarrifūnahu*) …
> So woe to those who write the Book with their own hands, then say, "This is from God" … (2: 75, 79; cf. 3: 78)

Although no precise account is given here of how (or when) such corruption of the earlier scriptures occurred, this is an accusation which at least begins to provide an explanation for the apparent discrepancy between these scriptures and the Qur'ān.[35] Elsewhere the Qur'ān seems to be dealing with the same problem in a different way by suggesting not that the texts of the earlier scriptures have been corrupted, but rather that the People of the Book are consciously evading the testimony in their scriptures to the truth brought by Muḥammad in the Qur'ān. This idea is vividly conveyed at 2: 101:

> When there has come to them a messenger from God
> confirming what was with them [i.e. their scripture],
> a party of them that were given the Book
> throw the Book of God behind their backs, as if they did not know.
> (cf. 3: 187)

In similar vein, other passages speak of those who "hide" the truth in the earlier scriptures (2: 174; cf. 2: 159). Such passages seem to imply that there is nothing wrong with the Torah and the Gospel in themselves, but that the problem lies with the way in which Jews and Christians approach these scriptures. This also seems to be the sense of passages calling on Jews and Christians to "observe" or "establish" (*aqāma*) the Torah and Gospel (5: 66, 68; cf. 5: 47), an appeal which implies a positive view of these scriptures in their existing form. Further variants on this general theme include the accusation of deliberate misreading ("twisting with their tongues," 4: 46; cf. 3: 78), and the ideas that the People of the Book only have "part of the Book" (4: 44, 51), or have forgotten part of their scriptures (5: 13).

It is difficult to systematise this range of explanations into one simple account of how the Qur'ān understands the scriptures read by Jews and Christians. For now, however, it is enough to observe that in the Medinan period the scriptures of the People of the Book are a subject about which the Qur'ān repeatedly indicates disquiet. Something has gone wrong, whether in the actual text of these scriptures or in the way they are being read, and this explains why Jews and Christians fail to acknowledge the Qur'ān as they should.

Christians

The two preceding sections have already given some impression of the portrayal of Christians in Medinan passages. We have seen that Christians are criticised for their view of Jesus and (along with Jews) for their corruption of the Bible, or at least for their failure to respond to its true message. Much else is said by way of criticism of them in the Medinan period. Christians (like Jews) arrogantly believe that only they will enter Paradise (2: 111, 120, 135) and presumptuously call themselves "God's children" (5: 18). As in Meccan passages, Christians are associated with disunity, divided among themselves (5: 14), and disputing with the Jews (2: 113). They are opposed to the message brought by Muḥammad, seeking in vain to extinguish the light of God (9: 32–3). Some of their doctrines and practices are seen as unbelief (*kufr*) and idolatry (*shirk*) (5: 72–3; 9: 29–31), terms usually applied to outright pagans.[36] Monasticism is a practice which God did not command (57: 27) and Christians are accused of idolatrously taking their monks as lords (9: 31); furthermore, monks and priests are greedy for gold and silver (9: 34–5). On the practical level, Christians are not to be taken as allies (*awliyā'*) (5: 51), and they are to be fought until, humbled, they pay a special tax (*jizya*, 9: 29).

But that is not the whole picture. For example, despite the negative image of monks just mentioned, there are a number of passages which imply a warm respect for Christian monasticism (e.g. 3: 113–15; 22: 40; 5: 82; possibly 24: 36–8); God has also placed tenderness and mercy in the hearts of those who follow Jesus (57: 27). Christians are seen in a more positive light than Jews (5: 82), and it is suggested that God has set Christians in power over Jews (3: 55; 61: 14), an observation which would correspond with the political realities of the day. Social intercourse between Christians and Muslims is made possible by regulations concerning food and marriage (5: 5). Finally, and perhaps most strikingly, godly Christians are promised that they will be rewarded on the Last Day (2: 62; 5: 69).

How, then, are we to explain the co-existence of this negative and positive material on Christians? This is perhaps the hardest question with which this study has to deal.[37] Here I will only mention certain possible approaches, indicating some of their strengths and limitations, but not claiming to arrive at a neat resolution. Although they come from different angles, these approaches need not be totally exclusive of one another.

One approach is to postulate the existence in Arabia of theologically distinct streams of Christianity whose adherents responded differently to Muḥammad and so are praised or criticised by the Qur'ān accordingly.[38] There may well be some truth in this approach, although it is necessarily somewhat speculative because of the difficulty involved in reconstructing exactly what kinds of Christians were encountered by Muḥammad.

Another approach would emphasise the chronological progression in Muḥammad's attitude to Christians. Waardenburg, for example, writes of the "remarkable change in [Muḥammad's] attitude toward the Christians and Christianity" in the latter part of the Medinan period.[39] Likewise, Caspar suggests that in Muḥammad's relations with both Jews and Christians there is, on different timescales, a progression from sympathy to conflict to "rupture," the total breakdown of relations.[40] In general terms, this seems undeniable; it is an analysis which also fits with the progression of thought outlined in the section on Jesus and Mary in Medinan passages, in which hostility to Christian doctrines is much more pronounced in the later Medinan period. However, it would be very difficult to date all positive verses about Christians as early Medinan and all hostile verses as late, so although we can recognise a broad trend from positive to negative attitudes, it may be necessary to think of different attitudes to Christians overlapping with one another to some extent.[41]

Another approach would argue that much or even all of the Medinan material which appears positive about Christians in fact refers specifically to Christians who are at some stage in the process of acknowledging the divine origin of the Qur'ān and joining the community of Muḥammad's followers.[42] This argument can appeal to texts such as 5: 82–5, which begins with positive comments about Christian priests and monks (5: 82), but then continues with this account of their reception of the Qur'ān:

> And when they hear what has been sent down to the messenger
> you see their eyes overflow with tears because of the truth they recognise.
> They say: "Our Lord, we believe; so write us down among the witnesses." (5: 83)

3: 199 is another passage in which the Qur'ān praises members of the People of the Book who believe in what has been revealed to Muḥammad. One could argue that such passages make explicit what is assumed throughout the Qur'ānic appeal to Christians, namely that the proper response of Christians to the Qur'ān is to acknowledge it as divine revelation and so become part of the Muslim community.[43] This approach suggests that behind the apparently conflicting positive and negative material on Christians there is a coherent Qur'ānic attitude: on the assumption that they are ready to believe in the Qur'ān, Christians are seen positively; where they disappoint that expectation, they are seen negatively. This approach has in its favour that it does full justice to what must be taken as a datum central to this enquiry, the fact that, as Khoury puts it: "The Qur'ānic polemic against Jews and Christians concentrates above all on the question of the acknowledgement of Muḥammad's prophetic mission and the genuineness of the Qur'ānic revelation."[44]

However, there are passages which do not fit easily with this approach. For example, the following verse, much quoted by those keen to establish a pluralistic understanding of Islam, appears to promise entry into Paradise not only for Muslims but also for godly Christians and other non-Muslims, and without obviously demanding their "conversion":

> Surely those that believe, and the Jews, and the Christians,
> and the Sabaeans, whoever believes in God and the Last Day,
> and does righteous deeds – their wage awaits them with their Lord,
> and no fear shall be on them, neither shall they sorrow. (2: 62; cf. 5: 69)

This verse certainly causes problems for the argument that it is only Christians who come to believe in Muḥammad and the Qur'ān who are seen positively. On the other hand, one must also question the approach of those who interpret verses such as 2: 62 and 5: 69 in isolation from their wider context. In both *sūras* 2 and 5 the wider concern is emphatically that the People of the Book should believe in the Qur'ān; the general impression given is certainly that "a Christianity not regarded as a harbinger of ... Muḥammad [is] not an acceptable creed in spite of its monotheistic foundation."[45] If this leaves us, as I said, without a neat resolution, that indicates the need for further study of this complex question, always bearing in mind that too neat a resolution might falsify some aspect of Muḥammad's evolving relationship with various Christians over a significant number of years.

CONCLUSION

As well as leaving certain questions unresolved, this chapter has left many questions largely untouched. As mentioned above, I have not explored the question of the sources of Muḥammad's knowledge of Christianity. I have also chosen neither to discuss the enigmatic Arabic version of the name of Jesus in the Qur'ān (*'Isa*), nor to comment in any detail on the significance of the various titles applied to him by the Qur'ān, nor to put together what one can of a "life of Jesus" from the Qur'ānic material. I have given little space to what might be thought crucial topics such as whether or not the Qur'ān teaches that Jesus died.[46] Such questions are of obvious significance to Christians; my concern, however, has been not so much to consider the questions which Christians may want answered about the Qur'ān, but rather to seek to understand the material on Christianity as it takes its place within the wider concerns of the Qur'ān. I hope that this chapter has shown that what the Qur'ān says about Jesus and Mary, the Bible and Christians is not an odd hotchpotch of narratives and other fragments, but rather makes very good sense within the patterns of the Qur'ānic understanding of God and humanity and against the backdrop of Muḥammad's developing relationship with the various groups which he addresses.

One way of summarising what has emerged from this study is to speak of the relationship between the *ideal* Christianity conceived of by Muḥammad and the *actual* Christianity which he encountered. This distinction is made well by Rahman:

> From the very start of his Call, the Prophet was convinced that his message was a continuation or, indeed, a revival of the earlier Prophets ... This attitude is, however, on a purely theoretical or ideal religious plane and has no reference to the *actual* doctrine and practice of the "People of the Book" and the two must be distinguished.[47]

At the heart of the Qur'ān there is a vision of religious history which includes an ideal form of Christianity. This consists of a Jesus and a Mary who are precursors of Muḥammad; a scripture which is a precursor of the Qur'ān; and Christians who are precursors of the followers of Muḥammad. Initially, this ideal understanding of Christianity is not greatly challenged, but gradually the ideal collides with the actual. The ideal of a Christianity which must find its proper goal in Muḥammad and the Qur'ān runs up against the actual forms of Christianity adhered to by the Christians encountered by Muḥammad.

Their failure to acknowledge Muḥammad and the Qur'ān reveals that such Christians are distortions of what followers of Jesus should be; that they hold a distorted understanding of Jesus and Mary; and that they have distorted the scripture brought by Jesus.

Christians hoping to understand how they and their faith appear to Muslims today may helpfully reflect on this relationship between the ideal and the actual in the Qur'ānic understanding of Christianity. They will find that in a range of different ways the ideal and the actual serve as lenses through which Christians and Christianity continue to be viewed. To varying degrees Christians will find themselves affirmed as "People of the Book," somehow connected to the ideal, the true religion. But to varying degrees they will also find their actual beliefs and practices regarded as distortions of what they should be.

NOTES

1 This approach implies a certain understanding of the relationship between Muḥammad and the Qur'ān. I take the Qur'ān as a reliable record of Muḥammad's preaching during the period 609–32 CE. I also accept, in broad outline, the account of Muḥammad's life during this period which is given by the traditional Islamic sources. It should be acknowledged that this approach is questioned by a number of Western scholars. For an introduction to some of the writers and issues involved in this debate see the "Excursus on Islamic Origins" in David Waines, *An Introduction to Islam* (Cambridge: Cambridge University Press, 1995) pp. 265–79. For further comments on the sense in which I take the Qur'ān as a historical source, and for a discussion of the approach assumed here to the dating of Qur'ānic passages, see chapter one of my study *God, Muhammad and the Unbelievers* (London: Curzon Press, 1999).

2 It is a comment on the need to be alert to one's presuppositions that I first defined this category simply as "Jesus." However, after further reflection on the Qur'ānic material I revised this to "Jesus and Mary" because, in contrast to the New Testament, the Qur'ān devotes not much less attention to Mary than it does to Jesus. Furthermore, the relationship between Jesus and Mary is constantly alluded to in the Qur'ān due to its repeated reference to Jesus as "the son of Mary."

3 These narratives are analysed in chapter three of my study *God, Muhammad and the Unbelievers.*

4 Translations from the Qur'ān are my own, but are based on Arthur J. Arberry, *The Koran Interpreted* (Oxford: Oxford University Press, 1964). However, the system of verse-numbering used here is that of the Egyptian official edition, which is followed by most recent translations but *not* by Arberry.

5 There is not space in this context to pursue the question of the sources of Qur'ānic narratives such as this, a question, incidentally, which is

incompatible with traditional Muslim understandings of the inspiration of the Qur'ān. Sources are discussed in works such as D. Sidersky, *Les Origines des Légendes Musulmanes dans le Coran et dans les Vies des Prophètes* (Paris: Librairie Orientaliste Paul Geuthner, 1933), and Heinrich Speyer, *Die Biblischen Erzählungen im Qoran* (Hildesheim: Georg Olms Verlag, 1971).

6 For further parallels between Muḥammad and Mary, see Neal Robinson, "Jesus and Mary in the Qur'an: Some Neglected Affinities," *Religion* 20 (1990), pp. 161–75.

7 See Heikki Räisänen's comments on p. 126 of "The Portrait of Jesus in the Qur'ān: Reflections of a Biblical Scholar," *The Muslim World* 70 (1980), pp. 122–33.

8 In the Qur'ān Jesus is described both as a prophet (*nabī*), as here, and as a messenger (*rasūl*, e.g. 3: 49; 5: 75; 61: 6). On the relationship between these two terms see W. M. Watt and R. Bell, *Introduction to the Qur'an* (Edinburgh: Edinburgh University Press, 1970), pp. 28–9. For a survey of the titles of Jesus in the Qur'ān see Geoffrey Parrinder, *Jesus in the Qur'an* (London: Faber and Faber, 1965), chapter four.

9 This is one reading of a famously obscure passage which Arberry translates "It is knowledge of the hour," with the reference of "it" unspecified. Paret supports the reading I have given; see Rudi Paret, *Der Koran: Kommentar und Konkordanz* (Stuttgart: Kohlhammer, 1989) fourth edition, ad loc. Eschatological significance also seems to attach to Jesus in a Medinan passage (4: 159).

10 See F. Buhl's discussion of the question "When did Muḥammad begin to criticise Christianity?," pp. 106–8 of "Zur Kuranexegese," *Acta Orientalia* 3, 1924, pp. 97–108.

11 For the former interpretation see Paret, *Kommentar*, ad loc; for the latter see Richard Bell, *A Commentary on the Qur'an* (Manchester: Manchester University Press, 1991) ad loc.

12 7: 157, which refers to the *injīl* (Gospel), is very probably Medinan; all other references to the *injīl* are definitely Medinan.

13 W. Montgomery Watt, *Muhammad at Mecca* (Oxford: Oxford University Press, 1953) p. 27. For a contrasting view see Fazlur Rahman's *Major Themes of the Qur'ān* (Minneapolis: Bibliotheca Islamica, 1989 (second edition)), chapter eight and the two appendices.

14 Richard Bell, *The Origin of Islam in its Christian Environment* (London: Macmillan, 1926) p. 147.

15 Others have seen the passage as depicting an eschatological scene. Watt defends the reading given above in his article "The Men of the Ukhdūd" in William Montgomery Watt, *Early Islam* (Edinburgh: Edinburgh University Press, 1990) pp. 54–6.

16 Bell, *Commentary*, ad loc. See also Paret's article on "aṣḥāb al-kahf" in *The Encyclopaedia of Islam* (second edition).

17 See Bell, *Commentary*, ad loc.

18 See William Montgomery Watt, *Companion to the Qur'ān* (Oxford: Oneworld, 1994) ad loc.

19 6: 20 has often been taken as a Medinan insertion into a Meccan *sūra* (e.g. *Tafsīr al-Jalālayn*, a traditional mediaeval commentary). The presence of

Medinan parallels in *sūra* 2 (particularly at v. 146, and also, to some extent, at vv. 89 and 144) might seem to bolster this argument. However, a Meccan origin for 6: 20 and 6: 114 is suggested by the contrasting ways in which *sūras* 6 and 2 apply the claim that the People of the Book recognise the Qur'ān/Muḥammad "as they recognise their sons." In *sūra* 6 this claim appears to be contrasted with the unbelief of the Meccan idolaters; the People of the Book are thus presented positively as witnesses in support of Muḥammad. In *sūra* 2, however, the fact that the People of the Book can see the truth about Muḥammad and the Qur'ān is set within a context of polemic against their refusal to acknowledge Muḥammad. The emphasis is on how perverse they are in their conscious evasion of the truth. The different use of the same image in these two different contexts is thus an illuminating comment on both the continuity in Muḥammad's fundamental assumptions about the People of the Book and also the disappointment he experienced in his actual encounters with them.

20 See *Major Themes*, e.g. p. 137.

21 See Buhl, "Zur Kuranexegese," pp. 106–8. Such anti-Christian polemic is explicit at 19: 34–5, the sequel to the narrative about the birth of Jesus. There are, however, strong stylistic grounds for believing that these verses are a later addition (see Paret, *Kommentar*, ad loc; Bell, *Commentary*, ad loc).

22 Readers of the New Testament will be familiar with the importance of the question "Who are the true descendants of Abraham?" See especially Paul's letters to the Romans and the Galatians.

23 Another interesting parallel between the experience of Muḥammad and Jesus is suggested in the description of the plotting of the Jews against Jesus: "and they schemed, and God schemed, and God is the best of schemers" (v. 54). Almost exactly the same words are used of Muḥammad's experience at 8: 30, admittedly referring in that context not to Muḥammad's conflict with the Jews but to God's deliverance of him from the murderous plots of the Meccans.

24 The passage immediately following this long narrative section (3: 59–64) is a polemic against Christian ideas about Jesus and is traditionally believed to date from very late in the Medinan period when Muḥammad argued with a deputation of Christians from Najrān (see Muhammad Asad, *The Message of the Qur'an* (Gibraltar: Dar al-Andalus, 1980) n. 48, p. 76; Bell, (*Commentary*, ad loc.) also suggests a later date.

25 Watt notes that "Aḥmad was not given as a name to Muslim children until a hundred years after the Hijra" (*Companion*, ad loc.), and elsewhere argues at greater length that at 61: 6 "*aḥmad*" should be taken as a comparative adjective (see his article "His Name is Aḥmad" in *Early Islam*, pp. 43–50).

26 For details see chapters 12 and 13 of Neal Robinson, *Christ in Islam and Christianity* (Albany: SUNY Press, 1991).

27 See Parrinder, *Jesus in the Qur'ān*, chapter 11, especially pp. 119–21.

28 Cf. David Marshall, "The Resurrection of Jesus and the Qur'an," in Gavin D'Costa (ed.), *Resurrection Reconsidered* (Oxford: Oneworld, 1996), pp. 171–5 and Jacques Jomier, *Bible et Coran* (Paris: Les Editions du Cerf, 1959), pp. 115–16.

29 See W. Montgomery Watt, *Muhammad at Medina* (Oxford: Oxford University Press, 1956), pp. 318–20; cf. Jacques Waardenburg, "Towards the Periodization of Earliest Islam according to its Relations with Other Religions," in Rudolph Peters (ed.), *Proceedings of the Ninth Congress of the Union Européenne des Arabisants et Islamisants* (Leiden: Brill), pp. 312–17.

30 The word translated as "son" at 4: 171 (*walad*) has associations with physical procreation. Disgust with the implications that this would have for understanding God may account in part for the Qur'ānic rejection of Christian beliefs about Jesus. Not too much weight should be placed on this argument, however, since in another passage attacking Christian beliefs equally emphatically (9:30) the Arabic for "son of God" (*ibn allāh*) does not have quite the same associations.

31 For examples of some such forms of Christian belief which may have been present in seventh century Arabia see Parrinder, *Jesus in the Qur'ān*, chapter 14.

32 See R. C. Zaehner, "The Qur'an and Christ," an appendix to *At Sundry Times: an Essay in the Comparison of Religions* (London: Faber and Faber, 1958), pp. 195–217, and Watt, "The Christianity Criticised in the Qur'an," in *Early Islam*, pp. 66–70. For a different angle (which, however, does not deal with the Qur'ān itself in any detail) see Adolfo Gonzalez Montes, "The Challenge of Islamic Monotheism: a Christian View" in *Concilium* 1994/3, pp. 67–75.

33 See Fazlur Rahman, *Islam* (London: Weidenfeld and Nicolson, 1966), p. 26.

34 The Qur'ān does not itself elaborate on this claim. However, Muslims have been particularly impressed by Deuteronomy 18: 15–18, which speaks of God raising up a prophet like Moses, and Jesus' promise in John 14 of the coming of the "Paraclete." Both these passages, as well as many others, are seen as referring to Muḥammad.

35 The Islamic exegetical tradition gave much attention to thinking through the implications of such passages; this led to various understandings of *taḥrīf*, the corruption of the Torah and the Gospel. For more on this topic see the article on "taḥrif" in the *Encyclopedia of Islam* (second edition).

36 Ahmad Von Denffer distinguishes between the theological, legal and societal aspects of the Qur'ānic view of Christians. In theological terms Christians are "kuffār" (unbelievers), and therefore implicitly on a level with pagans. In legal and societal terms, however, they are to be distinguished from other unbelievers (*Christians in the Qur'an and Sunna* (Leicester: Islamic Foundation, 1979) pp. 32–41). Toshihiko Izutsu makes a similar point, observing that although there is a complexity to the relationship between the People of the Book and the *umma*, ultimately the opposition between them is as great as that between the *umma* and pagans (*God and Man in the Koran*, Tokyo: The Keio Institute of Cultural and Linguistic Studies, 1964, p. 81).

37 See Faruq Sherif's candid acknowledgement of this difficulty in *A Guide to the Contents of the Qur'ān*, (Reading: Garnet, 1995), pp. 130–7, where he also gives a useful survey of the relevant material.

38 See, for example, Rahman, *Islam*, pp. 26–7.

39 Waardenburg, "Periodization," p. 312.
40 Robert Caspar, *Traité de Théologie Musulmane* [Tome 1] (Rome: PISAI, 1987), pp. 49–53.
41 Caspar himself acknowledges this, suggesting that the overlapping may reflect encounter with different Christian groups (*ibid.*, p. 52).
42 Jane Dammen McAuliffe's study *Qur'ānic Christians* (Cambridge: Cambridge University Press, 1991) illustrates that this is the mainstream approach of the Classical Qur'ān-commentaries.
43 Note should be taken, however, of the suggestion by Mahmoud Ayoub that the Qur'ān envisages Christians who remain Christians while at the same time believing in the Qur'ān and Muḥammad. He writes that certain Qur'ānic verses "confirm the People of the Book in their own religious identities and expect from them no more than the recognition of Muḥammad as a Messenger of God and of the Qur'ān as a genuine divine revelation confirming their own Scriptures" ("Nearest in Amity: Christians in the Qur'ān and Contemporary Exegetical Tradition," *Islam and Christian-Muslim Relations*, Vol. 8, No. 2, 1997, p. 158, cf. p. 155). For this intriguing argument to gain serious credibility as an attempt to understand the Qur'ān in its original context (rather than, primarily, as a proposal for contemporary Muslim-Christian relations) many further questions would need to be addressed. For example, it is not immediately clear how the religious identity of such Christians would differ from that of Muslims: so what would it mean to continue to call them Christians? It should also be kept in mind that, as Ayoub frankly acknowledges, his concern for interfaith relations today leads him to a deliberately selective reading of the Qur'ānic material (*ibid.*, p. 162).
44 Adel Theodor Khoury, *Toleranz im Islam* [second edition] (Altenberge: Christlich-Islamisches Schrifttum, 1986), p. 52. See also Willem A. Bijlefeld's argument that the decisive issue determining the Qur'ānic judgement on Jews and Christians is their response to the Qur'ān itself. See his "Some Recent Contributions to Qur'anic Studies: Selected Publications in English, French and German, 1964–1973," *The Muslim World* 64 (1974), pp. 94–5.
45 Sherif, *Contents*, p. 137.
46 As well as Parrinder's *Jesus in the Qur'ān*, see G. C. Anawati's article on ('Isa) in the *Encyclopaedia of Islam* (second edition) for useful surveys of such matters.
47 Rahman, *Islam*, p. 26 (his italics).

2

Christians in the *Ḥadīth* Literature

Marston Speight

The information given in this study comes from nine of the most well-known collections of *ḥadīth*, or reports of sayings, narrations and actions attributed to the Prophet Muḥammad or to his Companions.[1] All of these collections emerged from the ninth century AD,[2] and they represent the flowering of efforts by Sunni Muslims to capture in definitive and authoritative form the large number of reports that were circulating among the people. No particular chapter or section of the collections is devoted to the subject of "Christians," so a researcher faces the task of ferreting out texts pertaining to that subject found under a variety of headings and attributed to many different transmitters of *ḥadīth*. One of the reasons for restricting this study to the nine collections indicated is that they are the ones for which the research tool, A. J. Wensinck's *Concordance*,[3] provides an exhaustive number of references. The word for "Christians" in the *ḥadith* is *naṣāra* (sing. *naṣrānī*).[4] This word, together with the terms *Ahl al-Kitāb* (People of Scriptures), *Ahl al-Dhimma* (protected or subject people), *jizya* (poll tax) as indexed in the *Concordance* point to a large number of references reflecting the Muslim consciousness of and reaction to the Christian presence among them. In addition to Wensinck's work, another tool used for this investigation is the Sakhr *Ḥadīth* Encyclopedia on CD ROM,[5] also based on the nine collections and provided with an extensive search capacity. The analyses and conclusions of this study are based on an examination of approximately 500 *ḥadīth*, including many repetitions in variant readings. Although I do not claim to have found every relevant text in the literature, I believe that the ones presented here are broadly representative of the entire corpus of Sunni *ḥadīth*.

LITERARY FORMS OF *ḤADĪTH*

The *ḥadīth* conform to two general forms of expression. Usually they present sayings or actions attributed to the Prophet Muḥammad or to one of his Companions. The saying or action is either given simply without any supporting details, or it is enhanced by minimal rhetorical and narrative devices.[6] The other form is that of a historical or biographical report, attributed to the Prophet or to a Companion. It can be an unadorned statement or a more or less complex narration about events or persons. These two forms go by the names of *ḥadīth* (pl. *aḥādīth*), meaning "report," *khabar* or (pl. *akhbār*), meaning "piece of information," as well as by a third term, *athar* (pl. *āthār*), "trace" or "vestige." *Ḥadīth* is the more general term. The historical or biographical report was not only a form of *ḥadīth* but also a basic form of annalistic writing found outside the bounds of *ḥadīth* literature. Under the name of *khabar* this form in historical writing means "a piece of historical information."[7]

These forms of expression exist in *ḥadīth* collections completely separate from one another, each one furnished with its chain of transmitters, one of the criteria for its degree of reliability, depending on the personal qualities and scholarship of the various transmitters ranging from the purported first guarantor up to the individual compiler who finally included it in a comprehensive collection. Since the texts do not exist in any larger context of composition, each one must suffice alone to yield the information needed by an interpreter. Minimal help in understanding is afforded by the way many compilers gathered certain *ḥadīth* under particular subject headings, usually the rubrics of *fiqh*, or jurisprudence. Another key to explication is an analysis of the chains of transmission, the *asānīd* (sing. *isnād*), a technical process which is beyond the scope of this study. Only occasionally will I point out the significance of certain transmitters in the elaboration and preservation of a text. In general I have approached the literature with a synchronic viewpoint, attempting to determine how the texts in question functioned as a whole among the people to whom they were delivered in written collections. Because these collections come from one period of history it is scarcely possible to determine how they evolved over the century and a half that elapsed from the demise of the Prophet to the time of definitive collection. That evolution of the texts took place is obvious from the evidence of many variant readings. Viewed synchronically we can discern patterns of development in them without attempting to trace their historical development.

I have entitled this paper, "Christians in the *Ḥadīth* Literature" rather than "Christianity in the *Ḥadīth* Literature" because the literature is more concerned with social relationships between Muslims and Christians than with the doctrines of Christian faith. Even texts relating to Christ scarcely bear on our subject since the figure to whom reference is made in those texts is the Christ of Islam rather than the Christ of Christianity. The *ḥadīth* come from a period when Islam had won political authority over much of western Asia and North Africa. Christians and Jews were the principal religious groups with which Muslims of the ninth century had to do. In the *ḥadīth* the two communities are often called by a collective title, *Ahl al-Kitāb*, "People of Scriptures," and occasionally *Ahl al-Kitābayn*, "People of the two Scriptures." When the title, "*Ahl al-Kitāb,*" is used more often than not it refers to the Jews, and in some texts it is difficult to know whether Christians are included in that designation or not. G. Vajda, in *The Encyclopaedia of Islam*[8] observes that the *ḥadīth* literature reflects an attitude of mistrust toward the People of Scriptures and insists on the need of Muslims to differentiate from them. We shall see, upon examination of the texts, that this judgment is partially accurate but that, in the case of Muslim attitudes toward Christians, it needs to be nuanced. I have grouped the *ḥadīth* studied under five subject headings.

I. AFFIRMATIVE ATTITUDES

Ibn 'Abbās, a Companion of the Prophet, recounted a biographical recollection to the effect that Muḥammad preferred following the practices of the People of Scriptures in matters about which he had had no particular instruction.[9] The practice in question was the way men should arrange their hair and the immediate reference is to the Jews alone. However, when this report is taken along with the prophetic insight formulated in a startling metaphor and reported by Abū Hurayra, that "all prophets are brothers; their mothers are different, but their religion is one,"[10] it is obvious that Christians as well as Jews could, on occasion, be followed in their practice by the Prophet. This openness to the *Ahl al-Kitāb* and the concomitant affirmation of the unity of all prophetic religions serve to explain the many similarities between Islam and Christianity. *Ḥadīth* scholars have interpreted the metaphor, "one father – different mothers," as signifying the common monotheistic basis of prophetic religion and the varying "laws" (*sharā'i'*) or practices and codes of the particular faiths.[11]

The following text is a numerical saying, that is, a declaration whose various parts are arranged into an easily remembered and numbered list:

> The father of Abū Burda related that the Prophet (peace be upon him) said: "Three people will receive a reward twice. A person who, possessing a female slave, brings her up well, giving her a good education, then frees her and marries her, that person will receive a double reward. A believer of the People of Scriptures who believes in the Prophet (peace be upon him) and becomes a Muslim, that person will receive a double reward. And the slave who carries out his duty toward God and toward his owner."[12]

This saying contains elements that can be found elsewhere as separate statements. The opening promise of a double reward is found in the Qur'ān 28: 54. Also the slave owner who is kind to his female slave is found, as follows,

> Abū Mūsā al-Ash'arī related that the Messenger of God (peace be upon him) said, "Whoever owns a female slave and frees her and then marries her will have a double reward."[13]

The second element in the complex statement also exists independently, although I have found only one instance of it in the nine books of *ḥadīth*. Abū Umama related that on the day of the conquest of Mecca the Prophet pronounced this saying,

> "Whoever of the People of the Two Scriptures becomes a Muslim will have a reward twice over. Whatever rights and duties we have are his as well. Whoever of the polytheists becomes a Muslim has his reward. Whatever rights and duties we have are his as well."[14]

The third element specifying a faithful and religious slave as receiving a double reward is found in Bukhārī, *'itq*, 16, as well as in several variants in other collections. Then the first and third elements, the virtuous owner of a female slave and the faithful slave, are found together also in Bukhārī, *'itq*, 16. Since the three parts of the numerical saying exist separately and in partial combination it is tempting to assume that the one and two part readings represent earlier *ḥadīth* that were eventually combined into the full three part version. However, we are not warranted in so judging, for the ancient manuals of *ḥadīth* science point out that transmitters practiced varied means of rhetorical elaboration and condensation, so that both the combination of several elements into one whole and the breaking up of composite pieces into smaller units took place concurrently.

The three elements of the numerical saying are symmetrically arranged. In each case the person is promised a double reward for two acts:

1 Freeing and marrying a slave. The part about educating her is simply an elaboration of the two part structure. In comparison, the version in Ibn Ḥanbal, IV, 398, lacks such a detail.
2 Believing in a prophet from the past and believing in Muḥammad.
3 Fulfilling duty toward God and toward one's owners. Each pair of actions is graded from good to better, and they are given in that graded order, except for 3, where duty toward God is put first, out of reverence for the deity. Also the three cases represent basic institutions of early Muslim society, the family, the community of faith and slavery. Two attitudes toward Christians reveal themselves in this *ḥadīth*. First, since Christians are grouped together with slaves it appears that Christians were regarded as socially inferior. Nevertheless the text shows a certain positive appreciation of the Christian "prophet," since belief in him would make possible a double reward once faith was also confessed in Muḥammad.

Abū Mūsā al-Ash'arī is credited with the recollection of what the Prophet said and did when a funeral procession passed for one of the People of Scriptures. He stood out of respect and exhorted his followers to do the same.[15] The few variant readings of this recollection hint at the different degrees of acceptance of Christians and Jews by the Muslim community. As a reason for standing when a funeral procession of the *Ahl al-Kitāb* passes, the Prophet is said to have exclaimed: "Death is a fearful event (*faza'*), so when you see a funeral stand up."[16] Or: "We do not arise out of respect for the dead person, but for the angels who may be accompanying the procession."[17] Or: "It is a soul, is it not?"[18] 'Alī the Prophet's son-in-law, is quoted as saying that the Prophet only stood on one occasion for a funeral of the *Ahl al-Kitāb*.[19] These comments are unusual for the *ḥadīth*. Usually an exemplary action, such as standing for a funeral procession is recounted with little or no comment. The differing explanations of Muḥammad's gesture of respect indicate that the Muslim attitude toward Christians (and Jews) was neither uniform nor simple. In their definitive written form the *ḥadīth* reflect how prophetic dicta and actions were discussed and acted upon by the community.

Christians living under Muslim rule were subject as were the Jews to the *dhimmī* status as a protected religious minority. The early history of this status is unclear,[20] and the *ḥadīth* literature contains surprisingly little regarding it. As an example of affirmative attitudes toward *dhimmī* peoples here is an injunction attributed to ʻUmar, the second caliph:

> "I charge him according to the covenant of protection by God and His Messenger (peace be upon him) to observe faithfully the pact that was agreed upon with them, to defend them from harm and not to charge them with undue burdens."[21]

The collections of *ḥadīth* devote much space to dietary rules, but, regarding the *Ahl al-Kitāb*, there is little to differ from the liberal spirit of the Qur'ān, as seen in the verse, "The food of those who received Scriptures is lawful for you, and your food is lawful for them."[22] Once a conscientious Companion, Abū Thaʻlaba al-Khushanī, complained to the Prophet that in his relations with the People of Scriptures he and others were in doubt about using the cooking pots belonging to the non-Muslims, since they were likely to have used them to cook pork and to contain wine. The Prophet replied: "If you can find other pots eat and drink from them, but, if not, just wash them with water, then eat and drink."[23]

Qabīṣa b. Hulb is reported to have asked the Prophet about the food of Christians. He replied, "Don't let food worry you; that is the way the Christians do."[24] This warning is interpreted as being directed against the asceticism of certain Christians.[25]

II. ERRORS OF THE CHRISTIANS

The *ḥadīth* literature speaks of a settled Christian population in the midst of Islam, a permanent feature of the socio-economic scene. Christians were accepted without having to endure any pressure from Muslims to change their faith. By contrast, the impulse to bring Christians into Islam showed itself in the political and military policy of the earliest Muslim conquerers, as they applied the Qur'ānic injunction to call on unbelievers to surrender, and if they did not submit they should be forcibly subdued until peace should reign and the true religion of Islam prevail.[26] This policy was nuanced in the early days of Islam by offering unbelievers (including Christians and Jews) one of three choices: accept Islam; or refuse to accept Islam, thereby adopting the status of *dhimmī*, or protected minority carrying the obligation to pay a poll tax (*jizya*); or thirdly refuse either of the preceding and be obliged to defend themselves against the armed might of the Muslims.[27] The *ḥadīth* record a famous example of this policy of conquest as seen in the letter purported to have been written by Muḥammad to Heraclius the Byzantine emperor.[28]

As for the *dhimmī* population, it often figures in the *ḥadīth* as a foil to the Muslims with regard to religious and social behavior. The errors of Christians are noted, usually in order to serve as a warning to Muslims not to do likewise.

1 Embellishment of Churches

> The Messenger of God (peace be upon him) said, "I see that after I am gone you will exalt your mosques even as the Jews have exalted their synagogues and the Christians their churches."[29]

Al-Bukhārī often inserts quotations, without chains of authority, in the headings (*tarājim*) to his chapters. In the book on prayer he quotes 'Umar, the second caliph: "We do not enter your churches because of the statues and pictures. Ibn 'Abbās would pray in the church if there were no images in it."[30]

2 Clergy and Monasticism

When one of Muḥammad's Companions returned from a trip to Syria he bowed to the Prophet as he had seen the Christians bow down to their patriarchs and bishops in Syria. Muḥammad naturally disapproved strongly of such a practice.[31] Likewise he judged celibacy to be reprehensible. An unmarried man came to him once and when the Prophet asked him if he had sufficient wealth to marry, the man replied, "Yes." Then the Prophet said, "You are a brother of the devils. If you were a Christian you would be one of their monks. Ours is the way (*sunna*) of marriage. Bachelors are the worst of you all … "[32]

'Uthmān b. Maẓ'ūn, a Companion with ascetic tendencies, was rebuked by the Prophet for seeking to lead a celibate life. Muḥammad said, "We have had no directive regarding monasticism."[33] Another reputed saying is that "the monasticism of this people is struggle (*jihād*) in the way of God."[34]

3 Christians and God's Word

Even though Christians were recognized as People of Scripture the *ḥadīth* reflect the Qur'ānic judgment that they as well as the Jews were not faithful to the Word of God that was revealed to them.[35] Muḥammad warned once that religious knowledge (*'ilm*) would disappear. An astonished listener exclaimed,

> "How can religious knowledge disappear since we recite the Qur'ān, since we will recite it to our children and our children to their children even until the day of resurrection?" Muḥammad replied, "Ah! Are there not the Jews and the Christians who recite the Torah and the Gospel and yet do not observe what is said in them?"[36]

Not only did the People of Scriptures fail to obey the Word of God, but they also altered the sacred text by various means. In a report purported to have originated with Ibn 'Abbās, the famous exegete of the Qur'ān (hence, not a prophetic *ḥadīth*), it is said that the People of Scriptures divided their scriptural revelation into parts which they believed and parts which they did not believe.[37] Ibn 'Abbās also reported that they changed their Scriptures with their own hands.[38] These texts serve as examples of the Qur'ānic warning in *sūra* 15, verse 90, and, in a note to the last *ḥadīth* mentioned it is said that because of their having tampered with their Scriptures, they are not people from whom Muslims should seek information about God's Word. Besides, it is added, "I have not seen a single person (of the *Ahl al-Kitāb*) asking you (Muslims) about what has been revealed to you."[39]

Another non-prophetic text, this one from Ibn Mas'ūd, the famous reader of the Qur'ān, is found in a group of *ḥadīth* concerning the debate over whether to record the reports in writing or not. Ibn Mas'ūd, opposed to that practice and in favor of oral transmission, reported that "the *Ahl al-Kitāb* perished because they devoted themselves to the books of their scholars rather than to the Book of their Lord."[40]

4 Worship of Jesus

In a report obviously intended to forestall excessive veneration of the Prophet, 'Umar said that he heard Muḥammad say, "Do not extol me as the Christians extolled the son of Mary. I am a slave, so call me the slave of God and His messenger."[41] 'Alī reported a striking parallel drawn by Muḥammad, who said:

> "There is a similarity to be seen in 'Isā (Jesus). The Jews hated him so much that they defamed his mother, but the Christians loved him so much that they elevated him to a status that was not rightly his." Then

he said, "In my case two persons will be destroyed: the one who praises me inordinately and without reason, and the one who hates me to such a degree that he slanders me detestably."[42]

III. COMPARISONS BETWEEN MUSLIMS AND CHRISTIANS

Passing from relatively simple declarations of Christian errors we consider a number of texts in which comparisons between the Muslims and Christians function to strengthen Muslim behaviour and piety. First there is an overall perspective:

> Every child is born into the religion of human nature (*fiṭra*). Its parents make of it a Jew or a Christian. When a young camel is first born do you find any defect in it?[43]

In the following *ḥadīth* we find an echo of concern about the threat to Muslim unity, posed by differences in the recitation of the Qur'ān.

> Ḥudhayfa said to 'Uthmān, "O commander of the faithful, do something about this people before they differ over the Scriptures as the Jews and Christians did before."[44]

Extending the theme of disunity to the time of divine judgment, the following text is found in several versions:

> The Messenger of God said, "The Jews have divided into seventy-one sects. One of them will be in paradise and seventy in hell. The Christians have divided into seventy-two sects: Seventy-one will be in hell and one in paradise. And I swear that my people will divide into seventy-three sects. One will be in paradise and seventy-two in hell." Someone asked, "O Messenger of God, who are they (the ones in paradise)?" He said, "The *jamā'a.*"[45]

Whatever may have been the original setting for this saying it seems undeniable that this and similar versions emerged from the early times of religious and political dispute which resulted in sectarian activity and a strong reaction from the main body of Muslims called the *jamā'a*, or community, also commonly known as the *ahl al-sunna wa-l-jamā'a* (people of the prophetic example and the community).[46]

Next is a studied and ingeniously formulated metaphorical comparison, similar to the parable of Jesus found in Matthew 20:1–16. This text is found in a number of variant readings, but there are only two main versions. First,

> Ibn 'Umar reported that the Prophet (peace be upon him) said: "Your appointed time compared to that of nations past is like the time between mid-afternoon prayer and sunset. Your situation, compared with that of the Jews and the Christians is that of a man who hired workers, saying, 'Who will work for me half a day for one *qīrāt* as a wage?' The Jews worked thus. Then he said, 'Who will work for me from midday until the mid-afternoon prayer for one *qīrāt*?' The Christians worked thus. Then you (Muslims) are working from the mid-afternoon prayer until sunset for two *qīrāt* each. They (Jews and Christians) said, 'We have worked more and received less'. He said, 'Have I wronged you in any way?' They said, 'No.' He said, 'This is a favour on my part. I give it to whom I will.'"[47]

The foregoing text points to the superiority of the Islamic era, with the coming of Muḥammad and the revelation of the Qur'ān, all signified by the higher salary paid to the last group of workers. The Jews and Christians retort but not in anger. They are simply set in contrast to the Muslims, without any unfavorable judgment upon them. The second version is quite different:

> Abū Mūsā: The Prophet (peace be upon him) said, "The parable which may be applied to Muslims, Jews and Christians is that of a man who hired people to work for him a full day at an agreed wage. They worked until midday and then said, 'We do not need your money that you stipulated for us. What we have done is worth nothing.' He said to them, 'Don't stop. Finish the rest of your work and take your full wages.' They refused and went away. So the man hired other workers after them and said, 'Finish the day's work and I will give you the wage that I stipulated for the others' They worked until the mid-afternoon prayer and then said, 'What we have done is worthless. Keep the money that you promised to give us.' He said, 'Finish your work; there is only a little time left in the day.' But they refused. So he hired others to work for the rest of the day, until sunset. They received the full wage of the two preceding groups. This is analogous to the way that they have accepted this light."[48]

This text emphasizes the failure of the Jews and Christians. In the first story Islam's triumph was due to the sovereign favour (*faḍl*) of the Almighty. In the second the weakness[49] and irresponsibility of the first workers are given as reasons for their being supplanted. Those who "accepted this light" are the Muslims, who, in the similitude of assiduous workers, are faithful to the Prophet.[50]

A series of solemn warnings in several collections is based on a recollection of an event during the Prophet's lifetime:

> Abū Wāqid al-Laythī: When the Messenger of God went out to Ḥunayn[51] he passed by a tree called Dhāt Anwāṭ that was used by the polytheists to hang their weapons upon.[52] The Muslims said, "O Messenger of God, give us a Dhāt Anwāṭ such as they have." The Prophet (peace be upon him) said, "God is great! You have spoken as Moses' people did to him when they said, 'Give us a god, even as they have gods.'[53] I swear that you follow after the customs of those who were before you."[54]

There exist several warning statements based on this story, such as:

> Abū Hurayra: The Prophet (peace be upon him) said, "You follow the customs of those who were before you, span by span, and cubit by cubit, so that if they had entered the hole of a lizard, you would have entered it too."[55]

In other readings his hearers ask the Prophet to whose customs he is referring in saying that the Muslims follow them. One answer is, the Persians and the Greeks.[56] In another exchange the questioner asks, "Whom do you mean, the Jews and the Christians?" He replied, "Who else than they?"[57] Such occasional severity toward Christians reflects the growing attitudes of rivalry and antagonism which often marked the intercommunal life of the times.

Ritual life was an obvious point of comparison between the Muslims and Christians. A number of texts deal with the origin and development of Friday worship. On the one hand early records give no sign of controversy with other religious groups in the decision of Muslims to worship communally on Friday.[58] On the other hand the difference between the Muslim day and the days of the People of Scriptures became a concrete issue by which the separateness of the communities was dramatized. Hence the following etiological statement:

> Abū Hurayra: The Messenger of God said: "God ordained Friday for those who were before us, but they disagreed about it. Then God guided us to it, and people follow us with respect to the day, the Jews to the day after and the Christians to the day after that."[59]

Here is an example of how two independent reports are sometimes joined into a single text, or a composite report is broken into two or more parts by transmitters. First, a saying suggestive in phraseology of

Qur'ān 56:49 to affirm the priority of Islam, in spite of its late appearance in history: Abū Hurayra reported that the Messenger of God said, "We, the last in this world, will be the first in the hereafter."[60] By means of a connecting thought, "... although they (the former peoples) received Scriptures before we did ...," this affirmation is joined to the saying about Friday.[61] In another context it is said that the People of Scripture envied the Muslims because of Friday, and that they had strayed away from its observance.[62]

Another important part of ritual life for Muslims is the call to prayer, the manner of which was decided by the Prophet after listening to the discussion of his followers. According to one story the people suggested first one way to call the faithful to prayer and then another. The suggestions were made with reference to the Jewish customs (a fire or trumpet call) and the Christian custom (a clapper, or *nāqūs*, two pieces of wood struck against each other). In some readings 'Umar is said to have suggested a human voice. In another version 'Abd Allāh b. Zayd came forward to tell of a dream in which he saw a man trying to sell a *nāqūs*. 'Abd Allāh told the man he wanted to buy it to use as a call to prayer. The man then told 'Abd Allāh about a better way, using the human voice. These disparate elements are used separately and in various combinations to make up a large number of versions dealing with the way the call to prayer began and how Bilāl, the Abyssinian Companion, was first assigned the duty to pronounce it.[63]

Matters of dress and adornment figure often in the *ḥadīth*, but rarely do they serve to differentiate between the Muslims and the Christians. One of the practices of the *Ahl al-Kitāb* that the Prophet followed at first[64] was that of letting the hair hang loose. But later he started to part his hair.[65] Also the Christians and Jews had the habit of not dyeing their hair. According to a report from Abū Hurayra, Muḥammad ordered that Muslims should be different from them and dye their hair.[66] This contrast is a reversal of that seen in later literature where Jews and Christians are required by their Islamic rulers to dress differently from the Muslims.[67] The *ḥadīth* literature is silent on the requirements of distinctive dress for *dhimmī* people.

IV JUDGEMENTS AGAINST CHRISTIANS

Passing from comparisons in which Christians appear in an unfavorable light, we turn to *ḥadīth* in which eschatological judgments are pronounced against Christians because of their errors.

1 Tombs of the Prophets

'Ā'isha, the Prophet's wife is credited with this recollection:

> During the last illness of the Messenger of God (peace be upon him) he said, "May God curse the Jews and Christians! They have taken the tombs of their prophets as places of prayer."[68]

In another version of this report, 'Ā'isha is said to have added, "If he had not said that, his tomb would have been made a public place, and I am afraid that it would have become a place of prayer."[69] Another appended remark is, "In that way he warned his people about such practices."[70] The remarks appended to these versions of the curse show that this report played a part in the campaign against excessive grief at funerals and veneration of the dead.[71]

A different text on the same subject also adds a condemnation of image veneration:

> 'Ā'isha: Umm Salama[72] mentioned to the Messenger of God (peace be upon him) a church called Māriya that she had seen in Abyssinia that contained images. The Messenger of God (peace be upon him) said, "Those are people who, when a righteous person dies, build a place of prayer on his grave and fashion those images. In God's view they are the worst of creatures."[73]

2 Consequences of Rejection of Islam

Some strong condemnations can be understood as expressions of the offense felt by Muslims at the continued refusal of the People of Scriptures to accept Islam.

> Abū Hurayra: The Messenger of God (peace be upon him) said, "I swear that any from this community of Jews or Christians who hear of me and die without believing in my message will be among the people of hell."[74]

In a solemn foretelling of the future beatific vision in paradise, Abū Sa'īd al-Khudrī recounted that, according to the Prophet, people from the different religions will be asked on the day of resurrection, "Whom did you worship?" When the Christians are asked that question they will reply, "We worshipped Christ the Son of God." In reply the questioner, called a summoner (*mu'adhdhin*), will say, "You lie, for God has not taken a wife nor has He engendered a son." Then the Christians will fall into the fire of hell, even as will the Jews after failing the test of the summoner.[75] The severity of this judgment is mitigated slightly by the statement, toward the beginning of the account, that among those who will remain unscathed by the fire of hell are the worshipers of God, including "the remnant of the People of the Scriptures," presumably a reference to those Jews and Christians who had lived in earlier times and who had not falsified their revelation.

At the end of the first *sūra* of the Qur'ān, the *Fātiḥa*, worshipers plead that God would lead them in the straight path, not in the way of the "*maghḍūb alayhim*", those who have incurred wrath, nor in the way of the "*ḍālīn*", those who have gone astray. Although several interpretations have been given to these two expressions,[76] in a prophetic *ḥadīth* the Jews are designated as those who have incurred wrath, and the Christians as those who have gone astray.[77] This understanding of the verse has been dominant in the history of Qur'ān exegesis.

The last judgment *ḥadīth* selected here is a startlingly severe word:

> Abū Mūsā reported that God's Messenger (may peace be upon him) said, "When the day of resurrection comes God (may He be honoured and exalted) will hand over either a Jew or a Christian for each Muslim and He will say, 'This is your release (*fikāk*) from the fire of hell.'"[78]

This is an extreme judgment and seemingly goes contrary to the Qur'ān, which denies the possibility for the redemption of unbelievers in *sūra* 5, verse 36. As for believers there would be no need for a ransom from hell unless they were guilty of grave sins, in which case they would be consigned to temporary punishment.[79] Also, to consign Jews and Christians to hell as a ransom for Muslims goes much further than the previously cited judgment[80] which identifies them as people of hell because of their disbelief in Muḥammad. Another version of the present text says that some Muslims will come to the day of resurrection with sins "like mountains and God will grant them pardon, placing their sins upon the Jews and the Christians."[81] The transmitter adds his personal reservations about the report, saying, "I suppose (that is the way it went)." Another authority adds, "I do not know from whom the doubt came." Al-Nawawī, commenting on this text, links it with another which assigns each person a place in paradise and a place in hell. Then when believers go to paradise their place in hell is taken by the unbeliever according to what their unbelief deserves. Al-Nawawī goes on to say that God will only place the sins of Muslims on those Jews and Christians who bear themselves a corresponding weight of sin. So the latter will be put in hell for their own works, not really for those of the Muslims whose ransom they are.[82] Another explanation of the text is that it is a metaphorical expression meaning that space in paradise will be provided by the absence of Jews and Christians from it.[83] This rather uncertain exegesis shows that the report has proven difficult for Muslims. Nevertheless its presence in at least two of the collections[84] is evidence that it contributed to the growth of alienation between the Muslims and the Christians. In its several versions this report warrants further investigation. In one version[85] the Umayyad caliph ʿUmar b. ʿAbd al-ʿAzīz (d. 720) entered a discussion about the report and swore three times that Abū Burda's father, Abū Mūsā, really heard the judgment from the Prophet. Another version does not specify the Jews and Christians but states that people from the religions (*adyān*) will serve as ransom for the Muslims.[86] And finally still another *ḥadīth* attributed to Abū Mūsā and his son, Abū Burda, speaks of the ransom in a different way:

> The Messenger of God (peace be upon him) said, "When God gathers His creatures on the day of resurrection the people of Muḥammad will be permitted to bow down in prayer. They will bow in prayer for a long time. Then it will be said to them: 'Raise your heads. We have made your extended prayer a ransom for you from the fire.'"[87]

This text suggests a wider range of use for the rhetorical figure of a ransom than that seen in the judgment against Jews and Christians.

V. STRICTURES AGAINST CHRISTIANS

In the *ḥadīth* literature are found a number of texts referring to the events of early Muslim conquest, the social situations arising from interaction between Muslims and the peoples whom they conquered. In the provisions that were made for the protection of *dhimmī* people there were necessarily certain restrictions that had to be applied. These were codified in works of jurisprudence,[88] but the *ḥadīth* give occasional examples of them. Such reports do not constitute the best evidence of attitudes toward Christians since the restrictions, such as the poll tax (*jizya*) and the prescriptions about blood money (*diya*) applied to all *dhimmī* people regardless of their religion. A few relevant texts will be noted here.

1 Greetings

The Muslim greeting of peace (*salām*) plays an important part in worship and in everyday life.[89] It was inevitable that, given the sharp social and religious separation between Muslims and their subject peoples, there should be tension in the use of the everyday greeting of *salām*. The tension lay between the demands of ordinary good manners and the highly charged Islamic significance of the greeting. *Salām* is said to be the greeting given to those entering paradise.[90] The Holy Book also exhorts believers to greet each other with *salām*.[91] The expression, "Peace be upon you" (*al-salāmu 'alaykum*) is used constantly in the ritual life of Muslims.

According to a report attributed to Abū Hurayra the Prophet recommended that his people not greet Jews and Christians until they initiate the greetings. And when Muslims meet them on the road the subject people must move aside to let the Muslims pass.[92] This stricture seems to come from a desire to keep the *ahl al-dimma* in their place of social inferiority.

If, however, Jews or Christians greet Muslims, how should the latter respond? By a truncated form of the *salām* greeting: "And upon you," according to Anas b. Mālik, from the Prophet.[93] That settled the matter with regard to Christians, apparently, but with the Jews there arose additional complications. Once a group of Jews came to Muḥammad and greeted him insolently with the words, "*al-sāmu 'alayka.*" This expression, sounding somewhat like the authentic greeting meant, however, "May death be upon you." 'Ā'isha, the guarantor of this story said,

> "I answered them, 'Upon you be death and the curse.' The Prophet (may peace be upon him) said, 'O 'Ā'isha, God loves kindness (*rifq*) in every situation,' 'Ā'isha said, 'Didn't you hear what they said?' He replied, 'And I said, "And upon you."'"[94]

Finally the grandfather of 'Amr b. Shu'ayb reported that the Prophet ordered his people not to imitate the gestures used in their greetings by Jews, a sign with the fingers, or by Christians, a sign with the palm of the hand.[95]

2 Expulsion from Arabia

One of the best known strictures against Christians and Jews is their designation as persona non grata in Arabia. Although the *ḥadīth* and other records tell of their expulsion from the Arabian Peninsula history also reveals that in early times they never completely left the territory.[96] Nevertheless, using certain *ḥadīth* as justification, various legal authorities of Islam in subsequent centuries applied the stricture of exclusion with more or less severity. Following are some *ḥadīth* bearing on the subject.ʿĀʾisha is credited with this report:[97]

> The last thing the Messenger of God (peace be upon him) charged was that there should not be left two religions (*dīnān*) in the "Island of the Arabs" (*jazīrat al-ʿarab*).[98]

And again, this time according to Ibn ʿAbbās,

> The Messenger of God (peace be upon him) said, "There will not be two directions for prayer (*qiblatān*) in a single country."[99]

In other *ḥadīth* this saying is appended to other elements to form more complex compositions. It is used with reports of ʿUmar's expulsion of the Jews from Khaybar,[100] and Muḥammad's curse against Jews and Christians who make the tombs of their prophets into places of prayer.[101] In these cases the words about no two religions in one country seem to be for reinforcement for or justification of the measures taken or the curse pronounced. Some non-Muslim scholars have maintained that the saying about only one religion for the country was invented to justify ʿUmar's actions.[102] However, it could have been motivated by events such as the heated discussions with the Jews in Medina, reported in the *ḥadīth*. On one occasion, after the Battle of Badr, the Prophet addressed the Jews thus, the report attributed to Ibn ʿAbbās:

> "O assembly of Jews, accept Islam before something happens to you like what happened to Quraysh."[103] They said, "O Muḥammad, do not deceive yourself, for you did battle with a band of inexperienced Quraysh who did not know how to fight. If you had fought us you would have known who we are. You will not find our equal."[104]

Another *ḥadīth*, this one attributed to Abū Hurayra, reports a similar discussion. The Prophet said,

> "O assembly of Jews, accept Islam, and you will be safe." They said, "You have said it, O Abū Qāsim." [Then after repeating himself twice] he added: "Know that the land belongs to God and to His Messenger. I want to expel you from this land. If any one of you owns property he should sell it; otherwise know that the land belongs to God and to His Messenger (may peace be upon him)."[105]

The expression, "The land belongs to God and His Messenger" is suggestive of the more developed affirmation that there can be only one religion in the land.

Here are some of the varieties of expression found regarding this stricture against the Christians:

1 "Two religions cannot coexist in one land," occurring alone in at least two cases.[106]
2 After his conquest of Khaybar Muḥammad made a pact with the Jewish inhabitants permitting them to stay on the oasis and work the land in return for tribute. In the year 20/641 the caliph 'Umar revoked that pact, claiming that the unruly behavior of some Jews on the oasis had made it necessary to expel the inhabitants from Khaybar.[107]
3 Expulsion of Jews from Khaybar justified by the Prophet's declaration, "Two religions cannot coexist in one land."[108]
4 'Umar is said to have expelled the Jews and Christians from the Ḥijāz,[109] and sent them to the localities of Taymā' and Arīḥā'. Thus the report receives triple augmentation: Christians are added to the ones expelled; the place from which they were expelled is broadened – the Ḥijāz, a part of the Arabian Peninsula, and the destinations of the ones expelled are given. The Christians may have been added simply because the phrase, "Jews and Christians" recurs often representing the subject peoples. There is no record of Christians being expelled from the Ḥijāz, although 'Umar did expel most of the Christians from the city of Najrān in the southern part of Arabia,[110] supposedly because they practiced usury.[111]
5 In a *ḥadīth* from Ibn 'Abbās the Prophet is reported to have ordered on his deathbed the explusion of the polytheists (*mushrikūn*) from the Arabian Peninsula.[112] This elaboration of the Prophet's command could be a rhetorical interpretation or application of the more aphoristic saying, "Two religions must not coexist in one land." This is also said to have been one of the Prophet's last pronouncements. However, it is possible that such a descriptive setting was simply inserted into a version, an example of the common practice by transmitters of expansion (*ziyāda*).[113] The term *mushrikūn* is relevant to the subject of this study. Although Christians were often termed as *kuffār* (unbelievers) by Muslims the word "polytheists" was also applied to them because of their trinitarian beliefs.[114]

6 The famous Companion, Abū 'Ubayda, is credited with the report that one of the last commands of the Prophet was: "Expel the Jews of Ḥijaz and the people of Najrān from the Arabian Peninsula."[115] This order includes both Christians (people of Najrān) and Jews. However the meaning is rendered somewhat uncertain by another version, also from Abū 'Ubayda, which says: "Expel the Jews of the people of Ḥijāz and of the people of Najrān from the Arabian Peninsula."[116] This would seem to refer only to Jews from the two localities. Najrān had a strong Jewish presence in the period just before Islam, so there were probably still Jews there. However, whatever saying of the Prophet may have provided a basis for this report, one suspects that in the present version it was invented to justify 'Umar's measures of expulsion at Khaybar and at Najrān. And the same may be said for a report attributed to 'Umar himself, who heard the Prophet say: "If I live, God willing, I will expel the Jews and Christians from the Arabian Peninsula and I shall leave only Muslims in it."[117] In presenting these *ḥadīth* in the form of a progression of thought I do not mean to suggest that they represent a chronological progression. In the typically atomistic fashion of *ḥadīth* creation and transmission[118] these texts occur in collections which have little concern for strict historical sequence. It may be that a minute study of the chains of transmission would point to a closer cause and effect relationship between the texts, but the most that I claim is that all of the testimonies are affected by the meaning of Muḥammad's aphorism, "There will not be two religions in one country." Some texts have a narrow scope and others a broader one. Only in the last (6) is the scope comprehensive as regards Jews and Christians. And it is this last sweeping directive that has most influenced Muslim thought, so that the territory of Arabia became a hostile place to Jewish and Christian presence and remains so today.

CONCLUSION

Considering the foregoing evidence of Muslim attitudes toward Christians as seen in the *ḥadīth* literature, one has the impression that the affirmations, judgments, comparisons and restrictions in the texts functioned as a part of the Muslim expression of their identity on the world religious scene of the eighth and ninth centuries. The subject matter of the texts chosen is sometimes profound and sometimes banal. The *ḥadīth* show that, as the Islamic community marked its distinctive nature, it evoked scriptural and theological issues vis-à-vis the other religion, even if at a rudimentary level, and examined its social relationships with Christians. The reports testify as to how the dominant Muslim population found a place for Christians in the scheme of things by assigning them to the *dhimmī* status. The social and religious inferiority with which the Muslims regarded their *dhimmī* population is clearly delineated. And yet the accounts are not without certain touches of human warmth. Religiously, the ruling element isolated the Christians while at the same time acknowledging some ties with them. In general the *ḥadīth* served to strengthen the foundations of an exclusive theology which afterwards would set Muslims firmly apart from the People of the Scriptures.

NOTES

1 The collections of Al-Bukhārī, Muslim, Abū Dā'ūd, Al-Tirmidhī, Al-Nasā'ī, Ibn Māja, Al-Dārimī, Mālik Ibn Anas and Ibn Ḥanbal. See R. Marston Speight, "Attitudes toward Christians as Revealed in the *Musnad* of al-Ṭayālisī," *The Muslim World,* LXIII (1973), 249–68, for a similar study based on a single collection of *ḥadīth*. Some material for this investigation is taken from the earlier article.

2 The earliest compiler, Mālik b. Anas, died in 795, but recensions of his collection extended well into the ninth century.

3 A.J. Wensinck, *Concordance et Indices de la Tradition Musulmane: Les Six Livres, Le Musnad d'al-Dārimī, Le Muwatta' de Mālik, Le Musnad de Ahmad Ibn Ḥanbal.* 8 Vols. (Leiden: E.J. Brill, 1936–1988.)

4 *The Encyclopaedia of Islam*, New Edition, VII, 970–73.

5 Distributed by Digitek International, Falls Church, Virginia, USA.

6 A full typology of *ḥadīth* forms of expression may be found in R. Marston Speight, "The *Musnad* of al-Ṭayālisī: A Study of Islamic *Ḥadīth* as Oral Literature." (Ph.D. diss., Hartford Seminary Foundation, 1970.)

7 Régis Blachère, "Regards sur la littérature narrative en arabe au Ier siècle de l'hégire (=VIIe s.J.C.)," *Sémitica* 6 (1956): 86. Stefan Leder, "The Literary Use of the Khabar: A Basic Form of Historical Writing," in Averil Cameron and Lawrence I. Conrad (eds.), *The Byzantine and Early Islamic Near East*, Vol.1, *Problems in the Literary Source Material,* (Princeton: The Darwin Press, 1992), 277–315.

8 New Edition, s.v. "Ahl al-Kitāb."

9 Muḥammad b. Ismā'īl al-Bukhārī, *Ṣaḥīḥ al-Bukhārī*, 3 vols (Cairo: Dar wa-Maṭābi' al-Sha'b, n.d.), manāqib al-anṣār, 52, with variant readings in other collections. References to particular *ḥadīth* contain the compiler's name followed by the name of the section, or *kitāb*, and the number of the chapter *(bāb)*, or, in some cases, the number of the *ḥadīth*. For the collection of Ibn Ḥanbal references give the volume and page numbers.

10 Bukhārī, anbiyā' 48, with variant readings in several collections.

11 Ibn al-Athīr, *Al-Nihāya fī Gharīb al-Ḥadīth wa-l-Athar*, 5 vols. (Cairo: al-Ḥalabī, 1383/1963), III, 291.

12 Bukhārī, jihād, 145 with many variants. One version in Bukhārī, anbiyā', 48, specifies that if a believer in Jesus subsequently believes in Muḥammad he will receive a double reward.
13 Aḥmad b. Ḥanbal, *Musnad*, 6 vols. (Beirut: Dār Ṣādir wa-l-Maktab al-Islām, 1389/1969), IV, 398.
14 Ibn Ḥanbal, V, 259.
15 Ibn Ḥanbal, IV, 391.
16 Muslim b. al-Ḥajjāj, *Ṣaḥīḥ Muslim*, 5 vols., Ed. Muḥammad Fu'ād 'Abd al-Bāqī (Cairo: Al-Ḥalabī, 1955), janā'iz, 78.
17 Ibn Ḥanbal, IV, 391.
18 Muslim, janā'iz, 81.
19 Ibn Ḥanbal, IV, 413.
20 *The Encyclopaedia of Islam*, New Edition, s.v. "dhimma."
21 Bukhārī, jihād, 174.
22 Qur'ān 5:5.
23 Abū Dā'ūd al-Sijistānī, *Sunan Abī Dā'ūd*, 4 vols., ed. Muḥammad Muḥyī al-Dīn 'Abd al-Ḥamīd (Cairo: Maṭba'at Muṣṭafā Muḥammad, n.d.), aṭ'ima, 46 together with many variants in all nine books.
24 Abū 'Abd Allāh Muḥammad b. Yazīd al-Qazwīnī b. Māja, *Sunan*, 2 vols., ed. Muḥammad Fu'ād 'Abd al-Bāqī (Cairo: Al-Ḥalabī, n.d.), jihād, 26.
25 Muḥammad 'Abd al-Raḥmān al-Mubārakfūrī, *Tuḥfat al-Aḥwadhī bi-Sharḥ Jāmi' al-Tirmidhī*, 10 vols. Eds. 'Abd al-Wahhāb 'Abd al-Laṭīf and 'Abd al-Raḥmān Muḥammad 'Uthmān (Medina: Al-Maktaba al-Salafiyya, 1383/1963–1387/1967), V, 183.
26 Qur'ān 8:38,39.
27 Muslim, jihād, 2. In jihād, 1, a famous transmitter, Nāfi', is said to have written to an inquirer specifying that it was the practice in the early days of Islam to issue an invitation to accept Islam before engaging unbelievers in battle.
28 Muslim, jihād, 26, along with variants in several collections.
29 Ibn Māja, masājid, 2, and a variant in Abū Dā'ūd, ṣalāt, 12.
30 Bukhārī, ṣalāt, 54.
31 Ibn Māja, nikāḥ, 4 and Ibn Ḥanbal, IV, 381.
32 Ibn Ḥanbal, V, 163.
33 Abū Muḥammad 'Abd Allāh b. 'Abd al-Raḥmān b. al-Faḍl b. Bahrān al-Dārimī, *Sunan al-Dārimī*, 2 vols. (Beirut: Dār Iḥyā' al-Sunna al-Nabawiyya, n.d.), nikāḥ, 3; and Ibn Ḥanbal, IV, 381.
34 Ibn Ḥanbal, III, 266.
35 See Qur'ān 3:78; 5:14.
36 Ibn Māja, fitan, 26, with variants in other collections.
37 Bukhārī, manāqib al-anṣār, 52.
38 Bukhārī, shahādāt, 29.
39 *Ibid.*
40 Dārimī, muqaddima, 42.
41 Bukhārī, anbiyā', 48, along with variants in other collections.
42 Ibn Ḥanbal, I, 160.
43 Mālik b. Anas, *Al-Muwaṭṭa'*, 2 vols. Ed. Muḥammad Fu'ād 'Abd al-Bāqī (Cairo: Al-Ḥalabī, 1370/1951), janā'iz, 52, with variants in most of the collections. The *fiṭra* is Islam, and the comparative inferiority of the other

religions is highlighted by reference to a defect in the animal, absent at birth, but potentially a part of subsequent existence.

44 Bukhārī, faḍā'il al-Qur'ān, 3, with several variants.
45 Ibn Māja, fitan, 13, with variants in other collections.
46 See *The Encyclopaedia of Islam*, New Edition, s.v. "djamā'a," and W. M. Watt, *The Formative Period of Islamic Thought* (Edinburgh: University Press, 1973), 2, 3, with further references.
47 Bukhārī, faḍā'il al-Qur'ān, 17, and many variants. See remarks on this *ḥadīth* in Ignaz Goldziher, *Muslim Studies*, I, (London: George Allen & Unwin, 1967) 201–02.
48 Bukhārī, ijāra, 11.
49 In Bukhārī, tawḥīd, 47, a version uses the word *'ajaza* (to be weak) to describe the first workers.
50 Some readings of the parable combine the two versions, but in a way that does not show understanding of the difference between them, for example, Bukhārī, tawḥīd, 31,47; Ibn Ḥanbal, II, 121,129.
51 At the time of the Battle of Ḥunayn in the year 8/629.
52 A gesture of worship.
53 Qur'ān, 7:138.
54 Al-Mubārakfūrī, *Tuḥfat al-Aḥwadhī bi-Sharḥ Jāmi' al-Tirmidhī*, fitan, 16 with a fuller version in Ibn Ḥanbal, V, 218.
55 Ibn Ḥanbal, II, 511.
56 Ibn Ḥanbal, II, 527.
57 Ibn Ḥanbal, II, 257.
58 S.D. Goitein, "The Origin and Nature of the Muslim Friday Worship," *The Muslim World,* XLIX (1959), 195.
59 Ibn Ḥanbal, II, 236, with many variants.
60 Bukhārī, wuḍū', 68.
61 Bukhārī, jum'a, 1.
62 Ibn Ḥanbal, VI, 134–35.
63 Representative readings are: Bukhārī, adhān, 1; Abū Dā'ūd, ṣalāt, 27; Dārimī, ṣalāt, 3; Abū 'Abd al-Raḥmān al-Nasā'ī, *Sunan bi Sharḥ Jalāl al-Dīn al-Suyūṭī*, 8 vols. Ed. Ḥasan Muḥammad al-Mas'ūdī (Beirut: Iḥyā' al-Turāth al-'Arabī, 1348/1930), adhān, 1.
64 See p. 32.
65 Bukhārī, manāqib al-anṣār, 52 and several variant readings.
66 Ibn Māja, libās, 32, with many variants. See G.H.A. Juynboll, "Dyeing the Hair and Beard in Early Islam: a Ḥadīth Analytical Study," *Arabica,* XXXIII (March 1986): 49–75.
67 A.S. Tritton, *The Caliphs and Their Non-Muslim Subjects: A Critical Study of the Covenant of 'Umar* (London: Frank Cass, 1970) 115–26. Antoine Fattal, *Le Statut Légal des Non-Musulmans en Pays d'Islam* (Beirut: Imprimerie Catholique, 1958) 96–112.
68 Muslim, masājid, 19 and many variant readings.
69 Bukhārī, janā'iz, 62.
70 Bukhārī, anbiyā', 50.
71 Goldziher, *Muslim Studies* I, 209–38. Henri Lammens, *Fāṭima et les Filles de Mahomet* (Rome: Sumptibus Pontificii Instituti Biblici, 1912), 118–23.
72 One of the Prophet's wives.

73 Bukhārī, ṣalāt, 54 along with several variants in other collections.
74 Muslim, imān, 240; Ibn Ḥanbal, II, 317, 350; IV, 396, 398.
75 Bukhārī, tafsīr, sūra 4; Muslim, imān, 81.
76 Mahmoud Ayoub, *The Qur'ān and Its Interpreters*, Vol. 1 (Albany: State University of New York, 1984), 49–54.
77 Ibn Ḥanbal, IV, 378–79; V, 32–33, 77.
78 Muslim, tawba, 49. Another version, Ibn Ḥanbal, IV, 402, uses the word, fidā', "ransom" or "redemption."
79 *The Encyclopaedia of Islam*, New Edition, II, 382.
80 p. 42.
81 Muslim, tawba, 51.
82 Abū al-'Abbās al-Qasṭallānī, *Irshād al-Sārī li Sharḥ Ṣaḥīḥ al-Bukhārī*; in the margin, *Matn Ṣaḥīḥ al-Imām Muslim wa-Sharḥ al-Imām al-Nawawī 'alayhi*. 10 vols. (Bulāq: al-Maṭba'a al-Kubrā, 1304/1886), X, 197.
83 Muslim b. Ḥajjaj, *Ṣaḥīḥ Muslim*, trans. 'Abdul Hamīd Siddīqī (Lahore: Sh. Muhammad Ashraf, 1971–75), 1444, n.
84 In addition to the references in Muslim, see Ibn Ḥanbal, IV, 391, 398, 402, 407.
85 Muslim, tawba, 50 and Ibn Ḥanbal, IV, 398, 408.
86 Ibn Ḥanbal, IV, 408. Still another more general word is used (*milal*, "religions") in Ibn Ḥanbal, IV, 409–10.
87 Ibn Māja, zuhd, 34.
88 See A. S. Tritton, *The Caliphs and Their Non-Muslim Subjects*; Antoine Fattal, *Le Statut Légal des Non-Musulmans en Pays d'Islam*.
89 See *The Encyclopaedia of Islam*, New Edition, s.v. "salām."
90 Qur'ān 16:32.
91 Qur'ān 24:61.
92 Muslim, salām, 13, along with several variants.
93 Muslim, salām, 7, with variant.
94 Tirmidhī, isti'dhān, 12, with variants.
95 Tirmidh, isti'dhān, 7.
96 Abū 'Ubayd al-Bakrī, *Kitāb mu'jam mā 'sta'jama: Das geographische Wörterbuch des Abū 'Obeid 'Abdallah ben 'Abd el-'Azīz el-Bekrī*, 2 vols. in 1, Ed. Ferdinand Wüstenfeld (Göttingen: Deuerlich'sche Buchhandlung, 1876–77), I,9. Richard J. H. Gottheil, "Dhimmis and Moslems in Egypt," in *Old Testament and Semitic Studies in memory of William Rainey Harper*, Vol. 2, pp. 351–414 (Chicago: University of Chicago Press, 1908), 353. Fattal, *Le Statut Légal . . .*, xii, 35,88,90. Tritton, *The Caliphs and their Non-Muslim Subjects*, 175.
97 Ibn Ḥanbal, VI, 275.
98 The name given to the Arabian Peninsula.
99 Abū Dā'ūd, imāra, 28.
100 Mālik, jāmi', 18 and variants in several collections.
101 Mālik, jāmi', 17. See pp. 42. See also Ibn Ḥanbal, I, 223.
102 *The Encyclopaedia of Islam*, New Edition, IV, 1142.
103 Those defeated at Badr.
104 Abū Dā'ūd, imāra, 21.
105 *Ibid.*
106 See p. 46.

107 Bukhārī, shurūṭ, 14: Ibn Ḥanbal, I, 15. Abū Dā'ūd, imāra, 23. *The Encyclopaedia of Islam*, New Edition, s.v. "Khaybar."
108 Mālik, jāmi', 18 from Ibn Shihāb.
109 Bukhārī, ḥarth wa-muzāra'a, 17; fard al-khums, 19. Muslim, musāqāt, 6. These texts are attributed to Ibn 'Umar.
110 *The Encyclopaedia of Islam*, New Edition, s.v. "Nadjrān."
111 Aḥmad b. Yaḥyā al-Balādhurī, Futūḥ al-Buldān (Leiden: E.J. Brill, 1866), 66, 156.
112 Bukhārī, jihād, 176. Muslim, waṣīya, 20.
113 Al-Ḥasan b. 'Abd al-Raḥmān al-Ramahurmurzī, *Al-Muḥaddith al-Fāṣil bayn al-Rāwī wa-l-Wa'ī* (Beirut: Dār al-Fikr, 1391/1971), 530.
114 *The Encyclopaedia of Islam*, New Edition, s.v. "shirk" and "kāfir."
115 Dārimī, siyar, 55.
116 Ibn Ḥanbal, I, 195, 196.
117 Tirmidhī, siyar, 42, with slightly varying readings in Muslim, jihād, 63; Ibn Ḥanbal, I, 29,32; III, 345; Abū Dā'ūd, imāra, 28.
118 See Patricia Crone, *Slaves on Horses: The Evolution of the Islamic Polity* (Cambridge: University Press, 1980), 5.

3

Legal Exegesis: Christians as a Case Study

Jane Dammen McAuliffe

It is always an interesting classroom exercise to ask students to read the Qur'ānic references to Christians and Christianity as if these were the only information about this religious tradition available to them. Of course, a completely unprepared approach cannot be simulated; nevertheless, the conscious shift of perspective required to undertake this exercise usually provokes stimulating conversation. Read in textual order, the first mention of Christians under the Qur'ānic term al-Naṣārā occurs in the second *sūra* of the Qur'ān (2:62). The commentators frequently used this first occurrence to provide some etymological explanation or speculation about the term itself. Verses relevant to the Christians, however, cannot be confined to those in which this proper noun occurs. Frequently, less specific and more general phrases, such as "people of the Book" *(ahl al-kitāb)* or "those who were given the Book" *(alladhīna ūtū l-kitāb)*, are used to connote Christians as part of a larger religious configuration. Consequently, Qur'ānic material relevant to the Christians and Christianity can be found throughout the entire corpus and the subsequent exegetical tradition has expanded and refined the full extent of this depiction.

In some of my earlier work related to the present topic, my interest in such material has focused upon Christians as a religio-social group.[1] In other words, I have generally bracketed from consideration the passages that deal directly with Jesus, Mary or other figures in the Christian narrative.[2] Further, I have not concentrated upon the verses that challenge aspects of Christian doctrine, i.e. the well-known Qur'ānic rebuttals of such teachings as the Incarnation, the Trinity and Jesus' death by crucifixion. These matters have received, and continue to receive, the bulk of attention in both scholarly treatises and works of popular polemic and apologetic.[3] While all of these elements contribute importantly to the full Qur'ānic presentation of Christianity, less scholarly attention has been given to the wide range of verses that describe certain forms of Christian activity and practice, that praise or commend Christians, that criticise or condemn them and that provide various directives intended to guide Muslim behaviour toward them.

Not unexpectedly, it is that last-mentioned category, those behavioural directives, that have captured the most sustained attention from the commentators whose work I am about to consider. Verbal imperatives or their semantic equivalents constitute a primary preoccupation of legal commentaries and those verses that regulate Muslim conduct toward Christians ordinarily take this form. The legal commentaries themselves are but a subset of a much larger exegetical enterprise. Before concentrating upon this subset, it may be useful to mention some of the salient features of that larger endeavour.

A few years ago I walked into the Safeway grocery store in Amman, Jordan one Saturday afternoon to do some shopping. By that time of my life, I had been studying the Qur'ānic commentary (*tafsīr*) tradition for a number of years. I had some sense of the scope, both chronological and linguistic, of the exegetical effort that had been expended on explaining and clarifying the Qur'ānic text for more than a millennium. I was also well aware of the enduring importance of that exercise and of its productions, both classical and contemporary, in Muslim intellectual life. Nevertheless the sight at the entrance to the Amman Safeway came as something of a surprise. A small book display of literature for children and adults had been set up in the supermarket foyer, and placed squarely in the centre was a thirty-volume edition of the early tenth-century Qur'ān commentary by Abū Ja'far b. Jarīr al-Ṭabarī.

The memory of that scene has remained with me as a vivid reminder of the continuing religious relevance of even those Qur'ānic commentaries that predate the development of the medieval Christian university system in the West. While today's text-critical biblical scholars have largely lost sight of their patristic and medieval predecessors, except for their importance to historical theology, most Muslim scholars of the Qur'ān remain conceptually and methodologically connected to their ninth or eleventh or thirteenth-century counterparts. The names of al-Ṭabarī (d. 310/923), al-Zamakhsharī (d. 538/1144) and Fakhr al-Dīn al-Rāzī (d. 606/1210) continue to be found in the books and articles produced by Qur'ānic scholars in the contemporary Muslim world.

Consequently, such commentaries have been the subject of non-Muslim academic attention as well, studied not simply for their historical interest but for their continuing relevance in Muslim intellectual life. But one class of exegetical literature that has received very little treatment from North American or European scholars is that which focuses exclusively upon those Qur'ānic verses that have legal implications. This is known, in the standard subject classifications that Muslim scholars have produced for Qur'ānic commentary, as "legal commentary" (*al-tafsīr al-fiqhī*) or as "the commentary of the jurisprudents" (*tafsīr al-fuqahā'*).

Three Sunnī authors from the classical period produced works that have achieved the status of standards of this form of exegetical literature.[4] In university classes on "The Legal Precepts of the Qur'ān (*aḥkām al-Qur'ān*)" and in modern Muslim treatments of that subject, these are the most frequently-cited sources.[5] They are Aḥmad b. 'Alī al-Jaṣṣāṣ (d. 370/981), 'Imād al-Dīn 'Alī b. Muḥammad al-Ṭabarī Ilkiyā al-Harrāsī (d. 504/1110), and Abū Bakr Muḥammad b. 'Abdallāh al-Ma'āfirī, known as Ibn al-'Arabī (d. 543/1148). In their published form, the commentary of each of these is called simply *Aḥkām al-Qur'ān*. In an effort to broaden the scope of this survey, however, I am including some works that exceed the usual syllabus. Therefore I am adding to the consideration of these tenth and twelfth-century sources, an eighth-century work by Muqātil b. Sulaymān (d. 150/767) and a fifteenth-century one by the Shī'ī al-Miqdād al-Ḥillī.

Before presenting each of these authors it may be helpful to offer some comparative statistics that can clarify the distinction between their works and those of such figures as al-Ṭabarī and al-Rāzī. Quite simply the difference is one of verse selection and thematic emphasis. As Wael Hallaq has noted in a recent work on Islamic legal theory, there are about 500 verses in the Qur'ān with decidedly legal content.[6] These comprise less than 10% of the Qur'ānic total of 6236 verses[7] and, not surprisingly, the commentaries that devote themselves exclusively to such verses are considerably more compact than those that cover the entire Qur'ān.[8]

Further, the distribution of legal verses is not uniform throughout the text. Some *sūras* have dozens while others contain few, if any. A selective sampling from the commentary of Ibn al-'Arabī, who is actually more inclusive than his predecessors, should suffice to highlight these differences of scale. The third *sūra* of the Qur'ān, *Āl-'Imrān* contains 200 verses. Of these, Ibn al-'Arabī comments on 27 or about 13.5% of the total. The fifth *sūra*, *al-Mā'idah* includes 120 verses but Ibn al-ʿArabī's commentary deals with 41, i.e. 34% of the total. Again, the ninth *sūra*, *al-Tawbah*, ends with verse 129 and Ibn al-ʿArabī treats 55 verses from this *sūra*, i.e. 42.6%, or approaching half of the total. Of course, all three of these *sūras* are considered to be Medinan in the chronologies developed by both Muslim and Western scholarship, and therefore virtually by definition, could be expected to contain more prescriptive material.

Continuing further into the Qur'ānic text, representative sampling turns up similar variation. The sixteenth *sūra*, *al-Naḥl*, a largely late Meccan *sūra*, contains 128 verses but only, according to Ibn al-ʿArabī, 22 *aḥkām* verses. The twentieth-ninth *sūra*, *al-ʿAnkabūt*, one whose chronological placement is more contested, ends with verse 69 but only 5% of the total, i.e. 4 of its verses are treated. Finally, the sixtieth *sūra*, *al-Mumtaḥanah*, which is commonly considered late Medinan, contains but 13 verses yet 7 of them, or more than 50% receive consideration by Ibn al-ʿArabī.

Turning now to the specific works that I have selected for this brief survey, I will present them in chronological order, framing the three standard figures – al-Jaṣṣāṣ, Ilkiyā al-Harrāsī and Ibn al-ʿArabī – with the early text of Muqātil b. Sulaymān and the later one of al-Miqdād al-Ḥillī. For each I will provide some brief biographical information, as gleaned from the *ṭabaqāt* literature, and then an example of the kind of legal exegetical argument that each author has directed toward a verse relevant to the Qur'ānic attention to Christians.

MUQĀTIL B. SULAYMĀN

In twentieth-century scholarship on Qur'ānic exegesis, more attention has been paid to Muqātil b. Sulaymān than to those scholars whose works will be subsequently treated. A footnote in Ignaz Goldziher's *Muhammedanische Studien*, first published in 1889–90, cited Ibn Ḥajar al-ʿAsqalānī's *Tahdhīb al-tahdhīb* and al-Suyūṭī's *Itqān* as representative of the classical condemnation of Muqātil's exegetical output.[9] Thirty years later Louis Massignon offered more focused attention to Muqātil and his interest has been sustained, from varying perspectives, by Paul Nwyia, John Wansbrough, Isaiah Goldfeld and, more recently, Claude Gilliot.[10] Goldfeld has provided a helpful summary of the principal biographical notices dedicated to Muqātil and a brief note about his life can be drawn from these.

Muqātil was a Khūrāsānī, born and raised in that part of the Umayyad empire that now comprises parts of Iran, Afghanistan and beyond. While his birthplace was the more eastern city of Balkh, much of his early adult life is associated with Marw, where he served under a succession of rulers. Classical Muslim heresiographical sources ordinarily identify him with the Murji'ah and cite his exchanges with Jahm b. Ṣafwān (d. 128/745).[11]

During the last years of the Umayyad dynasty, Marw was a centre of Abbasid propaganda activity under the instigation of the astute strategist, Abū Muslim. In the inaugural years of Abbasid rule Muqātil b. Sulaymān, like many Khurāsānīs, migrated westward to the centres of political power in Iraq. Muqātil settled first in Baṣrah and then moved to Baghdād, whose foundation by al-Manṣūr as the caliphal capital is dated to within a decade of this scholar's death. Muqātil returned to Baṣrah at the end of his life and died there in 150/767.

The classical biographical sources give Muqātil a very mixed review. Rather scant praise is mingled with much criticism. Al-Dhahabī's *Ta'rīkh al-Islām* reproduces pages of recrimination, condemning his mendacity and his pretensions to scholarship.[12] This criticism, according to Paul Nwyia, collected itself chiefly around two accusations: first, that he incorporated material taken from Jewish and Christian informants into his exegetical works and, secondly, that he cited the interpretative *dicta* of his predecessors without full attribution, i.e. without *isnāds*.[13] These charges have coloured Muqātil's reputation among his successors and, apparently, continue to affect the accessibility of his works.[14]

Nevertheless, among scholars of the history of Qur'ānic *tafsīr* he remains a figure of importance and is regularly credited with having produced the first full commentary to come down to us.[15] Portions of that work were subsequently excerpted to form a legal commentary, perhaps the earliest of this genre, entitled *Tafsīr al-khams mi'at āyah min al-Qur'ān*. This work, which will be a focus of the present article, is ordered thematically, not according to verse sequence. For example, Qur'ānic passages pertaining to *ṣalat* are treated together, as are those that deal with *zakāt*, with *ṣawm*, with *ḥajj*, etc. A group of passages on the *ḥudūd* punishments follows a long section on Qur'ānic legislation about marriage and sexual conduct.

Among the earliest mentions of the Christians in Muqātil's *aḥkām* commentary is one to be found in the section devoted to *ḥajj* prescriptions. Q.7:31 begins with the imperative, *O children of Adam, put on your adornment near every masjid*. The "occasion of revelation" (*sabab al-nuzūl*) ordinarily associated with this verse describes a reputed pre-Islamic practice in which people circumambulated the Kaʿbah undressed, the men during the day and the women at night.[16] The rationale provided for this practice, in the usual narrative accounts, is one of divestment as a mark of disassociation. The pilgrims professed themselves unwilling to circumambulate the shrine in clothing worn during ordinary activity, during the days and times that sins had been committed. Although not explicitly glossed as such by Muqātil, the Qur'ānic mention of "adornment" (*zīnah*) quite clearly connects with clothing and body coverage. Nakedness, whether partial or total, in a place of prayer is proscribed and modest attire mandated.[17]

For Muqātil, however, unlike most later commentators, that mandate applies beyond specifically Muslim places of prayer. In addition to the mosque of Mecca and other mosques, he expands its prescriptive scope to include Christian and Jewish prayer spaces.[18] In this, as in many other parts of both his complete commentary and this compendium of legal verses, one perceives a porousness or permeability of religious categories. The boundaries between Muslim and Christian or Muslim and Jew seem more fluid and there is less need felt to draw sharp lines of demarcation. Of course, it is precisely this inclusiveness, this willingness to allow Christian and Jewish narrative and practice a hermeneutical function in the interpretation of the Qur'ān that drew the ire of subsequent generations of Muslim scholars.

In the closing pages of his *Tafsīr al-khams mi'at āyah* Muqātil addresses one of the central self-reflective verses of the Qur'ān, Q.3:7, a verse that supplies some key categories in the taxonomies of *ʿulūm al-Qur'ān* and one that has generated a significant amount of contemporary scholarship. One of these categories is that of *al-āyāt al-muḥkamāt*,[19] a designation related linguistically and semantically to the terminology of *aḥkām*. Unlike later commentators within the classical *tafsīr* tradition, Muqātil provides a sharply circumscribed explanation for this category. The *āyāt muḥkamāt* are, he says, three verses towards the end of *sūrat al-Anʿām*, i.e. Q.6:151–153. The first two verses of this group – which Muqātil cites in full – contain a core of Qur'ānic "commandments" and are often discussed in combination with the much expanded core to be found in Q.17:22–39.[20] The third verse rhetorically underlines these divine imperatives: *And this is My straight path, so follow it.*

For Muqātil these are an instance of the "fortified verses" (*āyāt muḥkamāt*), those which can never be subject to subsequent abrogation. And, consistent with his penchant for inclusivity, he does not limit this to Islam but gathers Christianity and Judaism into its scope: "Nothing in all the books abrogates these *muḥkamāt* verses. They are *muḥkamāt* for the entirety of the children of Adam, all of them. They are the *umm al-kitāb*, i.e. the *aṣl al-kitāb*. They are called the *aṣl al-kitāb* simply because they are written in *al-lawḥ al-maḥfūẓ* and in all of the books."[21]

This is an important assertion, one which throws the whole interpretative agenda into a cross-traditional perspective. Muqātil's hermeneutical horizon clearly includes not only the Qur'ān but such previous revelations as the Tawrāh and the Injīl, in fact, "all the books which God has sent down on all the prophets."[22] Unequivocally, he posits a revelatory core to which people of any religion will be held accountable. But Muqātil does not close his consideration of Q.3:7 on a note of unlimited inclusivity. As yet another instance of the *āyāt muḥkamāt* he mentions Q.5:3. I will quote this section of his commentary in full because it nicely exemplifies the way in which the legal orientation of his smaller *tafsīr* allows him to create intratextual connections in a sustained argument:

> He said, in the *sūra* in which the table is mentioned [Q.5:3], *Today I have perfected your religion for you.* That means that God prescribed for the Muslims in Mecca the confession of faith that "There is no god but God and that Muḥammad is the messenger of God;" as well as belief in the Resurrection, in the Garden and in the Fire; and the ritual prayer, two bowings of the head and body in the morning and two in the evening. Then, before his *hijrah*, the five-fold daily prayer was prescribed for Muḥammad and the compulsory almsgiving – which does not have a time mandate – as well as abstention from fighting [during the sacred months]. After the Prophet had emigrated to Medina, all the religious duties were prescribed for him.
>
> Before the conquest of Mecca, the Muslims were accustomed to make the Pilgrimage from Medina in the company of the Arab polytheists. After Mecca was conquered and Abū Bakr al-Ṣiddīq led the people on the Pilgrimage and the general populace of Arab polytheists made the pilgrimage as well, 'Alī b. Abī Ṭālib recited nine verses from the beginning of *sūrat al-Barā'ah* to the people.[23] He recited [Q.9:28] *The polytheists (mushrikūn) are unclean (najas) so do not let them come near the Mosque of Mecca (al-masjid al-ḥarām) after this year of theirs.* The following year, therefore, when the Prophet made the farewell Pilgrimage none of the polytheists were with him. Thus on the Day of 'Arafah,[24] the

> Friday, [Q.5:3] *Today I have perfected for you your religion* – meaning its commands and prohibitions (*amrahu wa-nahyahu*) – was revealed. After that no verses with legal prescriptions [lit. no *ḥalāl* or *ḥarām*, *ḥudūd*, or *farīḍah*] were revealed other than two verses at the end of [sūra] *al-Nisā'*, [i.e. from Q.4:176], *They ask you for a legal pronouncement; say 'God has pronounced for you concerning distant kindred'* up to the end of the sūra. God said [Q.5:3 continued] *and I have completed My favour for you* meaning Islam, since you made the Pilgrimage without a polytheist in your company and *I have chosen* – meaning and I have selected – *for you Islam as a religion*. No religion is more pleasing to God than Islam. Then this verse, that is in the sūra in which the cow is mentioned, was revealed: [Q.2:281] *Guard yourselves against a day in which you will be returned to God; then every soul will be paid in full* – meaning whether a pious person or an evildoer – *what it has earned* – meaning of good and evil – *and they will not be dealt with unjustly* in [the recompense of] their deeds, with nothing taken from their good deeds or anything added to their evil deeds. After [the revelation of] this verse, the Prophet lived for nine more nights. Then he died two nights before [the end of the month of] Rabī' al-awwal.[25]

This extract from Muqātil's legal commentary embodies both an adroit piece of narrative exegesis and a skillful statement about religious boundaries Q.5:3 exemplifies the *āyāt muḥkamāt* both substantively and semantically. The concepts of "completing" and "perfecting," in conveying notions of closure, are linguistically linked to the sense of "consolidation" and "fortification" that *muḥkam* connotes. To explain that closure, Muqātil provides an intratextual connection with Q.9:28, the verse about "uncleanness," and offers the narrative embellishment that makes exclusion a condition of closure. Exclusion of the polytheists – an exclusion which later commentators extend to all non-Muslims – renews and retains the purity of the sacred shrine. In Muqātil's reading, revelatory closure is made consequent upon physical enclosure. The boundaries of faith, captured in the concise citation of *shahādah*, *ṣalāt*, *zakāt* etc., replicate themselves in geographical boundaries and the physical reinforces the ideological.

AL-JAṢṢĀṢ

Although not a native of Baghdād, Abū Bakr Aḥmad b. 'Alī al-Rāzī al-Jaṣṣāṣ moved there as a youth and spent most of his sixty-five years of life in that city.[26] In legal studies his primary mentor was Abū 'l-Ḥasan al-Karkhī and he studied *ḥadīth* with noted scholars in both Nīshāpūr and Baghdād, including Abū 'l-'Abbās al-Aṣamm (d. 346/957), 'Abd al-Bāqī b. Qāni' (d. 351/962) and al-Ṭabarānī (d. 360/971).[27] Eventually his expertise in law and *ḥadīth* secured him the leadership of the Baghdādī Ḥanafīs of his generation. The biographical works consistently cite his reputation for asceticism (*zuhd*),[28] linking that to the most regularly-repeated event from this *faqīh's* life, i.e. his refusal to accept appointment as chief *qāḍī* of Baghdād.[29] Apparently his inclination to live a life of semi-seclusion prompted him to decline this invitation. Allusions in his writing to dreams and visions indicate, in the eyes of his biographers, the results or consequences of this ascetical reclusivity.[30] He died in Baghdād in 370/981 and Muḥammad b. Mūsā al-Khwārizmī (d. 383/993) led the funeral prayers for him.[31]

Unlike that of Muqātil b. Sulaymān, the legal commentary of al-Jaṣṣāṣ, *Aḥkām al-Qur'ān*, follows the *sūra* and verse order of the Qur'ānic text rather than a topical arrangement. Yet within this textual ordering he provides frequent excursus on topics prompted by the verse under consideration. For example, in commenting upon Q.2:106, a basic reference for the doctrine of abrogation, al-Jaṣṣāṣ brings other relevant verses into the discussion and then provides an excursus on "The abrogation of the Qur'ān by the Sunnah and mention of the various modes of abrogation."[32]

To represent the exegetical style of this commentator, I have selected Q.5:51: *O you who believe, do not take the Jews and Christians as associates* (*awliyā'*);[33] *they can be associates for each other. Those of you who associate with them are part of them. Truly God does not guide a wrong-doing people.* Within the overall structure of his commentary al-Jaṣṣāṣ ordinarily sections his discussion of particular verses, usually beginning with *asbāb al-nuzūl*, and for this verse he mentions three different *asbāb* on the authority of 'Ikrimah (d. 105/723), al-Suddī (d. 128/745) and 'Aṭiyyah b. Sa'd (d. 111/729), respectively. Although he indicates no preference among them, the citations are interesting because of the implicit signification that they provide for the key concept of *wilāyah*. The first of these targets Abū Lubābah b. 'Abd al-Mundhir, one of the most influential men in Medina, who tried to warn the Banū Qurayẓah of their impending massacre,[34] while the second mentions a group of people who, in the aftermath of the Uḥud debacle, feared that the unbelievers would gain ascendancy over them. Consequently, according to the version of this account reproduced by al-Jaṣṣāṣ, "one man said, 'I'll support (*uwālī*) the Jews' while another said, 'I'll do so with the Christians'."[35] The final *sabab* strikes a similar note in describing a situation where one man elects to extricate himself from clientage relationships with the Jews while another, fearing dire consequences (*al-dawā'ir*), does not.

Apprehension and treachery, then, are the emotions connected with "taking the Jews and Christians as *awliyā'*. The narrative portrayals are entirely negative, intent upon describing the dangers and liabilities of a Muslim's association with members of these religious groups. At no point is the quite common meaning of *wilāyah* as "friendship," either mentioned directly or even implied. Nor is a connection made with the Qur'ānic use of *mawaddah*, i.e. "affection," as, for example, Q.60:7. The assumed affiliation represented by the term *wilāyah* is clearly that of clientage or contractual alliance.

Proceeding from contextual to lexical analysis, al-Jaṣṣāṣ glosses the singular form, *walī*, as *nāṣir*, meaning one who helps or assists, especially against a common enemy.[36] This general concept is then given legal specificity with reference to particular relationships, e.g., the *walī* of a minor or that of a woman. Building a logical argument on the basis of this lexical explanation, this Ḥanafī commentator next makes several important pronouncements. First, no non-Muslim should ever exercise custodial authority over a Muslim nor should a Muslim accept non-Muslim collaboration against adversaries. Secondly, non-believers (*kuffār*) should be treated as enemies "since *wilāyah* is the opposite of enmity. Because of their disbelief, therefore, we are ordered to treat the Jews and Christians as enemies."[37] Thirdly, as disbelievers, Christians, Jews and other non-Muslims share a common status because "all disbelief is one religious grouping (*millah*) even if its forms of doctrine and practice differ (*wa-in ikhtalafat madhāhibuhu wa-ṭuruquhu*)."[38]

Continuing with his interpretation of this Qur'ānic imperative, al-Jaṣṣāṣ uses the phrase *they are associates for each other* as an explanation for the permissibility of marriage, commensality and inheritance among Christians and Jews. He further affirms the legal equivalency of Arab and non-Arab Christians: "The legal status (*ḥukm*) of the Christians of the Banū Taghlib is that of the Christians of the Banū Isrā'īl in terms of eating their sacrificial animals and marrying their women."[39] This latter point raises the interesting issue of the Taghlibī Christians and the question of whether ethnicity should be a factor in evaluating the legal status of non-Muslims.[40]

The final concerns occasioned by this verse centre, for al-Jaṣṣāṣ, on matters of apostasy and inheritance. These, in turn, are prompted by the rhetorical conundrum posed by the second sentence. Are the people being addressed by the declarative *those of you who associate with them are part of them* the same as those addressed at the beginning of the verse? If both are addressed to the believers, i.e. the Muslims, then the second sentence is a statement that Muslims who establish these forms of affiliation with Christians and Jews become, by that action, apostates. The legal consequences of apostasy, especially with regard to inheritance, thus enter the agenda.[41] If, on the other hand, this second sentence is addressed to the Arab polytheists, then the issue of their legal status upon conversion to Christianity or Judaism comes to the fore.

To further complicate the discussion, al-Jaṣṣāṣ points to the situation of someone within a particular religious tradition who holds unorthodox views. To use the example that he offers, what happens if a Muslim, without actually removing himself from the community, adheres to certain beliefs that could provoke the charge of *kāfir*? Can one still eat the meat that he has slaughtered or could a Muslim woman still marry him? Is a Muslim permitted to inherit from such a person? All of these questions are drawn from the imperative *do not take the Jews and Christians as associates* and from the implications of *they can be associates for each other*. Their suggestion and adjudication represent both the range and complexity of juridical detail that this Ḥanafī jurisprudent perceives in the Qur'ānic text.[42]

ILKIYĀ AL-HARRĀSĪ

'Alī b. Muḥammad b. 'Alī Ilkiyā[43] Abū 'l-Ḥasan al-Ṭabarī al-Harrāsī[44] was born in Ṭabaristān in 450/1058 and began his education there. For more advanced work, however, at the age of twenty he moved to Nīshāpūr.[45] There he studied *fiqh* with 'Abd al-Malik al-Juwaynī (d. 478/1085) at the Niẓāmiyyah *madrasah* that Niẓām al-Mulk had founded there for the Imām al-Ḥaramayn. Another of al-Juwaynī's students during this same period was Abū Ḥāmid al-Ghazālī (d. 505/1111) and this teacher is reported to have said about his students' debating talents that al-Khawāfī[46] excelled in precision (*taḥqīq*), al-Ghazālī in diction (*jarayān*) and Ilkiyā in exposition (*bayān*).[47] According to the biographical sources, Ilkiyā al-Harrāsī then spent some time in the Khurāsānī district of Bayhaq before a final move to Baghdād. There, in 493/1100, he received a teaching appointment at the Niẓāmiyyah, which he held until his death in 504/1110.[48] Among his more noted students were Sa'd al-Khayr al-Anṣārī, 'Abdallāh b. Muḥammad b. Ghullāb al-Anbārī and Abū Ṭāhir al-Silafī (d. 576/1180).[49]

Ibn al-Jawzī mentions that during his tenure at the Niẓāmiyyah in Baghdād, Ilkiyā al-Harrāsī was accused of Ismāʿīlī tendencies and was reproached for this. A group of his colleagues, however, sprang to his defence, including his older contemporary, the Ḥanbalī jurist, Abū 'l-Wafā' b. ʿAqīl (d. 513/1119).[50] In speaking of Ilkiyā's eventual exoneration, al-Subkī suggests that the situation originated in a confusion of names, i.e. that the Niẓārī Ismāʿīlī *dāʿī* Ḥasan al-Ṣabbāḥ, commander of the rock fortress of Alamūt, also bore the *laqab* Ilkiyā.[51]

In the introduction to his *Aḥkām al-Qur'ān* Ilkiyā al-Harrāsī extols the Shāfiʿī legal teaching as "the most apposite, most correct, most discriminating and most judicious of madhhabs."[52] He vigorously defends its positions throughout his commentary and, on occasion, takes issue with what he regards to be the misreading of al-Shāfiʿī to be found in the *Aḥkām* of al-Jaṣṣāṣ.[53] To exemplify his exegesis I have selected Q.9:29, which begins *Fight those who do not believe in God or the Last Day.* This verse ranks as the primary proof-text for classical justifications of a capitation (*al-jizyah*) levied upon the *ahl al-kitāb*.[54] Eligibility for such taxation is tied to the phrase *those who were given the book,* a common Qur'ānic expression for the Christians and Jews.[55] Ilkiyā al-Harrāsī's commentary on this verse provides neither *asbāb al-nuzūl* nor lexical specification as introduction but proceeds immediately to an intratextual argument. Al-Harrāsī reads Q.9:29 within the broader mandate of Q.9:5's command to *kill the polytheists* (*mushrikūn*). Pairing it with the Prophet's statement that "I was ordered to fight people until they say 'There is no god but God'" and with Q.8:39, *Fight them until there is no dissension* (*fitnah*) *and all religion belongs to God*, provides him with a tripartite proof for taking Q.9:5's imperative as predominant.

Fundamentally, the motivating concern is that of category formation. Do the Christians and Jews fall within the classification of the "polytheists"? This Shāfiʿī commentator would insist that they do. Further, he argues that the scope of Q.9:5 applies to the *ahl al-kitāb*, even if it is read in isolation from the other two supporting texts. To maintain this position, however, he must counter the objection that could be raised by those who want to give the verse a more restricted applicability. Basing themselves on Q.22:71's explicit listing of six classifications, i.e. *those who believe*, the Jews, the Ṣābi'ūn,[56] the Christians, and the Majūs, all of whom are mentioned in addition to the polytheists (*mushrikūn*), these exegetes would argue that the term *mushrikūn*, even in Q.9:5, must be restricted to those who actually worship idols.[57] Al-Harrāsī answers this with the assertions of those who make the charge of polytheism (*shirk*) against particular beliefs of these various religious groups. The Christians, for example, are *mushrikūn* because their "worshipping God involves worshipping the Messiah."[58]

Not unexpectedly, these positions are confirmed with a glance at the pages in which al-Harrāsī's treats Q.9:5 itself. This verse, which has been dubbed "the verse of the sword," is frequently cited in works about abrogation (*al-nāsikh wa-l-mansūkh*) because of the large number of verses that it is said to abrogate.[59] Al-Harrāsī begins his treatment of the phrase *kill the polytheists* (*mushrikūn*) by mentioning a number of these. Continuing his commentary, he underscores the obligation of killing "all the *mushrikūn*, such as the *ahl al-kitāb* and others (*qatl kāffat al-mushrikīn min ahl al-kitāb wa-ghayrihim*)" and connects the conditional clause in the second part of Q.9:5 with the qualifications that legitimate accepting the *jizyah*.[60]

Within the context of this intratextual determination, al-Harrāsī's Shāfi'ī interpretation of Q.9:29 takes shape around issues of inclusion and of justification. For example, since the phrase *those who were given the book* does not have the specificity of designations like al-Yahūd (the Jews) or al-Naṣārā (the Christians), how far can it be stretched? Can the Majūs, to take one particular case, be considered *ahl al-kitāb*? Given al-Harrāsī's geographical context and the long history and continuing demographic presence of Zoroastrianism in that region, it is not surprising that this subject would capture his attention. His elliptical remarks, clearly intended for an audience that was fully aware of the various positions on this question, finally focus on a decision that the Majūs cannot be included among the *ahl al-kitāb*. One proof text that he uses to support this stance is Q.6:156, *the book was only revealed to two groups before us*, the "two groups" being understood as a reference to the Jews and the Christians.[61]

The preoccupying debate to which al-Harrāsī is obviously responding in this commentary presses the limits of Q.9:29's applicability. *Kāfir* (unbeliever) as simply meaning a non-Muslim, is the most comprehensive category within which the debate is engaged. Aside from the Arab *mushrikūn* can the *jizyah* option be extended to include all other non-believers? No, replies al-Harrāsī, because the verse offers several qualifying descriptives about specific beliefs and behaviours. But this response, in turn, leads to the question of how the Christians and Jews could ever be described as not believing in God. Here the rejoinders fall into two groups. Either it is a matter of insufficient or inaccurate belief, i.e. belief that falls short of that held by Muslims, or the descriptive *who do not believe in God* is being used as a disparagement. For the latter, al-Harrāsī offers the example of Q.5:51, without actually citing this verse. Muslims who ally themselves with the unbelievers could be similarly denounced.

Beyond these matters of inclusion, of the range of applicability that can be legitimately tied to this verse, al-Harrāsī broaches the topic of justification. Put briefly, this dispute centres around the problem of conversion and what constitutes the conditions conducive to it. If some non-believers can pay a tax in lieu of embracing Islam, does this not leave them at the mercy of their unbelief and amount to the abdication of a primary Muslim responsibility? In defence of the *jizyah* this Shāfi'ī exegete argues that it is only an interim measure, one that presupposes the eventual conversion of those upon whom it is levied. The humiliation mandated to accompany its payment – *until they give the jizyah from/to hand* (*'an yadin*) *and/when they are humbled* (*ṣāghirūn*) – supplies powerful motivation for that conversion.[62]

IBN AL-'ARABĪ

Abū Bakr Muḥammad b. 'Abdallāh al-Ma'āfirī who is known as Ibn al-'Arabī was born in Seville in 468/1076 and received his early education from his maternal uncle, al-Ḥasan b. 'Umar al-Hawzanī, and various other Mālikī scholars in Andalusia. His father Abū Muḥammad, who was noted for his skill in rhetoric and composition, was a close associate of the Ẓāhirī theologian Ibn Ḥazm.[63] Ibn al-'Arabī himself, however, not only did not share his father's regard for Ibn Ḥazm but actively disliked him and spoke disparagingly of him.[64]

At the age of 17, Ibn al-'Arabī travelled east with his father to study in Baghdād and Damascus. Four years later he made the pilgrimage to Mecca and then returned to Baghdād where his teachers included the famous philosopher and theologian Abū Ḥāmid al-Ghazālī (d. 505/1111). According to some accounts he went home to Andalusia in 491/1098 at the age of 23, while other versions place his return somewhat later, after the death of his father in Jerusalem.[65] His modern biographers enjoy repeating the opinion, attributed to his contemporary 'Iyāḍ b. Mūsā (d. 544/1149), that Ibn al-'Arabī returned to Seville from his journey to the east with more knowledge than anyone who had ever made the trip before him.[66]

During his years in Seville, he was appointed *qāḍī*, serving with distinction in this position. Eventually, however, he left this post and, during the final years of al-Murābiṭūn rule, devoted himself to scholarly pursuits.[67] With the al-Muwaḥḥidūn conquest, Ibn al-ʻArabī was taken to North Africa for a period of imprisonment. He died there in 543, as he was leaving Marrakesh, and his body was taken to Fez for burial.[68]

As with al-Jaṣṣāṣ and Ilkiyā al-Harrāsī, the Mālikī commentary of Ibn al-ʻArabī covers the entire Qur'ān but treats only those verses that have legal implications. Unlike his predecessors, however, this commentator enumerates both the number of relevant verses within each *sūra* and the number of issues or topics for each verse that he treats. These topics can include the standard fare of any commentary, such as lexical identification and *asbāb al-nuzūl*, as well as the opinions of other Mālikī scholars or of those whom they seek to refute.[69]

Among the verses related to the Christians that this legal commentary includes is Q.9:28 and its reference to non-Muslim "uncleanness." Ritual purity is an important part of Muslim liturgical life and Q.9:28 speaks to the status of non-believers in this regard: *O you who believe, the unbelievers* (*mushrikūn*) *are unclean* (*najas*) *so do not let them come near the Mosque of Mecca after this year of theirs. If you fear becoming poor* (*ʻaylah*), *God will enrich you from his bounty, if He wills. Truly God is all-knowing and all-wise*. Ibn al-ʻArabī introduces his consideration of this verse with *asbāb al-nuzūl* that connect its imperative with Meccan trading practices.[70] Because the *mushrikūn* were a commercial presence in Mecca, the loss of revenue consequent upon their exclusion was, according to one account that he presents, compensated for by the collection of the *jizyah*.[71]

The more central considerations relative to ritual purity were, for Ibn al-ʻArabī those of legal definition and of juridical extension. First he clarifies the fact that the charge of "unclean" (*najas*), the status of "impurity" (*najāsah*), has nothing to do with a perceptible substance or essence; rather it is a legal valuation (*ḥukm sharʻī*).[72] He likens it to the status of minor or major *ḥadath*, a status that must be rectified before such ritual activity as the *ṣalāt*. As sparring partner for this point, Ibn al-ʻArabī uses the Ḥanafiyyah who have been, in his words, "befuddled" about this, confusing essential and legally-defined impurity.

Beneath this distinction lie certain jurisprudential concerns to which Ibn al-ʻArabī does not directly allude in his commentary on Q.9:28. Put simply, the problem is the status of those defined as "unclean" at the point of conversion to Islam. If the status were one of essence, as is the case with certain animals and bodily excretions, then conversion could not void it. Additionally, the question of contamination surfaced in the legal and exegetical literature. In his commentary on this verse Ilkiyā al-Harrāsī, for example, asks whether the touch of unbelievers can defile water or cooking utensils.[73]

But having settled the matter of definition, what about that of juridical extension? Does this legally-defined status prohibit entrance only to the Meccan sanctuary or is the restriction broader than that? Ibn al-ʿArabī argues analogically, by defining *najāsah* as the common attribute (i.e. the *ʿillah* or *ratio legis*), that a proper understanding of Q.9:28 must inevitably exclude the non-believers from all places that share the sacrosanctity of a *masjid* (*kull mawḍiʿ muḥtaram bi-l-masjidiyyah*).[74] All mosques, then, are off-limits to non-believers. Ibn al-ʿArabī does, however, mention other adjudications of this issue. While al-Shāfiʿī maintains the absolute prohibition against entrance to the central mosque of Mecca, according to him the non-believers can enter other mosques for reasons of necessity. Abū Ḥanīfah, as reported by Ibn al-ʿArabī, does not even impose the restriction of necessity.

Such views this Mālikī exegete dismisses as utterly mistaken and to underscore their absurdity, he offers a personal anecdote:

> In Damascus I used to see a strange sight. The large congregational mosque there has two doors, an eastern door, which is the Bāb Jayrūn, and a western door. People were in the habit of using the mosque as a pathway, walking through it all day long in their everyday affairs. When a *dhimmī* wanted to pass through, he would stop at the door until a passing Muslim went by. Then the *dhimmī* would say to him, "O Muslim, may I have your permission to go through with you?" The Muslim would respond positively so the *dhimmī* would enter with him, all the while wearing the badge (*ghiyār*), the sign of the *ahl al-dhimmah*. If the mosque custodian saw the *dhimmī* he would shout at him, "Go back, go back!" But the Muslim would tell him, "I have given him permission," and so the caretaker would leave him alone.[75]

AL-MIQDĀD AL-ḤILLĪ

Muḥammad Bāqir al-Khwānsārī, author of the Shīʿī biographical work, *Rawḍāt al-jannāt*, gives the full name of the final author to be discussed in this article as al-Miqdād b. ʿAbdallāh b. Muḥammad b. al-Ḥusayn b. Muḥammad al-Suyūrī al-Ḥillī al-Asadī. Beyond this and the usual list of honorifics, however, he provides very little detail about his life. Muḥammad b. Makkī al-ʿĀmilī, a noted scholar of *fiqh* and of *uṣūl al-fiqh* who is known as *al-Shahīd al-Awwal* (d. 786/1384), is mentioned as his principal teacher. In addition to his legal commentary entitled *Kanz al-ʿirfān*, the most frequently cited title among his many works is an expository treatise on *Nahj al-mustarshidīn fī uṣūl al-dīn* by the famous Shīʿī theologian ʿAllāma-i Ḥillī (d. 726/1325).[76] The biographical sources suggest that his *nisbah*, "al-Suyūrī," is derived either from one of the villages near Ḥillah, a town that lies midway between Baghdād and al-Kūfah, or from the plural form of the word "*sayr*", meaning a strip of leather.[77] These same sources place al-Miqdād al-Ḥillī's death and burial in Baghdād in 826/1423.

His work of legal exegesis, *Kanz al-ʿirfān*, gained an early and enduring reputation for this scholar. Subsequent works of this genre, like Aḥmad b. Muḥammad al-Ardabīlī's (d. 993/1585) *Zubdat al-bayān fī aḥkām al-Qur'ān*, claim indebtedness to it.[78] As with Muqātil's *Tafsīr khams mi'at āyah min al-Qur'ān*, the commentary with which this article began, al-Miqdād al-Ḥillī's work is arranged according to *fiqh* categories rather than according to the verse order of the Qur'ān. He occasionally introduces these discreet chapters, e.g. *al-ṣawm* or *al-ḥajj*, with a lexical and legal explanation of the term itself. For comparative purposes I will use the verse just discussed, i.e. Q.9:28, in order to explore the Shīʿī perspective that this commentary can provide. Al-Miqdād al-Ḥillī treats this verse in the first chapter, that on ritual purification (*al-ṭahārah*). What characterises his interpretation is comprehensiveness of both person and place.

He begins and ends his remarks on Q.9:28 with statements whose combined implication indicates that this proscription applies to all non-Muslims. There is no difference between the *mushrikūn* and the rest of the unbelievers with respect to their essential uncleanliness.[79] To emphasise this, he speaks specifically of the Christians and Jews in their joint status as *ahl al-dhimmah*. His argument follows the textual logic of word placement and selection. Starting with Q.9:30's accusation that *The Jews say ʿUzayr is the son of God and the Christians say the Messiah is the son of God*, al-Miqdād al-Ḥillī then ties this to the concluding phrase of Q.9:31, *may He be exalted above what they associate [with Him]*. Use of the verb "associate" (*yushrikūna*) gives him the lexical leverage to equate the Jews and Christians with the *mushrikūn*.[80]

Comprehensivity of person is matched in this Shīʿī commentator by comprehensivity of place. All mosques are off-limits to non-believers, not just the Meccan sanctuary. While basing this interpretation on unequivocal statements (*nuṣūṣ*) from the *ahl al-bayt,* especially 'Alī, al-Miqdād al-Ḥillī recognises divergent, albeit false, ways of reasoning about this. He particularly debates the stances adopted by al-Shāfi'ī and Abū Ḥanīfah, insisting upon the cogency of the most restrictive reading of this text. The inescapable connection between person and place could not permit him to rule otherwise.

For the uncleanliness of the non-believers is not a matter of legal status but of essence (*najāsah 'ayniyyah lā ḥukmiyyah*). Al-Miqdād al-Ḥillī notes that some jurisprudents view it as a function of major ritual impurity (*janābah*), such as seminal emission, or of contact with impure substances or even adopt a more metaphorical understanding by attributing this "uncleanness" to the pollution of bad beliefs. He, however, holds it to be intrinsic. The non-believers are, in effect, themselves an impure substance and, citing his quotation of al-Ḥasan al-Baṣrī, "Whoever shakes hands with a non-believer (*mushrik*) must perform the *wuḍū'*." Even "were they to wash their bodies seventy times" they could not rid themselves of this inherent pollution.[81]

CONCLUSION

Certainly, no comprehensive conclusions need be drawn from this series of case studies. The purpose of their presentation is primarily didactic and demonstrative. This genre of legally-focused exegetical literature has never been systematically studied, neither in its totality nor for the light that it could shed on the more specific subject of Muslim views of Christianity. That larger enterprise would require several lines of both synchronic and diachronic investigation. Source analysis and the historical contextualisation of individual authors and their works should be balanced with a comparative view of two larger bodies of Islamic literature, i.e. the full-scale *tafsīr* tradition and the library of classical *fiqh*. Yet the preliminary soundings that these case studies represent suggest some characteristic emphases to be found in this genre of legal commentaries.

The task of definition stands central. Upon it depends the applicability of particular Qur'ānic prescriptions. As these case studies repeatedly reveal, category formation pushes away from plurality toward binary opposition. For example, such status distinctions as Christians, Jews, *ahl al-kitāb*, *ahl al-dhimmah*, etc. dissolve into the undifferentiated classification of *kuffār* or *mushrikūn*. Like virtually the entire commentary tradition on the Qur'ān, this subgenre displays an air of authorial collectivity. While an individual name may grace the title page, the text itself carries both a cumulative and a dialectical quality. Cumulatively, it conveys the exegetical consensus of its *madhhab*, a consensus forged over generations. Dialectically, it engages with other *madhhabs* in pressing the legitimacy, if not the pre-eminence, of its own jurisprudential stance.

But, especially in the later works, the lines of competitive ideological engagement have become more pronounced and more elliptical. The broader contours of an issue need no longer sketched because sufficient background in both *tafsīr* and *fiqh* is presumed. By the time of Ibn al-ʿArabī, for instance, the debates were several centuries old and they were strictly intramural debates. As these legal exegetes reflect upon Qur'ānic references to Christians, they do so within a closed system. The task of definition, of assessing applicability, may be refined in the dialectical exchange of the various schools of law but it never breaches the binary boundary between believer and non-believer.

NOTES

1 Jane D. McAuliffe, *Qur'ānic Christians. An Analysis of Classical and Modern Exegesis* (Cambridge: Cambridge University Press, 1991) and "Christians in the Qur'ān and Tafsīr," in *Muslim Perceptions of Other Religions Throughout History*, ed. J. Waardenburg (New York: Oxford University Press, 1999) pp. 105–121.

2 The above-cited works contain relevant bibliography. Of recent interest is Yūsuf Khūrī, *'Īsā wa-Maryam fī-l-Qur'ān wa-l-tafsīr* (Amman: Royal Institute for Interfaith Studies, 1996) which reproduces Qur'ānic passages and their commentary as drawn from a wide selection of both classical and modern commentators.

3 Some quite recent British publications that exemplify this are Hugh Goddard, *Muslim Perceptions of Christianity* (London: Grey Seal, 1996), Kate Zebiri, *Muslims and Christians Face to Face* (Oxford: Oneworld, 1997), Ataullah Siddiqui, *Christian-Muslim Dialogue in the Twentieth Century* (London: Macmillan Ltd., 1997).

4 A fourth, the Mālikī Abū ʿAbdallāh Muḥammad b. Aḥmad al-Qurṭubī, (d. 671/1272), is ordinarily included with these others. His *al-Jāmiʿ li-aḥkām al-Qur'ān*, a very important work within the classical exegetical tradition with much legal interpretation, is actually a full-scale commentary, i.e. one whose scope comprehends the entire Qur'ān, not simply those verses with legal implications. Similarly *Zād al-masīr fī ʿilm al-tafsīr* by Abū l-Faraj ʿAbd al-Raḥmān b. ʿAlī, Ibn al-Jawzī (d. 597/1200), another full-scale commentary, is considered a source of Ḥanbalī legal exegesis

5 Cf. Muḥammad Ḥusayn al-Dhahabī, *al-Tafsīr wa-l-mufassirūn*, 3rd printing (Cairo: Maktabat Wahbah, 1405/1985), pp. 414–453; Fahd b. ʻAbd al-Raḥmān b. Sulaymān al-Rūmī, *Uṣūl al-tafsīr wa-manāhijuhu* (Riyadh: Maktabat al-Tawbah, 1413/1992), pp. 91–95; Mannāʻ Khalīl al-Qaṭṭān, *Mabāḥith fī ʻulūm al-Qur'ān* (Beirut: Mu'assasat al-Risālah, 1414/1993), pp. 377–380

6 Wael Hallaq, *A History of Islamic Legal Theories: An Introduction to Sunnī Uṣūl al-fiqh* (Cambridge: Cambridge University Press, 1977), p. 10.

7 This is the figure given in the introduction to the standard Cairo edition on the authority of such sources as *Nāẓimat al-zuhr* by Abū 'l-Qāsim al-Shāṭibī (d. 590/1194) and Shaykh Muḥammad al-Mutawallī's *Taḥqīq al-bayān.*

8 There is variation, of course, in the way that each of these legal exegetes defines his task and selects the specific verses that he will include in his commentary and it would be interesting, if time-consuming, to correlate the full selections made by all of these authors. Having done this for a total of sixty verses relevant to the Qur'ānic depiction of Christianity, I found considerable variation in coverage.

9 Ignaz Goldziher, *Muhammedanische Studien* (Halle: Max Niemeyer, 1888–90), 2:206; see also his *Die Richtungen der islamischen Koranauslegung* (Leiden: E.J. Brill, 1920), pp. 58–60.

10 Louis Massignon, *Recueil de textes inédits concernant l'histoire de la mystique en pays d'Islam* (Paris: Librairie Orientaliste Paul Geuthner, 1929), pp. 194–210; Paul Nwyia, *Exégèse coranique et langage mystique. Nouvel essai sur le lexique technique des mystiques musulmans* (Beirut: Dar El-Machreq, 1970); John Wansbrough, *Quranic Studies. Sources and Methods of Scriptural Interpretation* (Oxford:Oxford University Press, 1977); Isaiah Goldfeld, "Muqātil Ibn Sulaymān," *Arabic and Islamic Studies* (Bar Ilan) 2 (1978): xiii–xxx; Claude Gilliot, "Muqātil, grand exégetè, traditionniste et théologien maudit," *Journal asiatique* 279 (1991): 39–92.

11 Ibn Ḥazm, *al-Faṣl fī-l-milal wa-l-ahwā' wa-l-niḥal,* ed. Muḥammad Ibrāhīm Naṣr and ʻAbd al-Raḥmān ʻUmayrah (Riyadh: Sharikat Maktabāt ʻUkāẓ, 1402/1982), 2:269. In an earlier passage (2:235), Ibn Ḥazm mentions Muqātil in connection with flawed forms of *ḥadīth* collection and transmission.

12 Shams al-Dīn al-Dhahabī, *Ta'rīkh al-Islam*, ed. ʻUmar ʻAbd al-Salām Tadmurī (Beirut: Dār al-Kitāb al-ʻArabī, 1988), years 141–160, pp. 639–42.

13 Nwyia, *Exégèse coranique*, p. 27.

14 Gilliot, "Muqātil," p. 39, note 1.

15 Muqātil b. Sulaymān, *Tafsīr Muqātil b. Sulaymān*, ed. ʻAbdallāh Maḥmūd Shiḥātah (Cairo: al-Hay'ah al-Misriyyah al-ʻAmmah li-l-Kitāb, 1979), 1:25. C.H.M. Versteegh has described this as as "by far the most independent and interesting of the early commentaries." *Arabic Grammar and Qur'ānic Exegesis in Early Islam* (Leiden: Brill 1993), p. 130.

16 Ibn al-Jawzī, *Zād al-masīr*, 3:186–87; according to this account the woman would cover her private parts with a leather girdle. Further to this see E. Graf, *Jagdbeute und Schlachttier im islamischen Recht* (Bonn:

Orientalischen Seminars der Universität Bonn, 1959), pp. 29–33 and M.J. Kister, "Labbayka, Allāhumma, labbayka...: On a Monotheistic Aspect of a Jāhiliyya Practice," *Jerusalem Studies in Arabic and Islam* 2 (1980), p. 40.

17 Muqātil b. Sulaymān al-Balkhī, *Tafsīr al-khams mi'at āyah min al-Qur'ān* (ed). I. Goldfeld (Shfaram: al-Mashriq Press, 1980), p. 42.

18 Muqātil apparently understands *masjid* in this verse to mean simply "a place of worship."

19 This phrase, which can be provisionally translated as "secured/fortified verses," became, along with its correlate *al-āyāt al-mutashābihāt*, a prime focus of hermeneutical attention. Among the more important recent studies is that of Wansbrough, *Qur'ānic Studies*, pp.149–53. For the collected citation of earlier work see Rudi Paret, *Der Koran. Kommentar und Konkordanz* (Stuttgart: W. Kohlhammer, 1980), 60–61. Collectively, the following articles provide an extensive review of Muslim exegetical literature on this verse: Michel Lagarde, "De l'ambiguité *(mutašābih)* dans le Coran: tentatives d'explication des exégètes musulmans," *Quaderni di studi arabi* 3 (1985): 45–62; Leah Kinberg, "*Muḥkamāt* and *Mutashābihāt* (Koran 3/7): Implication of a Koranic Pair of Terms in Medieval Exegesis," *Arabica* 35 (1988): 143–72; Stefan Wild, "The Self-Referentiality of the Qur'an: Sura 3,7 as an Exegetical Challenge," in *With Reverence for the Word: Medieval Scriptural Exegesis in Judaism, Christianity and Islam*, ed. Jane D. McAuliffe et al. (New York: Oxford University Press, forthcoming). For a reading of this verse through the lens of contemporary critical theory, see Jane D. McAuliffe, "Text and Textuality: Q.3:7 as a Point of Intersection," in *Literary Structures of Religious Meaning in the Qur'ān*, ed. I. Boullata (London: Curzon Press, forthcoming).

20 Further to the Qur'ānic "decalogues" see Heinrich Speyer, *Die biblischen Erzälungen im Qoran* (1931; reprint, Hildesheim: Georg Olms, 1988), pp. 305–310 and W.M. Brinner, "An Islamic Decalogue," in *Studies in Islamic and Judaic Traditions*, W.M. Brinner and S.D. Ricks, eds. (Atlanta: Scholars Press, 1986), pp. 67–84.

21 Muqātil, *Tafsīr al-khams mi'at āyah*, p. 275.

22 On various aspects of intrascriptural relations see Jane D. McAuliffe, "The Abrogation of Judaism and Christianity in Islam: A Christian Perspective," *Concilium* (1994/3): 154–163; "The Qur'ānic Context of Muslim Biblical Scholarship," *Islam and Christian-Muslim Relations* 7 (1996): 141–158; "Ṭabarī's Prelude to the Prophet," in *Al-Ṭabarī: A Medieval Muslim Historian and his Work*, ed. Hugh Kennedy (Princeton: Darwin Press, forthcoming); "Assessing the Isrā'īliyyāt: An Exegetical Conundrum," in *Story-telling in the Framework of Non-fictional Arabic Literature*, ed. S. Leder (Wiesbaden: Harrassowitz Verlag, 1998) pp. 345–69.

23 If Q.9:1–9 is meant, this unit discusses treaty obligations with the *mushrikūn* and includes reference (Q.9:7) to treaties negotiated at *al-masjid al-ḥarām*.

24 The ninth day of the pilgrimage month.

25 Muqātil, *Tafsīr al-khams mi'at āyah*, pp. 275–77

26 al-Dhahabī, *Ta'rīkh al-Islām*, years 351–380, pp. 431–432. According to *Ta'rīkh Baghdād* he was born in 305 and moved to Baghdād in 325. Al-Khaṭīb al-Baghdādī, *Ta'rīkh Baghdād* (Beirut: Dār al-Kitāb al-'Arabī, n.d.), 4:314.
27 Shams al-Dīn Muḥammad b. Aḥmad al-Dhahabī, *Siyar a'lām al-nubalā'*, ed. Shu'ayb al-Arna'ūṭ et al. (Beirut: Mu'assasat al-Risālah, 1981–88), 16:340.
28 E.g. those already cited as well as Muḥammad b. 'Alī al-Dāwūdī, *Ṭabaqāt al-mufassirīn*, ed. 'Alī Muḥammad 'Umar (Cairo: Maktabat Wahbah, 1392/1972), 1:55.
29 al-Khaṭīb al-Baghdādī, *Ta'rīkh Baghdād*, 4:314.
30 al-Dhahabī, *Siyar*, 16:341 and *Ta'rīkh al-Islām*, years 351–380, p. 432.
31 al-Khaṭīb al-Baghdādī, *Ta'rīkh Baghdād*, 4:315.
32 Abū Bakr Aḥmad b. 'Alī al-Jaṣṣāṣ, *Aḥkām al-Qur'ān* (Beirut: Dār al-Fikr n.d.), p. 58f. For a discussion of al-Jaṣṣāṣ' exegetical methodology see Brannon Wheeler, *Applying the Canon in Islam: The Authorization and Maintenance of Interpretive Reasoning in Ḥanafī Scholarship* (Albany: State University of New York Press, 1996), pp. 109–113.
33 I have left the translation of *awliyā'* deliberately ambiguous so as not to prejudge the lexical specification that preoccupies commentary on this verse.
34 For the story of Abū Lubābah's betrayal and repentance, see Muḥammad b. Isḥāq, *Sīrat Rasūl Allāh* (recension of 'Abd al-Malik b. Hishām), ed. F. Wüstenfeld (Göttingen 1858–60), 1:686–87, trans. A. Guillaume, *The Life of Muhammad* (Oxford: Oxford University Press, 1955), pp. 462–63.
35 al-Jaṣṣāṣ, *Aḥkam*, 2:444.
36 For the frequent Qur'ānic linkage of these terms, see Q.4:45, 4:75, 4:73, 4:89, 9:116, 29:22, 33:17, etc.
37 Ibid.
38 Ibid. Further to this conception of unbelievers as one undifferentiated entity see the important new study by Y. Friedmann, "Classification of Unbelievers in Sunnī Muslim Law and Tradition," *Jerusalem Studies in Arabic and Islam* 22 (1998), especially pp. 164–65
39 al-Jaṣṣāṣ, *Aḥkām*, 2:444.
40 Cf. Friedmann, "Classification," pp. 170–77 and C. Gilliot, "Ṭabarī and les Chrétiens Taġlibites," *Annales du Département des Lettres Arabes (Université Saint-Joseph)* 6–B (1991–92):145–59.
41 Inheritance is the primary focus of the very brief comments that Ilkiyā al-Harrāsī (see following pages) makes on this verse. This Shāfi'ī jurisprudent states categorically, "*Those of you who associate with them are part of them* prevents the Muslim from inheriting from the apostate." Ilkiyā al-Harrāsī, *Aḥkām al-Qur'ān*, ed. Mūsā Muḥammad 'Alī and 'Izzah 'Alī 'Īd 'Aiyyah (Cairo: Dār al-Kutub al-Ḥadīthah, n.d.), 3:175.
42 For a discussion of Q.5:51 as interpreted by al-Ṭabarī, Fakhr al-Dīn al-Rāzī and the modern Shī'ī exegete, Muḥammad Ḥusayn Ṭabāṭabā'ī (d. 1982), see McAuliffe, "Christians in the Qur'ān and *tafsīr*." pp. 110–12 Ṭabāṭabā'ī departs significantly from the classical consensus on this verse.
43 Thus vocalized in al-Dhahabī, *Siyar*, 19:350 and *Ta'rīkh al-Islām*, years 501–510, p. 92–3, with the explanation that it is a non-Arabic word meaning a high-ranking person in a position of authority *(al-kabīr al-qadr, al-muqaddam)*. But cf. G. Makdisi, "al-Kiyā al-Harrāsī," *EI2*, 5:234.

44 Because of the close similarity of names, he is easily confused with the somewhat older *qāḍī* Abū al-Ḥasan 'Alī b. Muḥammad b. 'Alī al-Ṭabarī al-Āmulī. Ibn al-Ṣalāḥ, *Ṭabaqāt al-fuqahā' al-Shāfi'iyyah*, ed. Yaḥyā al-Dīn 'Alī Najīb (Beirut: Dār al-Bashā'ir al-Islāmiyyah, 1413/1992), 2:643 (no. 243) and 2:816 (of the appendix to it).

45 Ibn al-Dimyāṭī, *al-Mustafād min dhayl Ta'rīkh Baghdād lil Ibn al-Najjār*, ed. Muḥammad Mawlūd Khalaf (Beirut: Mu'assasat al-Risālah, 1406/1986), p. 348.

46 Aḥmad b. Muḥammad b. al-Muẓaffar al-Khawāfī, a Shāfi'ī jurisprudent. Al-Dhahabī, *Siyar*, 19:336, n. 4.

47 al-Dhahabī, *Siyar*, 19:351, as quoted on the authority of Ilkiyā's student, Abū Ṭāhir al-Silafī. In his biography of al-Ghazālī, al-Dhahabī cites another version of this: "Al-Ghazālī is an engulfing ocean *(baḥr mughriq)*, Ilkiyā is a quick-stalking lion *(asad muṭriq)* and al-Khawāfī is a scorching fire *(nār tuḥriq)*. *Siyar*, 19:336.

48 Ibn al-Dimyāṭī/Ibn al-Najjār, *Mustafād*, 348.

49 al-Dhahabī, *Ta'rikh*, years 501–510, p. 93.

50 'Abd al-Raḥmān b. 'Alīm, Ibn al-Jawzī, *al-Muntaẓam fī ta'rīkh al-mulūk wa-l-umam*, ed. Muḥammad and Muṣafā 'Abd al-Qādir 'Aṭā (Beirut: Dār al-Kutub al-'Ilmiyyah, 1412/1992), 18:122.

51 Tāj al-Dīn al-Subkī, *Ṭabaqāt al-Shāfi'iyyah al-kubrā* (Cairo: 'Īsā al-Bābī al-Ḥalabī, 1964–1976) 7:233.

52 Ilkiyā al-Harrāsī, *Aḥkām*, 1:20.

53 E.g. Ilkiyā al-Harrāsī, *Aḥkām*, 2:252f.

54 Further to this see Jane D. McAuliffe, "Fakhr al-Dīn al-Rāzī on *āyat al-jizyah* and *āyat al-sayf*," in *Conversion and Continuity: Indigenous Christian Communities in Islamic Lands, Eighth to Eighteenth Centuries*, eds. M. Gervers and R. Bihkazi (Toronto: Pontifical Institute of Mediaeval Studies, 1990), pp. 103–19.

55 For the different Qur'ānic expressions which, according to the commentators, provide direct or indirect allusion to the Christians and Jews, see McAuliffe, *Qur'ānic Christians*, pp. 2–4.

56 For identification theories and relevant bibliography see Jane D. McAuliffe, "Exegetical Identification of the Ṣābi'ūn," *The Muslim World* 72 (1982) 95–106 and Christopher Buck, "The Identity of the Ṣābi'ūn: An Historical Quest," *The Muslim World* 74 (1984): 172–186.

57 Ilkiyā al-Harrāsī, *Aḥkām*, 4:39.

58 *Ibid.*

59 David S. Powers, "The Exegetical Genre *nāsikh al-Qur'ān wa mansūkhuhu*," in *Approaches to the History of the Interpretation of the Qur'ān*, ed. A. Rippin (Oxford: Oxford University Press, 1988), pp. 117–138.

60 Ilkiyā al-Harrāsī, *Aḥkām*, 4:20.

61 Ilkiyā al-Harrāsī, *Aḥkām*, 4:39–40.

62 *Ibid* 4:43–47. For the views of F. Rosenthal, Claude Cahen et al. on the proper translation of *'an yadin* and *ṣāghirūn* see McAuliffe, "Fakhr al-Dīn al-Rāzī," pp. 108–10.

63 al-Dhahabī, *Siyar*, 19:130 for his biography.

64 al-Dhahabī, *Siyar*, 20:198.

65 al-Dhahabī, *Siyar*, 20:199. In another account (p. 201) his father's death is placed in Cairo at the beginning of 493/1100. Cf. J. Robson, s.v., *EI2*, 3:707.

66 Muḥammad al-Dhahabī, *al-Tafsīr wa-l-mufassirūn*, 2:469 and Muṣṭafā Ibrāhīm al-Mashnī, *Ibn al-'Arabī al-Mālikī al-Ishbīlī wa-tafsīruhu Aḥkām al-Qur'ān* (Amman: Dār al-'Ammār, 1411/1991), p. 24. Al-Mashnī (p. 26, n. 1) has collected more than two dozen references to this journey in Ibn al-'Arabī's commentary itself. His page numbers, however, do not correspond to the edition that I have used for this article but to an earlier Beirut edition issued by Dār al-Ma'rifah and edited by 'Alī Muḥammad al-Bajāwī.

67 Muḥammad b. 'Alī al-Dāwūdī, *Ṭabaqāt al-mufassirīn*, ed. 'Alī Muḥammad 'Umar (Cairo: Maktabat Wahbah, 1392/1972), 2:166.

68 al-Mashnī, *Ibn al-'Arabī*, p. 40.

69 For a comparison of Ibn al-'Arabī with other Andalusian exegetes, see Muṣṭafā Ibrāhīm al-Mashnī, *Madrasat al-tafsīr fī l-Andalus* (Beirut: Mu'assasat al-Risālah, 1406/1986).

70 For the probative value of the commentary tradition on this verse and relation to Q.2:198 (i.e. 2:194 in the author's use of the Flügel numbering), see Patricia Crone, *Meccan Trade and the Rise of Islam* (Princeton: Princeton University Press, 1987), p. 172.

71 Abū Bakr Muḥammad b. 'Abdallāh b. al-'Arabī, *Aḥkām al-Qur'ān*, edited by Muḥammad 'Abd al-Qādir 'Aṭā' (Beirut: Dār al-Kutub al-'Ilmiyyah, 1408/1988), 2:468.

72 Ibid., 2:468.

73 Ilkiyā al-Harrāsī, aḥkām, 4:36. Cf. Hava Lazarus-Yafeh, "Some Differences Between Judaism and Islam as Two Religions of Law," *Religion* 14 (1984): 183–84 and A. Kevin Reinhart, "Impurity/No Danger," *History of Religions* 30 (1990): 7–9.

74 Ibn al-'Arabī, *Aḥkām*, 2: 469.

75 Ibid., 2:470–71.

76 Muḥammad Bāqir al-Khwānsārī, *Rawḍāt al-jannāt*, ed. Asadullāh Ismā'īliyyān (Tehran: Maktabat Ismā'īliyān, 1390/1970), 7:171; Muḥammad b. al-Ḥasan al-Ḥurr al-'Amilī, *Amal al-āmil*, ed. Aḥmad al-Ḥusaynī (Baghdad: Maktabat al-Andalus, 1385/1965), 2:325.

77 The latter could imply some actual or ancestral connection to such trades as that of saddler or cobbler. al-Khwānsārī, *Rawḍāt*, 7:174.

78 Aḥmad b. Muḥammad al-Ardabīlī, *Zubdat al-bayān fī aḥkām al-Qur'ān* (Tehran: al-Maktabah al-Murtaḍawiyah, 1967), 703. See also Ḥusayn b. Muḥammad al-Kantūrī, *Kashf al-ḥujub* (Calcutta: Baptist Mission Press, 1912), 1:475, no. 2681.

79 Abū 'Abdallāh al-Miqdād b. 'Abdallāh al-Suyūrī al-Ḥillī, *Kanz al-'irfān fī fiqh al-Qur'ān* (Najaf: Dār al-Aḍwā', 1965), p. 40.

80 Ibid.

81 Ibid., p. 39–40.

4

The Doctrine of the Trinity in the Early Abbasid Era

David Thomas

In the centuries that followed the death of the Prophet Muḥammad in 632, Arab Muslim rule was extended over vast areas of the Middle East, North Africa, Spain, Persia and Central Asia. The empire that was administered successively from Medina, Damascus and Baghdad incorporated substantial populations of non-Muslims, among whom Christians were both numerous and often socially prominent. In some regions communities actually thrived under Islam, and were allowed to continue a semi-independent existence with their own religious hierarchies. In fact, for several centuries there were few signs of decline among the churches, and some indications that they enjoyed vigorous intellectual development.

In general, the first Muslim rulers accepted the existing social and administrative structures in the cities and towns which they occupied. This meant that in areas with largely Christian populations many middle- and high-ranking officials were Christian, and because bureaucratic positions were often passed down through families this situation persisted for generations. The example of the great theologian John of Damascus' family is well known: his grandfather, who as Byzantine governor surrendered Damascus to the Muslims in 635, his father, and John himself successively occupied senior posts in the administration of the Ummayad caliphs,[1] until John retired from public life in about 725, possibly under pressure from measures which were instituted by the caliphs partly in order to diminish the influence of non-Arabic speakers.[2]

There is also the example of Coptic officials in Egypt under the Fāṭimid caliphs of the tenth to twelfth centuries. These Christians were routinely removed from their senior positions in the state administration when a new ruler succeeded. But just as often they were brought back after an interval, for the plausible reason that they alone knew how to run the bureaucracy and they did not divulge their expertise outside their own families.[3]

By virtue of their knowledge and expertise, often as physicians, translators and teachers of science and philosophy, Christians were able to achieve respect and sometimes a measure of awe in Islamic society. The following complaint from the early ninth century Muslim author Abū ʿUthmān ʿAmr b. Baḥr al-Jāḥiẓ (d. 868) expresses exasperation at the way in which Christians in Baghdad seem to have taken advantage of the freedoms they were allowed and Muslims were only too ready to give them:

> As for the manifestations of the high social rank of the Christians, we know that they ride highly bred horses and dromedary camels, play polo, wear fashionable silk garments, and have attendants to serve them. They call themselves Ḥasan, Ḥusayn, ʿAbbās, Faḍl and ʿAlī, and also use their forenames; they have only now to call themselves Muḥammad, and to use his forename Abū al-Qāsim. And for doing this they are liked by the Muslims! Moreover, many of the Christians fail to wear their belts, while others hide their girdles beneath their outer garments. Many of their nobles refrain from paying tribute out of sheer pride. They return to Muslims insult for insult and blow for blow. But why should they not do this and even more, when our judges, or at least the majority of them, consider the blood of a patriarch or bishop equivalent to the blood of Jaʿfar, ʿAlī, ʿAbbās and Ḥamza?[4]

Even though there is probably a degree of exaggeration here, al-Jāḥiẓ's a complaint nevertheless suggests that Christians enjoyed a certain equality with their Muslim neighbours, who were quite unconcerned to stop them, even to the extent of applauding when they employed the names of revered early Muslim saints. His references to them hiding their girdles and refusing to pay the tribute relate to the legal requirements imposed upon Christians, who as technically client people, *Ahl al-dhimma* or *Dhimmīs*, were supposed among other things to distinguish themselves by wearing yellow belts (*zunnār*) and to pay tax in return for protection from their Muslim rulers.

With their occupation of positions of influence, and possession of knowledge and abilities that made them sought after, Christians in classical times frequently moved through Islamic society with a certain confidence. Of course, they were always subject to the legal restrictions imposed upon non-Muslims, and these were rigorously enforced from time to time. But it certainly appears that for about three or four centuries after the beginning of Islam they were not hampered or oppressed in any sustained or systematic way.[5]

In such circumstances as these, Christians and Muslims would have met for practical purposes on a more or less daily basis. And as well as matters of business, they must often have exchanged ideas and views about their respective religious outlooks. Certainly, by the late eighth century, when the first surviving records were written, each side had gained considerable knowledge of the other's main beliefs, and there was already an established tradition of refuting the points that seemed particularly repugnant. For Muslims there was no Christian teaching less palatable than the doctrine of the Trinity. The story of how Christians attempted to explain it in accessible forms, and their repeated failure to communicate, are both symptomatic of relations between Christians and Muslims in this period and indicative of how the one community was gradually absorbed intellectually into the thought world of the other.

Christians who lived within the boundaries of the Islamic empire were confronted by an alien faith expressed in what was to many of them a new language (there were, of course, Arabic speaking Christians well before the coming of Islam[6]), and according to strange modes of thought. They themselves were heirs to a long tradition of internal debates about the doctrine that stretched back through seven centuries, and the change in their circumstances was slow to exert an effect upon them. Hence, John of Damascus (died c. 748), whom we noted above, found it appropriate in mid-eighth century Palestine, where he withdrew from his public position at the Umayyad court, to express the doctrine of the Trinity in Greek in traditional formulations and vocabulary, as follows:

> In the Divinity we confess one nature (*physis*), while we hold three really existing Persons (*hypostaseis*). And we hold everything belonging to the nature and essence to be simple, while we recognise the difference of the Persons as residing only in the three properties of being uncaused and Father, of being caused and Son, and of being caused and proceeding. And we understand them to be inseparable and without interval between them, and united to one another and mutually immanent without confusion. And we understand them, while being separated without interval, to be united without confusion, for they are three even though they are united. For although each is subsistent in itself, that is to say is a perfect Person and has its own property or

> distinct manner of existence, they are united in their essence and natural properties and by their not being separated or removed from the Person of the Father, and they are one God and are so called.[7]

This gives in summary a statement that the Godhead is both one and three, simple and multiple, but it does not betray any awareness that an explanation is required of precisely how unity and plurality are possible in the same entity. It is evidently intended for an audience who share the author's presuppositions and technical vocabulary, and who seem to require no more than a brief description of the doctrine. John says at the beginning of the work in which this doctrine occurs: "I shall say nothing of my own, but I shall set down things which have been said in various places by wise and godly men."[8] He writes for fellow Christians in familiar forms and terminology, and is not aware of having to defend the doctrine at any length for anyone else.[9]

But other Christians did respond to the new situation, and began to look for appropriate ways of expressing the doctrine. At about the same time as John composed this account in Greek, one of the very first known attempts was being made to explain the Trinity in Arabic. The author of this work, the value of which has only recently been recognised,[10] is not known. But he was at ease in Arabic, and knew the Qur'ān well enough to quote from it. So he was clearly immersed in the thought and beliefs of the people among whom he lived. Like John, he was a Melkite.

This account of the Trinity is very different from John of Damascus' abstract brevity. The author quotes a number of passages in the Qur'ān and Bible from which divine plurality can be inferred, and illustrates the identity between one and three through analogies, such as the disk, rays and heat of the sun, the soul, mind and spirit of the human, and the body, branches and fruit of a tree.[11] These are his main forms of explaining the doctrine, rather than a technical exposition in theological language.

But though he does not make a detailed formulation of the doctrine, the author is evidently aware of having to express his beliefs in a way that may be understandable to people who do not accept them. For in addition to his quotations from Christian and Muslim scripture and the analogies, he also hints at a form of understanding the Trinity which Muslims might appreciate. In a number of places he says that God, the creative Word, *al-kalima al-khāliqa*, and the life-giving Holy Spirit, *al-rūḥ al-muqaddas al-muḥyī*, are one and indistinguishable,[12] by which he seems to indicate that God acts and expresses himself through his Word and Spirit, which are eternal and somehow intrinsic to his being. He indicates more clearly what he means when he says: God was always in his Word and Spirit, and his Word and Spirit were with God and in God, *wa-lākinna Allahu mundhu qaṭṭu bi-kalimatihi wa rūḥihi, wa-kānat kalimatuhu wa-rūḥuhu 'inda Allahi wa-bi-Allah.*[13] The notion of God being in his Word and Spirit and they being with him and in him recapitulates John of Damascus' description of the hypostases being "united to one another and mutually immanent," though there is a small but significant shift in understanding. For here the strict equality of the Persons in John has become the somewhat different form of God possessing Word and Spirit as functional qualities of his being. While John's insistence upon mutual co-inherence of the Persons is preserved, the Word and Spirit have here become more definitely subordinated to the being of God himself.

Towards the end of the eighth century the Nestorian Patriarch Timothy I of Baghdad (d. 823) wrote an account of a long discussion lasting two days which had been held in the year 791 between himself and the Abbasid Caliph al-Mahdī. The Caliph had asked him many searching questions about his faith, including some on the doctrine of the Trinity. In his replies Timothy takes slightly further the explanation offered above, when he says that the Word and the Spirit are inseparable from God, since otherwise God would not be rational and living:

> If one, therefore, ventures to say about God that there was a time when he had no Word or Spirit, such a one would blaspheme against God, because his saying would be equivalent to asserting that there was a time in which God had no reason and no life. If such adjectives are considered blasphemy and abomination when said of God, it follows that God begat the Word in a divine and eternal way, as a source of wisdom, and had the Spirit proceeding from eternally and without any beginning, as a source of life.[14]

Timothy makes it plain here that God's Word and Spirit endow his essence with the characteristics of reason and life which make him wise and living. Later in the discussion he amplifies this by explaining that the Father perceives and knows himself through his Word and Spirit, though because "the Father is in the Son and the Son in the Spirit" there is no separation between them, just as a human soul is in the reason and the reason in the mind, or the sun's disk is in its light and its light in its heat; in fact it is as impossible to conceive of God without his Word and Spirit as it is to think of the sun without light or a soul without reason and mind.[15] He suggests that the Word and Spirit are the means by which God is percipient, and are integral to his being as God.

This account is rather more than a description of the Christian doctrine. It is an attempt to explain how the divinity must necessarily be also plural, as having life and reason, if he is to be existentially viable. It thus introduces a new element into the articulation of the doctrine in making a connection between these characteristics and the Word and Spirit, which appear to function as eternal attributes within the being of the Godhead.[16]

Here and in the earlier anonymous account, the Trinity comprises Father as origin with Son-Word and Spirit-Life deriving from him and characterising him. This model places little emphasis on the substance or on equality of the hypostases, and seems primarily intended to preserve the strict unity of the Godhead as one being who possesses two attributes. Whether it was employing earlier Christian teachings about the doctrine,[17] or presenting an articulation that could be more easily explained and defended to Muslims is not clear. But we shall see shortly how other Arabic-speaking Christians developed it further, and continued this attempt to explain the Trinity in a Muslim context.

At the same time as Arabic-speaking Christians were making these attempts to explain and defend the Trinity, Muslim authors were recording the earliest surviving accounts of their own understanding of the doctrine. The difference in emphasis between them and these Christians is striking, for their versions were much closer to John of Damascus, as though they were aware only of the full classical formulation. It is instructive to look at what is said by three of these authors, who were all active in the early ninth century.

The Zaydī Imam al-Qāsim b. Ibrāhīm al-Rassī (d. 860) was a theologian whose interests extended beyond questions of Islamic thought to the beliefs of Christians and others.[18] His brief and incomplete *Al-radd ʿalā al-Naṣārā*, (*Refutation of the Christians*), which he wrote sometime at the beginning of the ninth century, contains extremely accurate accounts of Christian beliefs, including a very full description of the doctrine of the Trinity. In this he says that God is three individuals (*ashkhāṣ*) who are distinct as hypostases (*aqānīm*), and united as nature (*ṭabīʿa*) or essence (*dhāt*), and are equal in divinity, eternity and power.[19] He gives here a portrayal of the Godhead as three equal entities who share the same nature but are each distinct from one another. Its major emphasis is on the hypostases as individuals, unlike the Arabic speaking Christians who emphasise the identity between them, and it turns the Trinity into a community.

The same is true of al-Qāsim's contemporary Abū Yūsuf Ya'qūb b. Isḥāq al-Kindī (d. 864), the first major philosopher who wrote in Arabic. In a very short attack on the Trinity, also entitled *Al-radd 'alā al-Naṣārā* (*Refutation of the Christians*), he describes the doctrine in similar terms to al-Qāsim:

> three eternal hypostases (*aqānīm*) which exist eternally as one substance (*jawhar*); by the term 'hypostases' Christians mean 'individuals' (*ashkhāṣ*), and by 'one substance' that each hypostasis exists with its own specific characteristic (*khāṣṣa*); so the reality of the substance exists in each hypostasis, and they are all uniform in it (*wa-hiya fīhi muttafaqa*), and they each have a specific characteristic which distinguishes it from the others.[20]

With its emphasis upon the three Persons and their individuality this description also presents the Godhead as a community of separate and differentiated entities.

The third Muslim theologian from this period is the expert on religions Abū 'Īsā Muḥammad b. Hārūn al-Warrāq, who probably died in about 860.[21] His *Al-radd 'alā al-thalātha firaq min al-Naṣārā* (*The Refutation of the Three Christian Sects*) is the longest refutation of the three main Christian denominations that has survived from early classical times and the most detailed. At the beginning he gives an extensive description of the Trinity, which is worth quoting in full:

> The Jacobites and the Nestorians claim that the Eternal One is one substance and three hypostases, and that the three hypostases are the one substance and the one substance is the three hypostases. The Melkites, those who follow the faith of the king of the Byzantines, claim that the Eternal One is one substance which possesses three hypostases (*dhū thalāthati aqānīm*) and that the hypostases are the substance but the substance is other than the hypostases, though they do not acknowledge that it is numerically a fourth to them.
>
> The three sects, Jacobites, Nestorians and Melkites, claim that one of these hypostases is Father, another is Son, and the third is spirit, and that the Son is the Word and the Spirit is the Life – this is known among them as "the Holy Spirit." They all claim that the three hypostases are uniform in substantiality and differentiated in hypostaticity, that each of

> them is a specific substance, and that the one comprehensive substance is common to them. They claim that the Son is generated eternally from the Father, the Father generates eternally the Son, and the Spirit pours forth eternally from the Father.[22]

This account shows considerable knowledge about the details of Trinitarian doctrines, but like the two other Muslim descriptions it places strong emphasis upon the three hypostases as separate entities. In fact, Abū 'Īsā builds in an emphasis on both the oneness and the threeness in the Trinity as a preparation for the extensive arguments he employs against the doctrine in the attack that follows his introductory description.

We can readily see that these three early ninth century Muslim scholars are all thoroughly acquainted with the doctrine, and are familiar with the Arabic terms used in explaining it, among them *jawhar* which became the usual translation for the Greek *ousia*, "substance," and *uqnūm* which was transliterated from Syriac as the normal translation of the Greek *hypostasis*, "person." And they each present the Trinity as separate actualities within a communal Godhead. Al-Qāsim b. Ibrāhīm and al-Kindī make this point clear in their glosses upon *uqnūm* with the term *shakhṣ*, which means a solid, quantifiable individual.[23]

These and other Muslims were, of course, pre-disposed to think of the Trinity as a plurality of divinities because of the references to Christian beliefs about God which they found in the Qur'ān. The most obvious is a direct warning to the People of the Book in *sūra* 4: 171:

> O People of the Book! Commit no excesses in your religion: nor say of Allah aught but the truth. Christ Jesus the son of Mary was a messenger of Allah, and his Word, which he bestowed upon Mary, and a Spirit proceeding from him: so believe in Allah and his Messengers. Say not "Three" (*wa-lā taqūlū thalātha*): desist: it will be better for you: Allah is one God.

This is a straightforward denial that God is three. A second reference (in *sūra* 5: 73) gives the same warning slightly differently:

> They do blaspheme who say: Allah is the third of three (*thālithu thalāthatin*): for there is no god except one God.

This suggests that according to the doctrine God himself is only one of the three divine beings. A third reference (*sūra* 5: 116) maybe brings out what is implicitly contained here:

> And behold! Allah will say: "O Jesus the son of Mary! Didst thou say unto men, 'Worship me and my mother as gods in derogation of Allah'?" He will say: "Glory to thee! Never could I say what I had no right to."

This indicates Christians claimed that Jesus and Mary were divine together with God, and could be understood as parts of the Trinity.

These verses gave Muslims justification for detecting three discrete entities in the Christian Godhead, and formed a basis for *tathlīth*, the term usually used in Arabic descriptions of the doctrine. This is analogous to *tawḥīd*, the term used within Islam when referring to the oneness of God, and as *tawḥīd* literally means "to make one," so *tathlīth* means "to make three." The Muslim thinkers we have just examined were doing precisely that, finding where the triple nature of the Christian godhead lay.

The arguments used against the doctrine by these and other Muslims reflect a sense of incomprehensibility. Al-Qāsim questions whether the names "Father" and "Son," which in normal usage denote a relationship that has a beginning in time, can apply to God in his eternity, and can therefore have any reference to God himself rather than being human inventions; al-Kindī argues that if the hypostases are each both substance and specific characteristic they must be composite and therefore affected by an antecedent cause, and so they cannot be eternal; and Abū 'Īsā demonstrates at great length whatever way the doctrine is expressed, the attempt to identify three entities with one leads to confusion and incoherence. The fundamental problem which each polemicist differently raises is that since in any description of the doctrine more than one divine entity is listed, some form of plurality is entailed and the simple unity is obliterated. So the insistent claim made by the Christians that God is one becomes meaningless.

Yet this problem of unity and multiplicity was not peculiar to Christianity in the period we are discussing. Within Islamic thinking itself, the problem of how systematically to set down the teachings of the Qur'ān about God produced difficulties that, to many minds, itself affected the strict oneness of God's being in a way that parallels the issues concerned with the Trinity.

The matter of the divine attributes is very old in Islam. Some scholars think that it may, in fact, have been raised through discussions with Christians.[24] It arises from the problem of how to categorise the descriptions of God given by revelation and reason, whether these refer accurately to God's actual being or are human approximations of an unknowable divinity. At the beginning of the ninth century the debate was conducted mainly among thinkers associated with the Mu'tazilī principles of divine unity and justice, *tawḥīd* and *'adl*, for whom the strict oneness of God and the complete distinction between him and other beings were crucial matters of belief. And they were reluctant to refer to God in any way that appeared to suggest otherwise.

But this was the nub of the problem. According to the generally agreed perception at this time, the descriptions that could pertinently be made of a being were understood to refer to attributes that qualified the being itself. For example, if a being could be called living it was qualified by the attribute of life, and if it could be called seeing it was qualified by the attribute of sight. The attribute itself qualified the being as a whole, and in that respect was said to be of or in the being. This relationship between description and attribute was expressed according to the grammatical logic which was generally accepted at this time by paraphrasing a statement such as "he is living" *huwa ḥayy*, as *lahu ḥayāt*, "he has life," the two statements being regarded as equivalent. Thus, within the structure of this thinking to describe a being in any way was the same as saying that the being possessed attributes which were real and in some way additional to the being in its own actuality.

In applying these ideas to God, obvious problems arose. For if he possessed attributes which were both real and distinct from his being, he could not be the dense unity upon which the Mu'tazilīs insisted.

Some of them rejected the proposition that God subsisted in the same way as creatures, or that descriptions of him implied the existence of attributes. They said, for example, that the statement "God has knowledge" means no more than that there are things known (*ma'lūm*) to him.[25] But this avoidance of the problem raised more difficulties than it solved, since it entailed a necessary relationship between God and things outside him.

Another solution was offered by Abū al-Hudhayl al-'Allāf (d.*c.* 840) of the Baṣra Mu'tazilīs, who allowed that God is knowing by a "knowledge," but made this identical with God himself (*huwa 'ālimun bi-'ilmin huwa huwa*). He explains that as he sees it the descriptive statement "God is knowing" means that God has a "knowledge" which is himself, that he is not ignorant, and that there are present and future objects of his knowledge (*ma'lūm kāna aw yakūnu*).[26] He shows that he accepts the prevailing grammatical interpretations that the action of knowing derives from an attribute of knowledge, unlike many Muʿtazilīs and others,[27] but then he defines this attribute as identical with God himself (*huwa huwa*) in order to maintain the divine unity. This is an implicit rejection of the reality of the attribute, and in terms of the system renders statements about God as approximate expressions of belief rather than accurate logical propositions.

The other side of the debate was equally problematic, since those who maintained the reality of the attributes were confronted with the difficulty of explaining how God was one in any meaningful sense. Abū al-Hudhayl's contemporary ʿAbdallah b. Saʿīd Ibn Kullāb (d.*c.* 855) was a major representative of this side. From what we know of his thinking, he accepts quite readily that the meaning of the descriptive statement "God is knowing" is the same as "God has knowledge," and then he goes on to explain rather enigmatically that God's attributes are "of his essence, neither God nor other than him," (*li-dhātihi lā hiya Allah wa-lā hiya ghayruh*).[28] By means of this compressed formula he attempts to maintain that the attribute is actual, but also that it is not formally distinct from God's essence. This is his way of trying to say that God is not an unknowable mystery and that his mode of acting towards his creatures can be described with reliability. But the resulting problem is that since the attributes are not identical with God's essence but rather of it (*li-dhātih*) Ibn Kullāb cannot easily explain how the being of God is a simple unity.

The repercussions of this debate continued within Islam for many centuries and increased in complexity and sophistication. As we can see, however, even at this early stage it was accepted by leading theologians that any meaningful description of God logically involved the existence of attributes that were intrinsic to God, whether these were defined in negative terms, as by Abū al-Hudhayl, or positively, as by Ibn Kullāb.

For our purpose of tracing the way in which the doctrine of the Trinity was explained at this time, it is important to appreciate the dimensions of this debate and to see how Muslim theologians tried to maintain God's oneness while relating their descriptions of him to actualities in his being. For at exactly this time at the beginning of the ninth century we find Arabic speaking Christian theologians expressing the doctrine of the Trinity in precisely the same terms as these Muslim theologians. And it is difficult to deny that they were employing the logic of this debate in order to understand and defend the doctrine in the Muslim context in which they lived. A representative of this new development was the Nestorian 'Ammār al-Baṣrī.[29]

As with so many of the intellectuals active in the early ninth century Islamic world, we know very little about 'Ammār. In fact, until relatively recently we knew almost nothing, since we possessed only his name attached to two works on Christian doctrine.[30] But with the discovery of lost parts of Ibn al-Nadīm's *Fihrist*, the tenth century bio-bibliographical work, further information has come to light. For in recovered lists of the works of Abū al-Hudhayl (all of which have themselves been lost) there is one entitled *Against 'Ammār the Christian in Refutation of the Christians.*[31] This, together with the contents of the works themselves, gives a strong indication that 'Ammār was active in the early ninth century and that he was fully acquainted with the prevailing Muslim thought of the day. It even allows us to surmise that he debated with Abū al-Hudhayl and other Mu'tazilīs in Baṣra, and could have hammered out his own articulation of the Trinity on the tough to and fro arguing which characterised theological discourse in this time.

'Ammār gives the fullest explanation of the Trinity in his *Kitāb al-Burhān* (*The Book of the Proof*), which is the shorter of the two works ascribed to him. Beginning from the statement agreed by both Christians and Muslims that God is living, he argues that this description means that God must have life as something eternal in his essence (*lahu dhātiyya azaliyya*). This is because the participle (*ism*) "living" is derived from "life" and indicates its presence as a determinative reality (*ma'nā*) in a being.[32] And so, he explains somewhat innocently, when Christians talk of the Father, Son and Holy Spirit, they mean only the equivalent of the statement that God is living and speaking (*ḥayy, nāṭiq*) and that the Father has Life and Word (*lahu ḥayāt wa-kalima*).[33]

Although his technical terms are slightly different from those used by the Muslims we have discussed, the concepts he employs are clearly the same: "living" is derived from "life," and so the statement "God is living" means "God has life" as an actuality in his being. This logic enables 'Ammār to defend exactly the same model of the Trinity that we have seen above in the anonymous eighth century Arabic treatise and in the Patriarch Timothy's answers. But it goes further than his elder contemporaries in making use of the contemporary forms of explanation employed by Muslim theologians as a means of substantiating the doctrine.[34] His argument gives an example of how Christians at this time were coming under the influence of Muslim theological concepts, and appeared to find it congenial as well as apologetically advantageous to make use of them.

But just as there was some difficulty among Muslims in explaining how the attributes of God were not different from his essence, as we have seen, so ʿAmmār found problems in explaining how exactly the hypostases were one substance. He maintained that they were discrete and self-subsistent entities: "according to us the hypostasis is a thing which is complete rather than incomplete, not depending on anything other than itself for its continuation."[35] So, as well as claiming that the Trinity is only a way of describing God as living and self-expressing, he also said that it was one Creator who is known by three determinative realities (*maʿānīn*) with the substance encompassing (*yaʿummu*) the hypostases in the same way that the substance of humanity encompasses many human hypostases.[36] This comparison between separate human individuals related by their common humanity and the divine hypostases related by the substance suggests that the Trinity is a community of individuals, exactly the opposite of what ʿAmmār is trying to argue. He finds it very difficult to move away from the idea that although the hypostases are the forms in which the single Godhead expresses itself and communicates, they are nevertheless three realities. And here he differs from Ibn Kullāb. For the latter refuses to say any more than that the attributes are neither God nor other than him, allowing them a much less definite form of existence.

According to the logic of the system which both theologians employed, however, they faced similar challenges. For they acknowledged eternal entities in addition to the essence of God, whether these were self-subsistent as hypostases or less definite realities as attributes, and so had to answer the allegation of ascribing plurality to the Godhead. Each of them seems to have settled on a solution which comprehended a relative unity rather than the impenetrable denseness of Muʿtazilī teachings, in order to preserve the important principle that God can be ascribed certain characteristics that actually refer to his being. It is no co-incidence that among Muʿtazilīs, Ibn Kullāb and his followers were often regarded as pseudo-Christians.[37]

But the Christians faced another difficulty that Ibn Kullāb did not. For ʿAmmār was also forced to explain how God possessed only Life and Word as hypostases, and not other characteristics such as hearing, sight, knowledge and power. The Qur'ān refers to a number of descriptive characteristics of God, and the Muslim theologians listed as attributes rather more than the two upon which ʿAmmār insisted.

His response to this difficulty was to assert that Life and Word "form the basis of an essence and the constitution of a substance" (*min sūs al-dhāti wa-min binyati al-jawhar*) by which he meant that these attributes differ from others in characterising living and rational beings. Other attributes such as hearing and sight may or may not be present in such beings, but these two are necessary for the being in its existence and constitute the foundation on which other attributes rest.[38]

Although 'Ammār argues at some length about the distinction between these and other attributes, he and other Christians who employed similar arguments did not eventually succeed in explaining the doctrine in terms that convinced Muslims.[39] An examination of responses from two later ninth century Muslim theologians will show the nature of the persistent problems they found in the doctrine. These are the Baghdad Mu'tazilī Abū al-'Abbās 'Abdallah, known as al-Nāshi' al-Akbar (d. 906), and his better-known Mu'tazilī contemporary Abū 'Alī Muḥammad al-Jubbā'ī (d. 915), the leading scholar among the Baṣran Mu'tazilīs at this time. Although neither of them refers to 'Ammār or any other Christian by name, they were clearly refuting points made in works such as his, and they were possibly incorporating arguments from the refutation that Abū al-Hudhayl is known to have made.[40]

Incidentally, it is instructive to note that unlike the three early ninth century Muslims discussed above, these two Mu'tazilī theologians apparently knew the doctrine of the Trinity mainly in the form based on attributes doctrine presented by the Arabic speaking Christians. Writing some decades after the Christian and Muslim authors we have been discussing, al-Nāshi' al-Akbar describes the doctrine as follows:

> Among the Trinitarians are people who claim that the Creator is three hypostases and one substance: Father, Son and Holy Spirit, and the substance is the hypostases in a veiled way (*maghmūman*). They claim that of these the Father is the cause of the Son and Spirit, without preceding them in essence but being equal with them. They call the Son the knowledge of the Creator and the Spirit his life.[41]

The existence of the substance is merely acknowledged here, while the importance of the Father is repeatedly emphasised. Abū 'Alī al-Jubbā'ī gives a more or less identical description:

> The teaching of most Christians, except for a tiny minority, is that God the exalted is Creator of things, and the Creator is living and speaking.

> His life is the Spirit, which they call the Holy Spirit, and his speech is knowledge. Some of them say that the life is power. They claim that God, his Word and his Power are eternal.
>
> They claim the Word is the Son, and the one who possesses the Spirit and the Word is the Father. They claim that these three are one divinity and one Creator, and they are from one substance.[42]

Here the substance is hardly mentioned while the place of the Father, who possesses the Son and Spirit as attributes of his being, is central.

In a refutation of the Trinity which is separate from his main argument and may have been added, al-Nāshi' refers to recently expressed views (*wa-qad dhahaba qawm min muhdathīhum*) according to which the world gives proof of a maker who is knowing and living, and who must have knowledge and life, because no one who acts with wisdom in the observable world can fail to be knowing and living.[43] This summarises well the kind of reasoning typified by 'Ammār al-Baṣrī. But despite the fact that al-Nāshi' finds the thinking familiar, he is not convinced. Among his replies are: that a being who acts must be powerful, so according to their own reasoning the Christians must acknowledge power as an additional hypostasis; that no one who is living and knowing in the observable world comprises together with his knowledge and life one substance and three hypostases; that no one in the observable world differs from his life and knowledge by virtue of himself (*bi-nafsih*) rather than because of something outside himself; and that if the Creator is three hypostases and one substance, the substance must be a genus or species, according to the logic of "Christian" philosophers, because the hypostases are uniform with one another through it in the same way that individuals are consistent through their genus or species even though they differ in other ways.[44]

The second and third of these four rebuttals rather cheekily draw out impossible implications of the comparison between God and contingent beings which these Christians make. And the other points reveal weaknesses similar to those which 'Ammār had tried to defend. The first rebuttal, that there must be at least one further hypostasis, indicates that within Muslim theological circles the limitation of attributes to two fundamental characteristics of God was not thought convincing. And it is not easy to see how Christians might solve this difficulty. They could say that in order to be powerful and so on, a being must be living and also rational, as 'Ammār suggests.[45] But it may be said in response that without power a being could not subsist or act. Certainly there were Christians at this time who were thrown into confusion by this, since as we have seen above Abū 'Alī al-Jubbā'ī records some as saying that the hypostases are Word and Power, rather than Word and Life.[46]

This little point shows how difficult it was to translate a doctrine based upon Biblical teachings about the Son as Word-Logos of God and the Spirit as source of life into this new conceptual framework. For Muslims saw no reason to limit the attributes to two, because the Qur'ān and their own reasoning taught them that God must possess rather more than these in order to be the omnipotent and omniscient being they expected. For them the Christian limitation was arbitrary.

Al-Nāshi's fourth rebuttal raises the question of the ontology of the hypostases. The Christians evidently propose the idea that the hypostases are uniform with one another because they all come under the category of substance, and are differentiated because they are separate hypostases, recalling John of Damascus' description though schematising it drastically. This suggests to al-Nāshi' that the hypostases are therefore like individual members of a genus or species, as these are understood according to Aristotelian philosophy. He does not actually say they are individuals, but clearly their mode of existing allows them to be understood as such. In his mind their undeniable individuality distinguishes them from the substance, in a very different relationship from that between the attributes and essence in Muslim thinking. Thus the Christian Godhead can be described as a community of three similar but not identical individuals.

Al-Nāshi's exposure of these weaknesses is repeated by Abū 'Alī al-Jubbā'ī in some of the arguments quoted from him.[47] He argues that if Christians affirm three hypostases because God can only be active (*fā'ilan*) if he is living and knowing, then they must concede that he also has power (*qudra*) since acts are only possible for a being who is powerful. Similarly, God must have hearing, sight, and discernment, since a being who is living possesses these, and also will, since a being who is knowing and active must have this. He goes on to argue that there is no valid hierarchical distinction between the attributes, so that according to this logic the Godhead must either be a multiplicity of Persons corresponding to the descriptive adjectives that can be predicated of him, or a strict unity in which the attributes-Persons are all identical with the essence of God.

Abū 'Alī exposes a further complexity that arises from the understanding of how attributes functioned in the system of Islamic theology. He takes the example of "living" and argues that, logically speaking, within the Godhead either the Father alone is living or all three hypostases are living. If it is the Father alone then he alone is Creator and God, which destroys the doctrine. But if all three hypostases are living, then the hypostasis Life must be living as well as endowing the Father and Son with life. But this is impossible because within the system a cause cannot confer a condition upon itself as well as upon another, nor indeed upon itself alone. Here Abū 'Alī reveals the difficult and potentially embarrassing consequences of employing Muslim attributes theory to explain the Christian doctrine of the Trinity. For an attribute is the bearer of a characteristic within the being that it qualifies, not within itself. But if the hypostases Life and Word function as attributes, they cannot be both hypostases as the traditional doctrine of the Trinity sets out, and also function as attributes as the Muslim articulation requires.

This is a devastating point for the whole Christian enterprise. Its seriousness is underlined in an argument recorded by the tenth century Ash'arī theologian Abū Bakr Muḥammad al-Bāqillānī (d.1013), which indicates that Christians were aware of the difficulties their explanations had produced and were trying to salvage something. They ask him: 'Do you not say with respect to the attributes of God that they are neither identical with him nor distinct from him? So why deny that the divine substance is not identical with the hypostases but not distinct from them?' This question, which expressly compares the attributes of Muslim thought with the hypostases of Christian thought in both status and function, echoes the Ash'arī teaching about the divine attributes which is built upon that of Ibn Kullāb.[48] The Christians might presume that as a follower of al-Ash'arī, al-Bāqillānī would accept their comparison. But he does not and answers that in his thinking there is no proper distinction between the attributes and God himself, since he does not say they are other than God or identical with him.[49] In making this point he shows how he regards the hypostases as different from the attributes, and implies that their existence is more definite. To his mind, the Christians did not understand the Islamic concepts fully and their comparison was crassly inappropriate. Like al-Nāshi' al-Akbar and Abū 'Alī al-Jubbā'ī, he exposes the shallowness of the Christians' understanding of the attributes doctrine in which they attempted to express their own.

It is clear that in this important period of encounter between Christians and Muslims the doctrine of the Trinity occasioned much disagreement and misunderstanding. The basis of the problem was that to Muslim minds the mention of the three Persons meant three separate deities, as the Qur'ān clearly states. And Christian attempts to explain that their doctrine did not entail plurality failed completely. In whatever way they attempted to employ concepts borrowed from Islamic theology, and however well they themselves were satisfied with the new formulations in which they employed them, the end result was that they increased confusion rather than clarity.

It might have been easier for the Christians if they had found a suitable range of vocabulary. The usual term in Arabic for hypostasis was *uqnūm*, a transliteration of the Syriac *qnōmā*. This was often translated or glossed as "individual" (*shakhṣ*),[50] as we have noted above, a term which had the merit of safeguarding the distinction between the hypostases and allaying notions that they were no more than modes of the divine essence. But to Muslim minds this was much too crude: it conjured up ideas of three distinct beings,[51] or reminded them of "bodies" (*ajsām*) and "figures" (*ashbāh*), such as those they saw around them.[52]

And so the concept of "attribute," together with the structure of thought into which it fitted, must have appeared to 'Ammār and others as a true Godsend. For it denoted something which could formally be both a reality in itself and uniform with the being it qualified. But as we have seen, the total structure of Islamic thought about God proved more complicated than the Christians may have expected. In borrowing from it, they maybe failed to appreciate the complete conceptual context, and the consequences of what they did exposed the whole enterprise to scathing criticism and ridicule.

Despite these efforts of Arabic speaking Christians to explain the Trinity in terms borrowed from their neighbours, Muslims saw no reason to revise the accusation made in the Qur'ān that the doctrine of the Trinity was essentially tritheism. Christian attempts to uphold claims to the contrary confirmed their view that the doctrine inevitably led to confusion and incoherence. Such attitudes towards the doctrine changed little in subsequent centuries.

NOTES

1 D. J. Sahas, *John of Damascus on Islam, the 'Heresy of Ishmaelites'* (Leiden, 1972), pp. 17–45.
2 Sahas, John of Damascus, pp. 26 ff.; G. Hawting, *The First Dynasty of Islam* (London, 1986), pp. 63–6.
3 S. K. Samir, "The Role of Christians in the Fāṭimid Government Services of Egypt to the Reign of al-Ḥāfiẓ," *Medieval Encounters* 2, 1996, [pp. 177–92] pp. 190f.

4 J. Finkel, "A Risāla of al-Jāḥiẓ," *Journal of the American Oriental Society* 47, 1927, [pp. 311–34] pp. 328–9, a translation of al-Jāḥiẓ's "Al-radd 'alā al-Naṣārā," ed. J. Finkel in *Thalāth rasā'il li-Abī 'Uthmān ... al-Jāḥiẓ* (Cairo, 1926), p. 18.6–14.
5 A full account of relations between Muslims and the People of the Book, *Ahl al-kitāb*, who comprised Christians and other non-Muslim communities, is given in B. Lewis, *The Jews of Islam* (London, 1984), pp. 3–66.
6 I. Shahid, *Byzantium and the Arabs in the Fourth Century* (Washington D. C., 1984), pp. 556–8, argues for the existence of an Arab Church as early as the fourth century. See further his *Byzantium and the Arabs in the Fifth Century* (Washington D.C., 1989), pp. 520–8.
7 F. H. Chase Jr., *Saint John of Damascus, Writings* (Washington D.C., 1958), p. 277.
8 *Ibid.*, p. 10.
9 There are some references to Jews, but no extensive justification particularly for them. This apparent indifference accords with John's condemnation of Islam as nothing more than a Christian heresy in his *De Haeresibus*, where he shows basic but not extensive knowledge of Islam.
10 M. D. Gibson, *Fī tathlīth Allah al-wāḥid*, *Studia Sinaitica* vol. VII (London, 1899) pp. 2–36 (English), 74–107 (Arabic). S. K. Samir, "The Earliest Arab Apology for Christianity (c. 750)," in S. K. Samir and J. S. Nielsen, eds., *Christian Arabic Apologetics during the Abbasid Period (750–1258)* (Leiden, 1994), pp. 57–114, draws attention to shortcomings in this edition, and suggests a date of about 770. On the question of dating see also M. Swanson, "Ibn Taymiyya and the *Kitāb al-Burhān*: a Muslim Contraversialist Responds to a Ninth-Century Arabic Christian Apology," in Y. Haddad and W. Haddad, (eds.), *Christian-Muslim Encounters* (Gainsville, 1995), p. 103, n. 15.
11 Gibson, *Fī tathlīth Allah*, pp. 4 (English), 76. 1–19 (Arabic), summarised in Samir, "Arab Apology for Christianity," pp. 70–3.
12 Gibson, *Fī tathlīth Allah*, pp. 3–5 (English), 75.4f., 75.24–76.1, 77.10–13 (Arabic).
13 *Ibid.*, pp. 5 (English), 77.10–12 (Arabic).
14 A. Mingana, "The Apology of Timothy the Patriarch before the Caliph Mahdi," *Bulletin of the John Rylands Library* 12, 1928, [pp. 137–226] p. 159.
15 *Ibid.*, pp. 210–11.
16 Another early Arabic speaking Christian who presented arguments of this kind was the Melkite Bishop Theodore Abū Qurra (d. 825). For two examples of his explanation of the Trinity see C. Bacha, *Les oeuvres arabes de Theodore Aboucara* (Beirut, 1904), pp. 44.9ff., 79. 16ff. (Arabic). And see further, S. Rissanen, *Theological Encounter of Oriental Christians with Islam during Abbasid Rule* (Åbo, Finland, 1993), pp. 127–31. Theodore's views were widely known among Muslims in later years, and the early ninth century Muslim author Abū 'Īsā al-Warrāq may have given the earliest summary of his explanation of the Trinity; see D. Thomas, *Anti-Christian Polemic in Early Islam* (Cambridge, 1992), pp. 130–33, para. 106.
17 The Cappadocian Fathers had said something similar in the fourth century; see B. Studer, *Trinity and Incarnation* (Edinburgh, 1993), p. 146.

John of Damascus was evidently aware of the general principles involved, because he argues in his Chapter on Islam in the *De Haeresibus* that since God has a Word which is inseparable from him, "it is obvious that he is God as well," Sahas, *John of Damascus*, pp. 136 and 137.

18 W. Madelung, *Der Imām al-Qāsim Ibn Ibrāhīm und die Glaubenslehre der Zaiditen* (Berlin, 1965); B. Abrahamov, *Al-kāsim b. Ibrāhīm on the Proof of God's Existence* (Leiden, 1990), pp. 6f.

19 I. di Matteo, "Confutazione contro i Cristiani dello zaydita al-Qāsim b. Ibrāhīm," *Rivista degli Studi Orientali* 9, 1921–2, [pp. 301–64] pp. 314.23–316.3.

20 A. Perier, "Un Traité de Yaḥyā ben 'Adī," *Revue de l'Orient Chrétien* 22, 1920–1, [pp. 3–21] p. 4.10–13.

21 See Thomas, *Anti-Christian Polemics*, pp. 9–30.

22 *Ibid.*, p. 67.

23 See E. W. Lane, *Arabic-English Lexicon* (Cambridge, 1984) [1863–93], p. 1517.

24 Arguments in favour can be found in H. A. Wolfson, *The Philosophy of the Kalam* (Harvard, 1976), pp. 58–64, 112–32. Rissanen, *Theological Encounter*, pp. 11–17, gives a useful resume of the various positions for and against this claim.

25 Abū al-Ḥasan al-Ash'arī, *Kitāb maqālāt al-Islāmiyyīn*, ed. H. Ritter (Wiesbaden, 1980 [Istanbul, 1929–30]), p. 165.3f.

26 *Ibid.*, p. 165.5–9.

27 *Ibid.*, pp. 164.13–165.2.

28 *Ibid.*, p. 169.10–13.

29 The fullest account of his thinking currently available is S. Griffith, "The Concept of *al-Uqnūm* in 'Ammār al-Baṣrī's Apology for the Doctrine of the Trinity," in K. Samir (ed.), *Actes du premier congrès international d'études chrétiennes, Goslar, Septembre 1980*, [*Orientalia Christiana Analecta* 218], (Rome, 1982), pp. 169–91.

30 M. Hayek, ed., *'Ammār al-Baṣrī, apologie et controverses* (Beirut, 1977).

31 Hayek, *'Ammār al-Baṣrī*, p. 19; B. Dodge, *The Fihrist of al-Nadīm* (New York, 1970), p. 388.

32 This term is most thoroughly explained by R. M. Frank, "Al-Ma'nā: some reflections on the technical meanings of the term in the Kalām," *Journal of the American Oriental Society* 87, 1967, pp. 248–59.

33 Hayek, *'Ammār al-Baṣrī*, pp. 46–8.

34 Another Christian who employed these thought forms in the same period was the Jacobite Ḥabīb Ibn Khidma Abū Rā'iṭa, *Die schriften des Jacobiten Ḥabīb ibn Hidma Abū Rā'iṭa [Corpus Scriptorum Christianorum Orientalium 130]*, ed. G. Graf (Louvain, 1951), esp. pp. 7.15ff. See also Rissanen, *Theological Encounter*, pp. 131–4.

35 Hayek, *'Ammār Baṣrī*, p. 50.4.

36 *Ibid.*, p. 51.20–22.

37 See e.g. Dodge, *The Fihrist of al-Nadīm*, p. 448; 'Abd al-Jabbār, *Sharḥ al-uṣūl al-khamsa*, ed. 'A. K. 'Uthmān (Cairo, 1996 [1965]), pp. 294.14–295.3.

38 Hayek, *'Ammār al-Baṣrī*, pp. 52.13–53.4.

39 Among later Muslims who knew about this explanation were al-Ḥasan Ibn Ayyūb (a tenth century convert from Christianity), quoted in Ibn

Taymiyya, *Al-jawāb al-ṣaḥīḥ li-man baddala dīn al-Masīḥ* (Cairo, 1905), vol. II, p. 355.5–9; Abū Bakr al-Bāqillānī, *K. al-tamhīd*, ed. R. J. McCarthy (Beirut, 1957), p. 79.6–10; and the Andalusī Abū Muḥammad ʿAlī Ibn Ḥazm, *K. al-fiṣal fī al-milal* (Cairo, 1317), vol. I, p. 50.18ff., who reports the intriguing detail, not supported by evidence of the Eastern authors discussed here, that some Christians say the identification of God's knowledge as his Son is dictated by the Latin language *(al-lugha al-lātīniyya)* "in which the knowledge of the knower is said to be his son."

40 See n. 31 above.

41 *Kitāb al-awsaṭ fī al-maqālāt*, ed. J. van Ess, *Frühe muʿtazilitische Häresiographie* (Beirut, 1971), p. 76.12–16 (Arabic).

42 Quoted in ʿAbd al-Jabbār, *Kitāb al-mughnī*, vol. V, ed. M. M. al-Khuḍayrī (Cairo, 1958) p. 80.5–8, 13–15 (in 1.14 read *al-ab* instead of *al-ibn* in the text).

43 Al-Nāshi', *Kitāb al-awsaṭ*, p. 87.1ff (Arabic).

44 *Ibid.*, p. 87.4–19 (Arabic).

45 Hayek, *ʿAmmār al-Baṣrī*, pp. 53.6ff.

46 Quoted in ʿAbd al-Jabbār, *Mughnī*, vol. V, p. 80.6f.

47 In *Mughnī*, vol. V. pp. 91.13–95.11; for similar arguments from later Muslim theologians, see also al-Ḥasan Ibn Ayyūb in Ibn Taymiyya, *Jawāb al-ṣaḥīḥ*, vol. II, p. 355.9–15; al-Bāqillānī, *Tamhīd*, pp. 79.10–81.2; Ibn Ḥazm, *Fiṣal*, vol. I, p. 51.5ff.

48 See M. Allard, *Le problème des attributs divins dans la doctrine d'al-Ashʿarī et de ses premiers grands disciples* (Beirut, 1965), pp. 232f.

49 Al-Bāqillānī, *Tamhīd*, pp. 84.13–85.3.

50 E.g. al-Qāsim b. Ibrāhīm, *Radd*, pp. 314.24, 315.24; al-Kindī, *Radd*, p. 4.11; Abū ʿĪṣā al-Warrāq, *Radd*, p. 68.9; al-Ḥasan Ibn Ayyūb in Ibn Taymiyya, *Jawāb al-ṣaḥīḥ*, vol. II, p. 354.13; al-Bāqillānī, *Tamhīd*, p. 86.7; ʿAbd al-Jabbār, *Mughnī*, vol. V, p. 82.3–8.

51 Al-Kindī, *Radd*, pp. 4–10; al-Ḥasan Ibn Ayyūb in Ibn Taymiyya, *Jawāb al-ṣaḥiḥ*, vol. II, p. 354.13–15.

52 See e.g. Abū ʿĪṣā al-Warrāq, *Radd*, p. 180.9ff. According to al-Ashʿarī, *Maqālāt*, p. 155.4, this was the understanding common among the Muʿtazila.

5

Christianity as Portrayed by Jalāl al-Dīn Rūmī

Lloyd Ridgeon

Jalāl al-Dīn Rūmī, also known to Iranians as *Mawlānā* (Our Master), is considered to be one of, if not *the* greatest of Islamic and Persian poets. English translations of the works of this thirteenth century mystic have become remarkably popular in the contemporary Western world to the extent that Rūmī is "reputedly the best-selling poet in America today."[1] Such an attraction is surprising given the negative and misinformed understanding of Islam that is found in both the popular media and public opinion of Europe and the United States of America.[2] Indeed after the collapse of communism, 80% of the British public believed the greatest threat to the West came from Islam.[3] There are several reasons which help to explain the popularity of Rūmī's works in the West. First, Islam is the fastest growing religion in many parts of Europe, and it is only natural that believers will investigate the myriad literary manifestations of their faith, including Rūmī's mystical masterpieces. Second, the West has become aware of Rūmī's poetry through performances of Sufi dancing (*samā'*) by members of the *Mawlawiyya* order which regards Rūmī as its founder. The members of the *Mawlawiyya* order are the "whirling dervishes" (whose *samā'* is accompanied with recitations and singing of Rūmī's verse) and they tour major Western cities on a regular basis.[4] Casual curiosity about other cultural traditions often leads to the discovery of their foundations and ideals, so it is a quick step from the *samā'* to Rūmī's poetry. Third, one of the general messages of Rūmī's poetry is the need to transcend the boundaries that conceal the reality of things, and leave only the forms visible. Likewise, many people in the West are seeking a remedy for the alienation, social dislocation and spiritual void that they feel in the post-modern age. And it is within Rūmī's works that such readers find verses which parallel their desire to transcend the restrictive barriers that their own cultures and environment have wrapped around them.

This third point, the need to cross over from the form of things to the underlying reality is a common theme in Rūmī's works. The following is a typical example:

Lo, for I to myself am unknown, now in God's name what must I do?
I adore not the Cross nor the Crescent, I am not a Magian nor a Jew.
East nor West, land nor sea, is my home; I have kin not with angel nor gnome;
I am wrought not of fire nor of foam, I am shaped not of dust nor of dew.
I was born not in China afar, nor in Saqsin[5] *and not in Bulghar;*
Not in India, where five rivers are[6]*, nor 'Irāq nor Khurāsān I grew.*
Not in this world nor that world I dwell, not in Paradise neither in Hell;
Not from Eden and Riẓwān[7] *I fell, not from Adam my lineage I drew.*
In a place beyond uttermost place, in a tract without shadow or trace,
Soul and body transcending I live in the Soul of my Loved One anew.[8]

Verses of this nature that endorse an "inclusivist" religion, however, provide a somewhat distorted picture of Rūmī's whole message. One problem related to understanding the totality of Rūmī's world view, which is particularly relevant to contemporary Western readers, has been highlighted by Schimmel: "Modern people tried to select from often very vague secondhand translations only those verses that speak of love and ecstacy, of intoxication and whirling dance. The role that the Prophet of Islam plays in Mawlana's poetry is hardly mentioned in secondary literature."[9]

Rūmī was first and foremost a Muslim who viewed Islam as the perfect religion, indeed, *sūra* 5: 3 states that Muḥammad was sent to perfect religion, and *sūra* 2: 111–13 implies that Islam, as a universal religion, is superior to Christianity and Judaism. If one investigates Rūmī's voluminous poetical works, it becomes clear that his understanding of Christianity reflects such Islamic tradition. Rūmī's "orthodoxy" was described by Jāmī, the celebrated Persian theosopher and poet of the fifteenth century[10], who portrayed Rūmī's *Mathnawī* (a masterpiece composed of twenty-five thousand rhyming couplets) in the following manner: "Whoever recites the *Mathnawī* in the morning and evening, for him Hellfire be forbidden! The spiritual *Mathnawī* of Mawlānā is the Qur'ān in Persian tongue."[11] Moreover, this divinely inspired work almost raised Rūmī to the rank of prophethood: "Although he is not a prophet, he has a book!"[12]

This chapter examines Rūmī's attitude towards Christianity, and this should inform us of the extent of his "inclusivist" religion. One of the problems in analysing Rūmī's understanding of Christianity concerns the role of Jesus. Jesus is a multi-dimensional character in Rūmī's works: sometimes he is the historical Islamic prophet; at other times he is the trans-historical reality within man; and occasionally Jesus is the Christian Son of God. Therefore, in order to yield a comprehensive view of Rūmī's Christianity, not only is it necessary to analyse the explicit references that Rūmī makes to Christian doctrine and practice, but a thorough investigation of the passages and verses that relate to Jesus is required.

There are four sections in this chapter. The first section examines Rūmī's knowledge of both the Christian understanding of Jesus and the Islamic understanding of Jesus. In the second section, Muḥammad and Jesus are compared, and this leads us into the third section that highlights Rūmī's critique of Christianity. The fourth section then investigates the nature of mystical experience and Sufi pluralism, and the extent to which the Christian can realise Unity.

I. JESUS IN RŪMĪ'S WORKS

This section is divided into two. The first focuses upon Rūmī's knowledge of the Christian Jesus, and the second investigates his portrayal of the Islamic Jesus. The second section contains four sub-sections which highlight the various dimensions of the Islamic Jesus.

The references in Rūmī's works to Jesus that bear resemblance to events described in the Gospels, but which do not appear in the Qur'ān are not very numerous. There is a striking similarity between Rūmī's story of Jesus not being allowed to remain in the jackal's den, causing him to proclaim, "Lord, the jackal's whelp has a shelter, but the son of Mary has no shelter, no place where he may dwell,"[13] and Matthew 8: 20: "Foxes have holes and birds of the air have nests but the Son of Man has nowhere to lay his head." Another example can be found in Rūmī's advice, "When you get one blow on your cheek, go and seek another blow,"[14] which repeats Matthew 5: 49. Mention must also be made of the association Rūmī makes between Jesus and the donkey, a pairing which re-appears frequently in his works.[15] The donkey symbolises man's body while Jesus – referred to as the spirit of God (*rūḥallāh*), breath, word, and wind – represents man's higher faculties, such as reason or spirit. Jesus' entry into Jerusalem is evoked for Christians when Rūmī comments that Jesus rode on a donkey out of humility: "How else should the morning breeze ride on the donkey's back?"[16]

Other examples of Rūmī's knowledge of Christian stories and incidents which are not mentioned explicitly in the Qur'ān include the raising of Lazarus,[17] and Jesus' walking on water.[18] Christian images can be read into other pieces of Rūmī's poetry, yet it is necessary to be very careful not to miss the possible Islamic origin of such verses. For example, when Rūmī exclaims "O seize the hem of his kindness!"[19] or "Lay hold of his skirt!"[20] the Christian reader might see associations of this with the story found in the Gospels when a women touches the edge of Jesus' cloak, seeking a cure for her illness.[21] However, most Sufis would be aware of the Islamic meaning in spiritual blessing (*baraka*) that can be derived from contact with sacred objects[22], while for Rūmī it also refers to touching Joseph's shirt of the spirit,[23] manifestly an Islamic image derived from the Qur'ān (12: 25–28). In addition, the phrase is a Persian idiom meaning "to seek protection."[24]

Turning now to the Islamic understanding of Jesus, it is clear that Jesus is much more an Islamic Prophet in Rūmī's works than the Christian saviour and Son of God. But Rūmī is not content to list Jesus' miracles as portrayed in the Islamic tradition, rather he breathes new life into these stories, resurrecting them by unveiling a multitude of new meanings and insights which teach the Sufi path and lead the individual towards self-realisation and intimacy with God. Rūmī's portrayal of Jesus as an Islamic prophet is classified into four categories.

First is Rūmī's discussion of Jesus as "Spirit of God" (*rūhallāh*). Jesus' miracles are frequently associated with this name, derived from *sūra* 21: 19 which tells of God's spirit being blown into Mary who subsequently conceived Jesus. Likewise, Jesus is able to breathe life into objects, as *sūra* 3: 43–9 describes, he moulded a handful of clay into the form of a bird, and then animated the clay bird by blowing into it. Rūmī interiorises this idea by describing how the Sufi shaykh can mimic the Messiah's act by transforming the spiritually dead Sufi aspirant through a single kiss on the lips.[25]

Rūmī's unceasing search for the realities behind forms, seeking to transform the dross into gold, leads him to use Jesus as Spirit of God with life-giving power as a symbol applicable to each and every individual. In fact, this connection is suggested in *sūra* 32: 7–9 which states that the Prophet Adam was created from a mixture of earth and

God's spirit therefore there is a degree of similarity between Adam and Jesus.[26] The name "Adam" (*Ādam* in Arabic) means "man," and Adam is considered the archetypal human being. So, if there is a degree of similarity between Adam and Jesus, there must also be a similarity between Jesus and each individual. The connection between Jesus and human beings lies of course in the spiritual dimension, and Rūmī contrasts the divine realm (*lāhūt*) in which the spirit has its origin with the creaturely, corporeal realm (*nāsūt*):

> *O my soul! You are like Jesus. O* [what] *good fortune you are for the Christian.*
> *You show the eternal realm of* lāhūt *through the realm of* nāsūt.[27]

Rūmī compares man's spirit to Jesus and his body to Mary; the pains of the body (i.e. the pains that the body endures through spiritual effort such as fasting or devotional prayers) guide man towards the purpose of his creation, which is the meeting with God. If man does not engage in spiritual and religious effort (such as the *dhikr*, a verbal or non-verbal remembrance of God),[28] then there is no chance for the Jesus of the spirit to develop:

> The body is like Mary. Every one of us has a Jesus within him, but until the pangs manifest in us, our Jesus is not born. If the pangs never come, then Jesus rejoins his origin by the same secret path by which he came, leaving us bereft and without portion of him.
>
> *The soul within you is needy, the flesh without is well fed:*
> *The devil gorges to swelling, Jamshid*[29] *lacks even for bread.*
> *See now to the cure of your soul while Jesus is yet on earth;*
> *When Jesus returns to heaven all hope of your cure will have fled.*[30]

Aside from having reviving power, Jesus, or the spirit, is also utilised by Rūmī as a metaphor for rationality and gnosis, which seems somewhat contradictory given that the Sufis believed there was a certain tension between the finite capacity of reason and the infinite scope of mystical knowledge. Rūmī states that Jesus' donkey lived in the same station as the men of reason, because Jesus (reason) took control of the donkey (the body) and made it lean. However, the person who has a weak reason will find his or her donkey turning into dragon.[31]

In contrast, the scope of the spirit is so great in acquiring knowledge that even eminent rational philosophers, such as Avicenna and Galen, are left completely bewildered. Indeed, Avicenna would be like "a donkey on ice" if he tried to understand the forms that appear "fatherless like Jesus" in one's breast.[32] Furthermore, even though Galen possessed thousands of medical skills, they were pitiful compared to the healing powers of Jesus' breath.[33]

The second category in this section concerns Rūmī's understanding of the crucifixion and ascent of Jesus. The Qur'ān states that God caused another individual to take on the "likeness" of Jesus, who was in fact taken up before his death to heaven.[34] Rūmī follows the Islamic tradition of placing Jesus in the fourth heaven.[35] (According to the eleventh century Ismā'īlī theosopher Nāṣir-i Khusraw, Jesus ascended to the fourth heaven because it contains the Sun, the heart of the universe since it emanates light and heat which are the sources of life. Likewise, Jesus is a source of life because he revives the dead.[36]) Rūmī reveals the spiritual reality that Jesus' "ascent" holds for each person. Through religious effort, ascetic discipline and the cultivation of reason, the spirit is able to shake free from the shackles of the body (personified by the donkey), and like Jesus, soar upwards into the heavens even before bodily death:

> The situation of man is like this. They took the feathers of an angel, and tied them to the tail of a donkey, that haply the donkey in the ray and society of the angel might become an angel. For it is possible that he may become of the same complexion of the angel.
>
> *Reason lent to Jesus pinions, and to heaven he flew and higher;*
> *Had his donkey had half a wing, he would not have hugged the mire.*[37]

The following is another example of how Rūmī gives every-day relevance to the images of Jesus and the fourth heaven, and the donkey and the stable. He compares a tyrannical king who orders the seizure of donkeys for forced labour with a just king who is concerned with the owners of donkeys:

> *But the king* [i.e. God] *of our city does not take at random. He is discriminating. He is seeing and hearing.*[38]
> *Be a man! Be not afraid of those who steal donkeys: You are not a donkey. Don't be afraid, O Jesus of this age.*
> *Moreover the fourth heaven is filled with your light: God forbid that your station is in the stable.*
> *You are higher even than the sky and the stars, though for a good reason you are* [temporarily] *in the stable.*
> *The master of the stable is one thing and the donkey another: not everyone who has entered the stable is a donkey.*[39]

The third category in this section is a discussion of Jesus' miracles. Rūmī describes Jesus' power to cure the deaf and blind,[40] and this ability to heal the sick is mentioned in the Qur'ān in the same breath as Jesus restoring life to the dead (5: 110). In addition, Rūmī speaks of the lame, the palsied, and those clothed in rags who gather outside Jesus' cell every morning in the hope of a miracle, and return home with their requests granted.[41] Another Qur'ānic miracle is Jesus' ability to speak while still a baby, for which "the most satisfactory parallel" is the Gospel story of Jesus lecturing in the temple when he was only twelve years of age.[42] Rūmī adapts Jesus' Qur'ānic words in *sūra* 19: 30–31: "Lo! I am God's servant; God has given me the book and made me a prophet," to demonstrate the real meaning of human perfection, personified in the following by the Sufi shaykh. Rūmī plays on the double meaning of the Persian word *pīr*, which as an adjective means old, and as a noun means a venerable person, or a Sufi shaykh:

> *Who is a "shaykh"? He is* pīr, *that is to say, white haired. Do you understand the meaning of this hair, O hopeless one?*
> *If self-existence remains within man, then it is shown by the black hair* [of existence].
> *When his self-existence vanishes, man is* pīr *whether he is black-haired or just greying.*
> *The existence of black hair is the attribute of man; it is not the hair of the head or beard.*
> *Jesus in the cradle cries out, "Without having become a youth, I am a shaykh and* pīr*!"*[43]

The subject of colour introduces another of Jesus' miracles which Rūmī presents in the *Mathnawī*. Jesus inserts a multi-coloured garment into a vat of dye and then draws out the same piece of clothing from the vat as pure and unicoloured. (This episode appears in the apocryphal Gospel of Philip when Jesus entered the dye works of Levi and threw seventy-two colours into a vat).[44] Rūmī's intention is to illustrate that the different forms of doctrine all have an underlying unity.[45]

The fourth and final category in this section concerns Rūmī's stories in *Fīhi mā fīhi* about Jesus that provide a possible juxtaposition of the Islamic concepts of divine mercy and divine wrath. Sufis of Rūmī's era, such as 'Azīz Nasafī (d. c. 1300), frequently expressed the mystical idea of the *coincidentia oppositorum*, where opposites become fused, or, all attributes are gathered together in one person who manifests each attribute at the appropriate time.[46] This is the reality of the Perfect Man, in this case Jesus.

Taking divine mercy first, Rūmī reports a discussion between Jesus who laughed much and John the Baptist who wept much. John questioned whether Jesus laughed because he had become secure against subtle deceits, and in return Jesus asked whether John had forgotten God's kindness and graces. At this point, one of the Friends of God wondered which of the two possessed the higher spiritual station. God replies to this enquiry in the words of a *ḥadīth*: "He who thinks better of Me – that is to say, 'I am where My servant thinks of Me.'"[47] This is explained further in a discussion which is related to the Sufi understanding of the imagination (see below). God is the servant of each individual for he appears in the form that any particular person has of him. It is better therefore if God is imagined in the purest manner possible.[48]

Divine wrath is the subject of a question addressed to Jesus concerning the greatest and most difficult thing for a man in this world and the next. The answer given by Jesus is "divine wrath" from which man can save himself by mastering his own wrath and rage.[49] The connection of Jesus with God's wrath also occurs in the *Mathnawī* when Jesus is found fleeing up a mountain side in an attempt to escape from a fool. Since Jesus has power over all things the fool could not comprehend why he was running away, and asks: "Who do you fear?"[50] (This episode has been likened to Jesus' temptation in the desert.[51]) While still attempting to escape from the fool, Jesus explains that folly is caused by divine wrath which brings rejection in its wake. Rūmī's intention in this story is to urge the spiritually minded to seek their own kind, and to stay away from fools who do not exercise their reason which can lead the individual towards God.

The discussion concerning God's wrath and mercy is intriguing because one wonders whether or not Rūmī intentionally meant to convey a teaching by juxtaposing these two attributes of God in narratives about Jesus. The answer would have to be negative if Arberry's opinion about *Fīhi mā fīhi* is correct, for he believed that it "represent[s] the impromptu outpourings of a mind overwhelmed in mystical thought, the multifarious, and often arrestingly original and beautiful images welling up unceasingly out of the poet's overflowing unconscious."[52] The stories themselves probably have no historical truth, and so Rūmī could just as easily have used any other Islamic prophet, or combination of prophets to convey his teachings.

II. MUḤAMMAD AND JESUS COMPARED

The Qur'ān states that all the prophets are fundamentally the same, and that there is no distinction between them (2: 136). So they can be considered as perfect men who manifest the appropriate attribute at the correct time. Given this, Rūmī poetically describes the perfect man of his age (such as Shams-i Tabrīz, who was one of Rūmī's spiritual mentors) as "the Jesus of the age"[53], and he also employs the term "the Moses of the age."[54]

However, Islamic tradition came to revere Muḥammad over and above all other prophets since he was honoured with the revelation of the perfected religion. He is considered as the most perfect "perfect man," and this "idealised" Muḥammad is very different from the Muḥammad that emerges from a literal reading of the Qur'ān. Indeed, it may be argued that after a literal reading of the Gospels, Jesus appears as a more remarkable prophet than Muḥammad due to the detailed portrayal of the miraculous events of the former's life. Perhaps influenced by contacts with Christians, there developed certain traditions about Muḥammad which are not mentioned specifically in the Qur'ān.[55] Rūmī, like other Muslims of his era, ascribed miracles to Muḥammad, perhaps to counter those attributed to Jesus. Although the Qur'ān states that Muḥammad is merely a man who does not perform miracles, and that the only miracle of Islam is the Qur'ān itself, Rūmī's works are littered with references to the Prophet's miracles such as the splitting of the moon[56] and God acting through Muḥammad when he threw dust against his enemies.[57] Rūmī also makes his comparison between Muḥammad and Jesus explicit when he states that God honoured and brought Jesus before him, indicating to his creatures that whoever serves Jesus also serves God, however, God also did the same to Muḥammad, "manifesting by his hand all that he manifested by Jesus' hand and more."[58]

Jesus' "inferior" rank compared to that of Muḥammad is referred to several times by Rūmī. He compares all the prophets to fish in the ocean of meaning (the reality of which is love), however, Muḥammad is the pearl in this ocean. Indeed, Muhammad sits alone, separate from the rest of the prophets who are paired together, such as Jesus and Moses, and Jonah and Joseph.[59] Mention is also made of Jesus' ascent to the fourth heaven which seems insignificant when compared to that of Muḥammad who passed all the heavens, and spoke to and witnessed God, and then returned back to Earth to continue his prophetic mission.[60] Furthermore, Rūmī compares Muḥammad's "Night

Ascent" to walking through the air, whereas Jesus could only walk on water (an element considered to be grosser than air in the elemental hierarchy of the classical period). He describes the situation of a thirsty man who is carried along in the water of life:

> *He is like Jesus, for the water carries him on its surface, since there is safety from drowning in the water of life.*
> [But] *Aḥmad* [Muḥammad] *says, "Had* [Jesus'] *certainty been greater, the air would have been his carriage and he would have been secure,*
> *Like me, a passenger upon the air on the Night Ascent and sought divine communion."*[61]

The reason that Jesus could not progress higher than the fourth heaven is explained by Rūmī as a result of Jesus' possession of a needle. Although Jesus is portrayed as an ascetic who renounces all needs, and prefers seclusion in a cave or on a mountain, owning a needle reveals his lack of complete reliance on God for all earthly needs.[62] Not all Sufis regarded Jesus' needle in such a negative manner. Hujwīrī (d. 1063) relates that a certain shaykh was told by Jesus that the lights on his cloak were the lights of necessary grace. In other words, Jesus sewed upon his cloak each patch through necessity and God turned into a light every tribulation that he inflicted upon his heart.[63] Again, Muḥammad's superior nature over that of Jesus is confirmed by Rūmī who reports that 'Alī (Muḥammad's son-in-law and cousin) said that his soul had been delivered from spiritual death due to the completion of Muḥammad's prophetic mission. This was a feat which neither two hundred mothers, nor Jesus could achieve. Although Jesus revived the dead such as Lazarus, ultimately they perished once again.[64]

In fact Muḥammad is able to ascend to the highest rank because he is the Islamic logos, created by God before time as a perfect spiritual existent containing all things within him. This is the so-called Muḥammadan Light. All prophets possess some degree of Muḥammad's perfection, but cannot be said to encompass the completeness of the first and last prophet.[65]

> *The Muḥammadan Light was* [divided] *into a thousand branches ...*
> *If Muḥammad unveils even one branch,*
> *A thousand monks and priests will rend* [their Christian] *belts.*[66]

The interpretation of the rending the "*zunnār*" belt (which Christians were obliged to fasten around their waists to indicate their religion) may take several forms. On one level Muḥammad's revelation causes monks and priests to accept Islam, and thus cast aside the "*zunnār*" belt. On another level, it may be a criticism, not of Christianity itself, but a rejection of Christian monastic practice and celibacy.[67]

Finally, mention should be made of Rūmī's criticism of Jesus' practice of solitude or seclusion which he implies is the origin of "monkery" (to be discussed in the next section). A comparison is made between Jesus' solitude and God's command to Muḥammad to be a guide for the community, for the latter is a second Noah, and is "the deliverer of every ship" for the journey. Therefore he should not "practice solitude like [Jesus] the Spirit of God," rather, he should put a stop to "seclusion and solitude."[68]

III. RŪMĪ'S CRITICISMS OF CHRISTIANITY

Although Rūmī's intention is not to criticise Jesus, he does include verses which disparage Christians. For example, Rūmī refers to the malicious nature of some Christians in his narrative about the "hypocrites" mentioned in *sūra* 9: 108–9, who built a mosque in Medina as a centre for spreading their anti-Islamic sentiments: "When have Christians or Jews sought the welfare of the [true] religion?"[69] In addition, Rūmī cites the Qur'ānic story of the table in which the apostles ask Jesus for a table of food to be sent down from heaven since this miracle would increase their faith.[70] God warns them that those who disbelieve after this miracle will be chastised. Some Christians fail to show respect when the table descends, for they hurriedly snatch away the viands, despite Jesus' pleas for them to restrain themselves, for the food is "lasting."[71] Rūmī sees God's chastisement of these people in *sūra* 5: 65: "And He turned them into apes and swine."[72]

Aside from the malicious nature of Christians, Rūmī's main criticisms of Christianity can be classified under three headings: a mistaken understanding of the nature of God, deficient practices, and falsification (*taḥrīf*) by Christians of the holy texts that God had sent down.

1 The Christian Understanding of God

The monotheism that is so explicitly affirmed in the Qur'ān is contrasted by Rūmī with the Christian concept of the Trinity that is described in *sūra* 5: 73. The Islamic mystical understanding of monotheism portrayed all existence as one (thus the boundaries delimiting the existence of man and God are erased). There is no concept of absorption, since absorption occurs between two things.

On achieving "enlightenment," the Sufi comes to recognise that ontological unity has existed all the time. This startling realisation often causes profound joy in the Sufi, and results in some mystics such as Ḥallāj to reveal the secret of unity that contradicts the belief of those Muslims who see an utter ontological chasm between man and God. In the following, Rūmī associates multiplicity with Christianity, since multiplicity maybe manifested in the form of the Trinity, or duality (an "orthodox" Islamic criticism of Christianity, since Muslims held that Christians believed that Jesus had both a divine and also human spirit in one body).

Become placeless in the Unity, take your place in the essence of annihilation;
put on a Christian neck every head which possesses duality.[73]
My heart and soul has been filled with the essence of the meaning of "He" [God]; *He is – even though He said he is not – the third and second to me.*[74]

The proximity of God, or the "Unity," is expressed in the following verses by Rūmī, in which he appears to criticise Christians for not understanding that God is within the individual. There is no need for a priest to act as an intermediary between man and God. Although God exists within each individual, the divine cannot be encompassed, and this explains why God can initiate the attraction, or "pulling" (see below), which draws the individual to the divine, or in other words, assists him or her to recognise Unity. Once this is realised, the water of life cascades from a once stone-like heart:

The Christian confesses to the priest the sins of the year – fornication, malice, hypocrisy,
So that the priest will forgive those sins, for he regards the priest's forgiveness as God's forgiveness.
[But] *that priest has no knowledge of sin or recompense ...*
When My pull is set in motion from [My] *direction,* [the Christian] *does not see the priest intervening between* [us].
The Christian is craving forgiveness for his sins and transgressions from God's kindness behind the veil.
When a spring gushes out of a rock, the rock disappears in the spring.
After that, no one calls it a "stone," since such a precious substance gushes forth from the stone.[75]

Rūmī's main criticism, however, remains with the Trinity. His remarks about the priest are designed to draw the reader's attention to his fundamental point, which is to realise Unity through love.

Although Christian images are utilised in the above verse, Rūmī also makes the same point with reference to the Islamic jurist (*faqīh*) who considered his task as analysing which human acts were legally permitted under Islamic law: "Faqīh! For God's sake, learn the science of love, for after death, where are 'lawful', 'unlawful' and 'obligatory acts'?"[76]

The Christian mis-understanding of the nature of God and Jesus appears in Rūmī's criticism of Christians in seeking help from Jesus who could not even save himself from crucifixion: "See the ignorance of the Christian appealing for protection to the Lord who was suspended [on a cross]."[77] This verse highlights Rūmī's limited appreciation of the Christian understanding of Christ as Son of God. (Of course, Muslims have no need to believe in the crucifixion – which for Christians is necessary in order for man's sins to be absolved – since the concept of original sin is a Christian one).

Likewise, Rūmī asks that after ascending to the fourth heaven, what can Jesus do for the Church? This is contrasted with the effect of Shams-i Tabrīz's advent in the world which causes the bedstone of the water mill to be set in motion.[78]

2 Christian Practices

Aside from criticisms on the nature of the Christian God, or existence, Rūmī focuses his aim upon Christian practices. One of these, "Monkery," was singled out in both the Qur'ān 57: 27 and *ḥadīth* as a practice which was never prescribed by God. Rūmī argues that monasticism is not sanctioned by God because religion is of a communal nature and faith is strengthened in a crowd. Despite their base nature, donkeys are exhilarated in a group and exert themselves. But when they stray alone, the road seems long and they become weary.[79] In an explicit criticism of monasticism, Rūmī spells out the communal duties of prayer, enjoining the good and forbidding evil, bearing the affliction that other people cause and conferring benefits on others.[80] Rūmī then warns that the person who wishes only for bread is a donkey and companionship with such a person is the essence of monkery.[81] Indeed, Rūmī contrasts the seclusion that he associates with monasticism with the warfare that is encouraged in some situations by Islam:

... Jihād occurs when a highwayman ... is on the road,
The valiant man enters the unsafe road to protect, help and battle.

The root of manhood becomes apparent when the traveller meets his enemies on the road.
Since the Messenger was the Prophet of the sword, his community is [composed of] *heroes and champions.*
In our religion, war and terror are expedient; in the religion of Jesus [solitude in] *cave and mountain is expedient ...*
Generally a wolf seizes [its prey] *when a lamb strays alone from the flock.*
... He who has renounced the Sunna with the [Muslim] *community, has he not drunk his own blood in the lair of wild beasts?*
The Sunna is the road of the community and is like a friend: without the road and without a companion you will fall into dire straits.[82]

Monasticism is associated in Islam with celibacy which is considered in an unfavourable light. After all, writing does not come about unless it is through the union of ink and pen, and rush mats cannot exist until straws are woven together.[83] Moreover, according to Rūmī, monasticism does not resolve the problem of temptation because it is necessary to come face to face with temptation in order to master it:

Don't tear out your feathers [O peacock], *but detach your heart from them because the enemy is the necessary condition for this jihād.*
When there is no enemy, the jihād is inconceivable; if you have no lust, there can be no obedience [to the Divine Command].
There can be no patience when you have no desire; when there is no adversary, what need for your strength?
Don't be hasty! Don't castrate yourself, don't become a monk; for chastity depends upon the existence of lust.
Without sensuality it is impossible to forbid sensuality: heroism cannot be displayed against the dead.[84]

A similar message is provided in *Fīhi mā fīhi*, where the trials of the communal nature of Islam are compared with the problems encountered by Christian ascetics:

> The way of the Prophet now, God bless him and give him peace, was this. It is necessary to endure pain, ridding oneself of jealousy and manly pride, pain over extravagance and clothing one's wife, and a hundred other pains beyond all bounds, that the Muḥammadan world may come into being. The way of Jesus, upon whom be peace, was wrestling with solitude and not gratifying lust; the way of Muḥammad, God bless him and give him peace, is to endure the oppression and agonies afflicted by

men and women. If you cannot go by the Muḥammadan way, at least go by the way of Jesus, that you may not remain altogether beyond the pale.[85]

Other Christian practices which Rūmī disdains include idol-worship: "Infidels are content with the figures of the prophets which are painted and kept in churches."[86] Rūmī also has much to say about the consumption of wine which is forbidden by Islamic law. Perhaps because wine is not permitted to Muslims, Persian mystical poets frequently utilised the image of a Christian wine-bearer who offers the intoxicating brew. As a result of this wine of love, intoxication became a common theme in Sufi literature, and the metaphor was extended by describing the actions of the drunk who is unable to control his actions and ecstatic utterances (*shaṭḥ*), such as the "I am the Truth" uttered by Manṣūr al-Ḥallāj (executed in 922):

O wine-bearer of the spirit! Fill that ancient cup, that highwayman of the heart, that ambusher of religion!
Fill it with the wine that springs from the heart and mixes with the spirit, the wine whose ferment intoxicates the God-seeing eye.
That grape wine is for Jesus' community – but this "Ḥallājiyan" wine is for the community of Yā Sīn [Muḥammad].
There are vats of that wine and vats of this. Until you break the first you will never taste of the second!
That wine drowns sorrow from the heart for but an instant, it can never eliminate sorrow, it can never uproot malice.[87]

The metaphor of the drunk and wine is continued in the following, in which Rūmī identifies himself as the Christian wine-bearer, and his spirtual mentor, Shams al-Dīn al-Tabrīzī (literally the Sun of Religion of Tabrīz), is the person who understands the secrets of wine:

The actions of a drunk are caused by wine.
What appears in water is nothing but [the reflection of the moon] *from above.*
At last, a cup from him, Tabriz, the Sun of Religion!
Come, won't you tell just one secret to that Christian wine-bearer.[88]

The intoxicating effects of spiritual wine, as mentioned above, were often associated with Ḥallāj, and it is worthy to note that both Muslim and non-Muslim scholars have drawn two main connections between Ḥallāj and Christianity. First, Hallāj was accused of advocating incarnationism (*ḥulūl*), the infusion of two spirits within one body, a doctrine which Muslims held to be the Christian understanding of Jesus (that is, a divine spirit and a human spirit). Comprehending the message that Ḥallāj wished to convey is problematic, but as Ernst has indicated, lines such as "My spirit mixes with your spirit, in nearness and distance, so that I am You, just as You are I" were criticised by Ḥallāj's own friends because they seemed to "imply a semi-Christian doctrine of incarnation (*ḥulūl*)."[89] The second reason for the association between Jesus and Ḥallāj is that whereas the former is believed by Muslims to have escaped the cross, the latter met his end through crucifixion. Rūmī contrasts the Christian belief in Jesus' crucifixion with the Sufi ideal of killing all non-Godly concerns associated with the lower-self, or ego, which separates man from the divine:

> *The* [Muslim] *believer does not have that idea which the Christian carries, that* [God] *is killing the Messiah on the cross.*
> *Every true lover is like Manṣūr* [al-Ḥallāj], *for they slay themselves.*[90]

The reasons for Ḥallāj's execution remain somewhat obscure, although his controversial lifestyle, based on his interpretation and practice of Sufism, combined with the political intrigues of the 'Abbasid court certainly contributed to his execution by crucifixion.[91] It seems that Ḥallāj himself was well aware of the consequences of his actions and the circumstances of his times, as he predicted: "My death will be in the religion of the cross."[92] Thus, parallels have been drawn by Western scholars such as Massignon and Mason of Ḥallāj's readiness "to become a powerless victim, to suffer condemnation and death like Jesus, for the purification of his Community."[93]

Rūmī also makes a parallel between Ḥallāj's ecstatic statement, "I am the Truth," and the story of Jesus who placed into a vat clothes of various colours, and which were heard to exclaim, "I am the vat."[94] Both Ḥallāj and the garments experienced the Islamic baptism mentioned in *sūra* 2: 138, which leaves all things in their primordial nature.

3 Falsification (*taḥrīf*) of the Scriptures

The falsification of the texts was, and continues to be, one of the major topics of discussion between Muslims and Christians. *Sūra* 2: 75 accuses the People of the Book (Jews and Christians) of writing the Book with their own hands in order to sell it for a small price. The Qur'ān does not offer specific examples of this, however, Islamic tradition identified the censorship of Muḥammad's name from the Gospels as one instance of *taḥrīf*. In one of his narratives, Rūmī claims that the name of Muḥammad did indeed appear in the Gospels, in addition, the real Gospels foretold his battles, fasting and eating. This was recognised by a party of Christians who "would bestow kisses on that noble name and stoop their faces towards that beauteous description."[95] However, another group of Christians held the name of the Islamic prophet in contempt, and the corruption of their scrolls perverted the genuine laws and religion that God had sent down.[96] It has been suggested that this narrative alludes to the traditional Muslim belief that Muḥammad is referred to in verses fourteen and fifteen of John's Gospel.[97] Christians read *parakletos*, or advocate, whereas the Islamic belief is that the word revealed by God was *periklutos*, which means much praised, a name similar to the Arabic "Muḥammad" meaning "one who is praised."

Rūmī's narrative of the appearance of Muḥammad's name appearing in the Gospels is part of a lengthy explanation of how diversity appeared in the Christian community.[98] In this story, Rūmī described the antics of an evil Jewish king and his vizier who failed to see the underlying unity between the religions of Moses and Jesus. Aside from their attempts to discredit Christianity in numerous ways, they killed hundreds of thousands of Christians. In one episode, the vizier pretended to be a Christian and claimed that he possessed the true message of Christianity. Once he was accepted by the Christians as Jesus' deputy (*nāyib-i 'Īsā*), this wolf in sheep's clothing handed to each leader of the twelve Christian communities a scroll which presented the "pristine" version of the Gospels. The contents of these scrolls contradicted each other, and in addition, the vizier privately appointed each of the twelve Christian leaders as his vicegerent (*khalīfa*). The vizier then commited suicide, throwing the Christian community into dissent and turmoil since each of the twelve communities regarded their scrolls as genuine, and twelve individuals emerged claiming to be the true *khalīfa* of the vizier. Muslims prior to Rūmī were familiar with this story of the vizier and the Christians, the former being identified as Saint Paul. (It has been argued that this identification was probably derived from Christian theologians favourable to Saint Peter).[99] One of the messages in the story above is that Christianity in its true form is a genuine revelation from God, and the twisting of the texts has caused the squabbles among the various denominations (reflecting *sūra* 19: 34–6) who fail to cross over from the form of religion to the inner meaning.

IV. CHRISTIANITY AND SUFI PLURALISM

The essence of Rūmī's message is the need to cross over from the form to the reality, thus he speaks of "a thousand Gabriels within man" and "the Messiahs within the donkey's belly," and "a thousand Kaʿba's concealed in a church."[100] Religions too have their form and reality, including both Islam and Christianity. This belief is the foundation of Rūmī's pluralist worldview which is based upon his mystical epistemology (derived in part from the writings of Ibn Sīnā). The knowledge that man obtains from this world through his five senses is stored in his memory, and can then be utilised by his imagination to give forms to abstract ideas. The imagination also plays a vital role for man in his understanding of knowledge which has its origin in the divine realm.[101] Such knowledge may be a self-disclosure of God (who is described as light in *sūra* 24: 35), and it may be revealed by angels who are created by God from light. It is impossible for man to perceive God's light, and it is the imagination which enables him to make sense of God's self-disclosures and angels, since the imagination provides this light with a form. The imagination then is the store of forms that man has actualised during his life in this world, and the forms of the self-disclosures and angels will necessarily reflect his culture and upbringing. Rūmī describes this process in *Fīhi mā fīhi* by comparing the human imagination to a vestibule of a house. Once the divine knowledge has entered the vestibule it can then become manifest in the world.[102]

Since the culture and experience of each individual is unique, Rūmī could not logically limit God's self-disclosure through the imagination to one form alone. Because the spirit transcends form, God is portrayed by Rūmī as appearing in one form which is annihilated once it becomes an idol. Indeed, Sufis of Rūmī's era including ʿAzīz Nasafī, compared God's appearance through forms to the waves on a billowing ocean. Such a view affirms God's infinite creative power, ultimate incomprehensibility, and Sufi pluralism:

> *Hold on to the skirt of His grace, for suddenly He will flee; but do not draw Him as an arrow, for He will flee from the bow.*
> *What images does He play at, what tricks contrive! If He is present in form, He will flee by way of the spirit.*
> *Seek Him in the sky, and He shines from the water like the* [reflection of] *the moon; jump in the water and He flees up to heaven.*
> *Call Him from the placeless and He points you to place; seek Him in place, and He flees to the placeless.*[103]

To understand how Rūmī considers pluralism, it is necessary to investigate the imagination further, and fortunately he offers many insights into this topic by employing themes which are relevant to Christianity. Several important features of the imagination appear in his explanation of the annunciation, an account of which appears in *sūra* nineteen of the Qur'ān. Islamic tradition holds that the spirit spoken of in the Qur'ān refers to Gabriel who appeared in the likeness (*tamaththala*) of a man to Mary. In his discussion of the annunciation, Rūmī has Gabriel explain that he is manifest to Mary through her imagination, and such forms which come from the unseen realm of God cannot be set aside, unlike the fantasies that derive from the transient human realm:

> *Look well Mary, for I am a difficult form* [to understand]. *I am both the new moon and also the image* (khayāl) *in the heart.*
> *When an image enters your heart and establishes* [itself there], *it remains with you wherever you flee*
> *Unless it is an insubstantial, false image that sinks like the false dawn.*
> *I am like the true dawn* [created] *from the Lord's light: no night prowls around my day.*[104]

This appearance of Gabriel is merely the means by which God discloses himself. This occurs through the imagination, not in the realm of sense perception (termed the stable):

> *All perceptions* [ride] *upon lame donkeys. He* [i.e. God's self-disclosure] *rides upon the wind, flying like an arrow ...*[105]
> *The eye of a child, like that of a donkey, falls upon the stable* (ākhur), *while the eye of a man of reason takes account of the next world* (ākhir).[106]

At first, Mary did not understand the reality of this spiritual manifestation, and naked and fearful, she sought protection in God.[107] Gabriel has to explain that although the external appearance of Mary's "imaginalisation" is of a beautiful youth (thus the full-moon) the inner reality is a manifestation of the divine attributes. Her fear and seeking protection in God are meaningless:

> *I am that seclusion that was* [your] *deliverance. You take refuge, yet I am that refuge.*
> *There is no greater calamity than not recognising* [the Truth]*: You are with the Friend but you don't know how to make love!*
> *You fancy that the Friend is a stranger. You have placed the name of sorrow upon a joy.*

> *This date palm, which is the kindness of our Friend, is our gibbet* (dār), *if we are robbers.*[108]

The above is full of allusions to the Qur'ān: "seclusion" refers to Mary seeking isolation from her people before the advent of the spirit (19: 17); "refuge" is Mary's cry at the appearance of the spirit in 19: 18; the "date-palm" is mentioned in 19: 23–25, when the pangs of childbirth drove Mary to a date-palm where she was able to eat and drink. It is interesting that Rūmī also mentions a gibbet in the same sentence as the date-palm, and one wonders if Rūmī is making an association with this tree and a crucifixion upon a tree? If God's self-disclosure through the imagination is not understood for what it is, then we are like robbers taking something that does not belong to us, thus God's mercy turns to wrath, or the date-palm becomes the cross. (The connection between "imaginalisation" and the crucifixion is offered by Rūmī when he describes a devious prince who desired to steal Jesus' crown. However the prince was crucified (literally, he became the crown of the gibbet *[tāj-dār])* instead of Jesus.[109])

Rūmī was not the only Sufi of the medieval period to discuss God's self-disclosure appearing through the imagination. Indeed, on the basis of this kind of epistemology, Persian Sufis including Suhrawardī (d. 1191)[110] and 'Azīz Nasafī held that experiences of non-Muslims were legitimate manifestations of reality. However, there were other mystics who claimed that the mystical experiences of non-Muslims were deficient. For example, Najm al-Dīn Rāzī (d. 1256) held that Hindus, Christians and Philosophers experienced the reality of the spirit "whereas Muslims witness the lights and attribute of unity."[111] His position was reflected in the writings of another Persian mystic, Alā al-Dawla Simnānī (1261–1336) which record a hierarchy of seven spiritual centres within man, that is, seven levels of being which are differentiated by the "spiritual witnessing" of colours.[112] These rankings reflect the hierarchy in the heavens, and Simnānī places Jesus in the sixth heaven which is also the level attained by Sufis such as Ḥallāj. Simnānī discusses the Christian mistake of believing that Jesus is God, and that of Ḥallāj which prevents further progression to the seventh station. For Ḥallāj, the experience of "I am the Truth," that is, annihilation in God, caused him to think actual material absorption had taken place in the Godhead. The reverse is the case for Christians who believe that the Godhead was absorbed into the human. For Simnānī, the reality of the sixth heaven is the appearance of the ego, or in other words, the breath which God blew in to man, a reality which Ḥallāj and Christians mis-interpret. The highest rank is the Muḥammadan level, for here man realises the nature of his essence, which is derived from God's spirit. In other words, man is similar to yet also distinct from God, a seemingly paradoxical situation that reflects the Islamic teaching of God's similarity and incomparability (or to use Christian terms, immanence and transcendence) with man.

Yet the position of Najm al-Dīn Rāzī and Simnānī restricts God's absolute power; the famous light verse of the Qur'ān (24: 35) states, "God guides to His light whomever He pleases." The Sufis held that ultimately, regardless of the individual's actions, it is God that "pulls" or attracts man to him, "pulling" (*jadhba*) being one of the technical terms of the Islamic mystics. Numerous Sufis cited a *ḥadīth* which supported this view: "A single pulling of God equals all the works of *jinn* and men."[113] Rūmī also cites this *ḥadīth* in a story of the famous lovers Layla and Majnūn. In Rūmī's portrayal, Layla symbolises God, Majnūn represents the spirit of the wayfarer searching for God, and a third party, namely a she-camel is introduced, signifying the body of this wayfarer. Majnūn is a lover of God, but the she-camel cares for nothing except her baby camel. Whereas Majnūn desires to progress forward towards God, the she-camel wants to return to her infant, and since he can no longer control the camel, Majnūn flings himself off the animal's back, but in so doing he breaks his leg. It is at this point that Majnūn realises that even after his spiritual effort he has to rely on God for any further progress, for "such is the extraordinary voyage which transcends the utmost effort of the *Jinn* and mankind."[114] Yet, in some passages Rūmī implies that God's pull is more likely to occur if the divine commands and prohibitions are followed.[115] Christians also have divine commands and prohibitions revealed to them, and therefore it is possible that God will draw them to himself. But for this to happen, one assumes that the Christian must follow the pristine commands and prohibitions, or he or she must become a Muslim. Once divine unity has been realised, and existence is understood in a mystical mode that is not comprehended through the senses, then all forms are transcended, and only pure Islam remains.

> *I slept under the shadow of fortune; you* [God] *opened a way for me beside the five senses.*
> *On that road it is possible to go east and west, without feather, without head or foot.*
> *On that road is no thorn of free will; no Christian, no Jew.*

The soul, beyond the circumference of its blue sky, is escaped from blueness and blindness.
Why do you weep? Go to the laughing ones! Why do you tarry? Go to the same place where you once were![116]

CONCLUSION

This chapter has focused on Rūmī's portrayal of Jesus and Christianity, which demonstrates that his inclusive interpretation of Islam must be re-assessed. Certainly, there are many verses within Rūmī's works that appear to confirm an inclusive understanding, such as the following, which explains that God may be manifested to believers of all traditions through the perfected individual:

Sometimes, through your face you bestow love and impatience on reason;
sometimes through your eyes, you play the Messiah to the sick.
Sometimes, with your tresses you give the image of God's cord[117] *to the believer;*
sometimes through twisted curls you give a cross to the Christian.[118]

The above describes how reality appears in different forms, which is, perhaps, the major theme in Rūmī's works, as he exclaims, "So long as the *form* of the Beloved's image is with us, for us the whole of life is a joyful festival."[119]

Despite his inclusivist veneer, it must be remembered that Rūmī considered the Islamic form of religion was superior to that of others because the comprehensive nature of Islam extends into all spheres of life as a communal religion. In this respect Rūmī is an "orthodox" Muslim, convinced that the form of religion was perfected with God's revelation that was sent to Muḥammad, for *sūra* 5: 3 states: "Today I have perfected your religion for you, and I have completed My blessing upon you, and I have approved Islam for your religion."

For Rūmī, everything in existence has a form and reality, and such an understanding can also be applied to Jesus. The form is the Jesus of the Qur'ān, both a remarkable prophet who performed miracles and also a spiritual master aware of the realities of the age. This Jesus is a saviour in as much as he calls people to the sacred law that God has revealed. To speak of Jesus in terms of salvation is meaningless for "orthodox" Muslims because the Qur'ān offers a version of Adam's fall and an interpretation of the nature of sin which are different from those in the Bible.[120] It is necessary to interiorise the teachings of the prophets which can guide man to the reality within himself. Merely accepting the historical Jesus as a prophet will not result in man being admitted to paradise. For Sufis, it is the form of Jesus that Christians perceive in the Incarnation – an understanding in the sensory realm, not in the imagination.

The reality is the Jesus to whom Rūmī refers as the "Spirit of God," the "Messiah within the donkey," in other words, it is man's spiritual dimension. This Jesus can provide salvation since he has the power to master the body and is the creative source that must be reflected in a mirror. Therefore, it is necessary to witness the "Jesus of your being" in the suprasensory realm, the imagination. Each individual must become a mirror where the Truth can be witnessed as a theophany, just as light takes a form by shining through stained glass. This, according to Corbin shows how "the Godhead is in mankind as an Image is in a mirror. The *place* of this Presence is the consciousness of the individual believer, or more exactly, the theophanic Imagination invested in him. His time is lived psychic time. The Incarnation, on the other hand, is hypostatic union. It occurs in the flesh."[121]

NOTES

1 See C. Ernst, *The Shambhala Guide to Sufism* (Boston & London: Shambhala, 1997), p. 170.

2 See F. R. van der Mehden, "American Perceptions of Islam," in J. Esposito (ed.), *Voices of Resurgent Islam,* (Oxford University Press, 1983), pp. 18–31. See also R. Fisk's article "US Media Mirror Distorts Middle East," in *The Independent*, 10.06.98, p. 14.

3 Cited by A. Ahmad, *Postmodernism and Islam* (London: Routledge, 1992), p. 37.

4 In December 1994, I attended a *samā'* of the whirling dervishes in the Cathedral Church of St John the Divine in New York.

5 *Saqsin*, according to Nicholson, *Selected Poems from the Dīvāni Shamsi Tabrīz* (Cambridge: Cambridge University Press, 1898) p. 282, was a city in the land of the Khazars whose territories extended from the Crimean to the Caspian Seas.

6 In Persian, *Panj āb*, or *Punjāb*, means the five rivers.

7 *Riẓwan* is the door-keeper of Paradise.

8 Rūmī, from *Dīwān-i Shams-i Tabrīz*, trans. R. A. Nicholson in *Rūmī, Mystic and Poet* (London: George Allen and Unwin, 1950), p. 177. The difficulty in translating in verse led Nicholson to a less literal version, which appears in his *Selected Poems from the Dīvāni Shamsi Tabrīz*, p. 125. Schimmel has implied that this verse may not have been composed by Rūmī at all since it is not found in the critical edition of the Kulliyāt-i Shams, but resembles in its tenor the works of later Persian and Turkish poets. See *The Triumphal Sun* (London & the Hague: East-West Publications, 1980), p. 389.

9 A. Schimmel, foreward in J. Renard, *All the King's Falcons* (Albany: SUNY Press, 1994), p. x–xi.
10 'Abd al-Raḥmān Jāmī (d. 1492), a great Sufi poet in his own right and commentator on the works of Ibn 'Arabī.
11 Cited by A. Schimmel, *The Triumphal Sun*, p. 367.
12 *Ibid*., p. 369.
13 *Fīhi mā fīhi*, trans. A. J. Arberry as *Discourses of Rūmī*, (Richmond: Curzon reprint, 1993), p. 54. The moral of Rūmī's story is that by forcing Jesus from one place to another, he is in fact being drawn closer to God. All subsequent references to *Fīhi mā fīhi* are taken from Arberry's translation.
14 *Mathnawī-yi Ma'nawī*, edited and translated R. A. Nicholson, with commentary, 8 volumes (London: Luzac & Co), VI: 930. The translations in this article are my own, although heavily based on Nicholson's.
15 The donkey is still regarded with disdain and ridicule in areas such as Iran and Turkey, perhaps because of the descriptions found of the donkey in the Qur'ān. For example, 31: 19 states, "the most hideous of voices is the donkey's," and 62: 5 describes a people who do not understand God's revelations as donkeys that carry books. Rūmī cites this verse in *Mathnawī.* I: 3447.
16 *Dīwān-i Shams*, ed. B. Furūzānfar (Tehran: Amīr Kabīr, 1957–66) no. 35583.
17 *Mathnawī*, V: 275–76.
18 *Mathnawī*, I: 1185; II: 571–72.
19 Cited by A. Schimmel, *Deciphering the Signs of God* (Albany: SUNY Press, 1994), p. 103.
20 *Mathnawī*, I: 424; II: 344.
21 Matthew 9: 20, Mark 5: 29, Luke 8: 44.
22 See Schimmel, *Deciphering the Signs of God*, p. 103.
23 *Mathnawī*, VI: 4118.
24 See A. J. Arberry, *Mystical Poems of Rūmī 2* (Chicago: Chicago University Press,1991), p. 164.
25 *Dīwān-i Shams*, no. 1826, line 19180.
26 Qur'ān 3: 58, "Jesus in God's sight is like Adam; He created him from dust, then He said to him: 'Be', and there he was."
27 *Dīwān-i Shams,* no. 2617, line 27726.
28 The advantages of engaging in *dhikr* were described by many medieval Islamic mystics, including Najm al-Dīn Kubrā (d. 1220–1) who listed eleven benefits, but his tenth is worth citing here:

> The tenth benefit [of remaining silent except for reciting the *dhikr*] is becoming similar to Mary, the mother of Jesus, since [she said], "I have vowed to the All-Merciful a fast, and today I will not speak with any man" [19: 26]. When the period of silence had passed, the Truth Most High caused Jesus to speak in infancy: "Lo, I am God's servant; God has given me the book" [19: 30] Is it not a marvel that when someone of the [Sufi] path refrains from talking nonsense, the Jesus of his heart begins to speak?

Najm al-Dīn Kubrā, *Al-sā'ir al-ḥā'ir*, ed. M. Qāsimī (Tehran: Kitābfurūshī Zawwār, 1361), p. 24. Rūmī also describes these circumstances, based on *sūra* 19: 25–30:

Sometimes, like Jesus, we have all become tongue;
Sometimes, like Mary, we have a silent heart.

Diwān-i Shams, no. 21030, translated by A. Schimmel in Y. Y. Haddad & W. Z. Haddad (eds.), *Christian-Muslim Encounters*, (Gainesville: University of Florida Press, 1995), p. 154.

29 Jamshid was a pre-Islamic Iranian king, famous for his love of pleasure. He was instrumental in introducing wine-drinking into Iran.
30 *Fīhi mā fīhi*, p. 33. Quatrain attributed to the Persian poet Khāqānī (d. 1200).
31 *Mathnawī*, II: 1858–60.
32 *Diwān-i Shams*, line 35277.
33 *Mathnawī*, I: 528.
34 See *Mathnawī*, VI: 4364–70, based on the Qur'ān 4: 154–9.
35 *Mathnawī*, I: 649. In some cases, the Islamic tradition holds that Jesus abides in the second heaven, and Ibn Iṣḥaq (d. 773) cites a *ḥadīth* to this effect (see *The Life of Muḥammad*, trans. A. Guillaume [Oxford University Press, 1955], p. 186).
36 See S. H. Nasr, *The Islamic Intellectual Tradition in Persia* (Richmond: Curzon Press, 1996), p. 18. Medieval Islamic cosmology held that there were seven heavens (each one containing a planet) arranged around each other like the layers of an onion, with Earth at the centre. Beyond the seven spheres was the sphere of the fixed stars, and encompassing them all was the Sphere of Spheres. See M. Fakhri, *A History of Islamic Philosophy* (London: Longman, 1983), p. 171–2. The idea of a living cosmos is found in the works of Plato and Plutarch, the latter argued that the sun pumped out heat and light like blood. See S. Sambursky, *The Physical World of the Greeks* (London: Routledge, 1987), p. 213.
37 *Fīhi mā fīhi*, p. 118. The verse is by Sanā'ī, *Dīvān*, p. 497.
38 "He is seeing and hearing" is a reference to *sūra* 17: 1.
39 *Mathnawī*, V: 2547–50.
40 *Mathnawī*, III: 2585.
41 *Mathnawī*, III: 298–307.
42 G. Parrinder, p. 79 referring to Luke, 2: 49. The story of Jesus speaking as a baby appears to have developed by Rūmī's time from its Qur'ānic form. Marco Polo relates a variant of this story that he heard from some Perians based in Saba (or Sāvah – some fifty miles south-west of Tehran). From the city of Saba, the three kings, Jaspar, Melchior and Balthazar went to worship a prophet that had been born in a distant land, carrying with them the gifts of gold (befitting for an earthly king), incense (worthy of God), and myrrh (a suitable gift for a physician). On reaching the place where the child had been born, the kings went into see this prophet one by one. On each occasion, the child appeared to each king as his own age. For the full version of this story, see *The Book of Ser Marco Polo, the Venetion*, pp. 73–6.
43 *Mathnawī*, III: 1790–94.
44 *The Gospel of Philip*, trans, R. Wilson (London: A. R. Mowbray & Co., 1962), p. 39.
45 *Mathnawī*, I: 500–1. The root of transmission of this story may have been

the Arabic Infancy Gospels (the dates of which have yet to be established, although it has been speculated that they might have been written in 400 C. E.). See G. Parrinder, *Jesus in the Qur'ān* (Oxford: One World, 1995) pp. 27–29. From there, it may have passed into the *Qiṣas al-anbiyā* of Tha'labī (d. 1036) in which Jesus drew several garments out of the vat one by one and each was a different colour. The Sufi inspired poet Sanā'ī (d. 1131) offered an alternative in which Jesus dyed many coloured garments in his vat and all the clothes became pure and white, see J. Renard, op. cit. p. 187–8 n. 46.

46 See L. Ridgeon, *'Azīz Nasafī* (London: Curzon Press, pp. 171–78.

47 *Ḥadīth*, see W. Graham, *Divine Word and Prophetic Word in Early Islam* (The Hague: Mouton, 1977), p. 130.

48 *Fīhi mā fīhi*, p. 60–1. This discussion also appears in *Dīwān-i Shams*, no. 1211.

49 *Ibid.*, p. 239.

50 *Mathnawī*, III: 2581.

51 James Roy King, "Jesus and Joseph in Rūmī's Mathnawī," *The Muslim World*, 80:2 (April 1990), p. 84.

52 Arberry, *Discourses of Rumi*, p. 9.

53 *Dīwān-i Shams,* no. 1156, line 12274. *(Shams-i Tabrīz, 'Īsā-yi 'ahdī).* Other expressions include *'Īsā-yi rūzgār,* no. 707, line 7394.

54 *Dīwān-i Shams,* no. 2220, line 23553.

55 As A. Jeffrey comments: "As pre-existence was ascribed to Christ, so it was to Muḥammad. As Gabriel announced Jesus to the Virgin Mary, so he did to Amina, the mother of Muḥammad. As the angel gave the name of Jesus before he was born, so in the case of Muḥammad. As Jesus in infancy was presented in the Temple, so was Muḥammad in the national sanctuary of Arabia. As Jesus in the beginning of his ministry had to pass through an ordeal of Satanic temptation, so did Muḥammad. As Jesus chose twelve apostles, so Muḥammad chose twelve companions. As Jesus ascended into heaven, so did Muḥammad; and so on." See "Muḥammad: Real and Unreal," in the *International Review of Missions*, vol. XVIII, 1929, pp. 393.

56 Muslims believe that *sūra* 53: 1 refers to this.

57 Muslims believe that *sūra* 8: 17 refers to this. Rūmī discusses many other miracles performed by Muḥammad, see chapter eight of J. Renard.

58 *Fīhi mā fīhi*, p. 136.

59 *Dīwān-i Shams,* no. 1700, lines 17805–6.

60 *Dīwān-i Shams*, no. 341, line 3685.

61 *Mathnawī*, VI: 1186–88.

62 *Dīwān-i Shams*, 2550, line 27055. See also Schimmel, *The Triumphal Sun*, pp. 182, 438 n. 56.

63 Hujwīrī, *Kashf al-Mahjub*, ed. Zhukovski (Tehran: Kitabkhana-yi turi, 1375), p. 56.

64 *Mathnawī*, V: 274–76. Rūmī repeats the same idea in IV: 1064–68.

65 *Mathnawī*, IV: 524–9.

66 *Dīwān-i Shams*, no. 1137, line 12051–2.

67 With regard to the *zunnār*, we can cite the following lines from Rūmī:

O Jesus, the conjoiner [of nāsūt and lāhūt]*! The healing of great suffering.*
Don't guard the zunnār for the sake of two or three Christians.

(Rūmī, Dīwān-i Shams, no. 2220, line 23554).

68 *Mathnawī*, IV: 1458–62.
69 *Mathnawī*, I: 2859.
70 As Parrinder comments, it is not clear whether this Qur'ānic tale parallels the story in the Gospels of the feeding of the five-thousand or the Last Supper. See G. Parrinder, *Jesus in the Qur'ān* (Oxford: One World, 1995), p. 87. Mentioned by Rūmī in the *Dīwān-i Shams,* no. 1739.
71 *Mathnawī*, I: 80–89. See the Qur'ān, 5: 65.
72 *Mathnawī*, V: 2591–99.
73 *Dīwān-i Shams*, no. 1876, line 19763.
74 *Dīwān-i Shams,* no. 207, line 2315.
75 *Mathnawī*, V: 3257–84.
76 *Dīwān-i Shams,* no. 2705.
77 *Mathnawī,* II: 1401.
78 *Dīwān-i Shams,* no. 114, lines 1283–5.
79 *Mathnawī*, VI: 514–15.
80 *Mathnawī*, VI: 480–1.
81 *Mathnawī*, VI: 485.
82 *Mathnawī*, VI: 490–502.
83 *Mathnawī*, VI: 521–23.
84 *Mathnawī*, V: 574–78.
85 *Fīhi mā fīhi*, p. 99.
86 *Mathnawī*, V: 3599.
87 *Dīwān-i Shams*, no. 81, lines 929–933. Rūmī also tells a story in which Christian wine is considered in a spiritual light: "In that [Christian's]wine there is a [hidden] spiritual substance, even as [spiritual] sovereignty is [hidden] in the dervish-cloak." *Mathnawī*, V: 3448.
88 *Dīwān-i Shams*, no. 2617, lines 27734–5.
89 Cited in C. Ernst, *Words of Ecstasy in Sufism* (Albany: SUNY Press, 1985), p. 27.
90 *Dīwān-i Shams,* no. 728, lines 7642–3.
91 See L. Massignon, *Hallaj: Mystic and Martyr*, translated, edited and abridged by H. Mason (Princeton University Press, 1994), pp. 204–6. For Ḥallāj's trial, see Ernst, *Words of Ecstacy in Sufism*, pp. 102–110.
92 Ernst, *Words of Ecstacy in Sufism*, p. 69.
93 H. Mason, *Hallaj* (Richmond: Curzon Press, 1995), p. 17.
94 *Mathnawī*, II: 1347.
95 *Mathnawī*, I: 730.
96 *Mathnawī*, I: 727–36.
97 J. Renard, op. cit., p. 145.
98 For a discussion on this narrative see H. Dabashi, "Rūmī and the Problems of Theodicy: Moral Imagination and Narrative Discourse in a Story of the *Masnavī*," in Banani, Houannisian and Sabagh (eds.), *Poetry and Mysticism in Islam*, (Cambridge University Press, 1994), pp. 112–135.

99 See Nicholson, *Mathnawī of Jalālu'ddin Rūmī: vol. I & II Commentary*, pp. 34–6.
100 *Mathnawī*, VI: 4584–87.
101 According to the Sufis, *sūra* 18: 65 refers to this knowledge *('ilm ladunnī)*.
102 *Fīhi mā fīhi*, p. 148–49.
103 *Dīwān-i Shams*, no. 900, line 9434.
104 *Mathnawī*, III: 3773–6.
105 *Mathnawī*, III: 3721.
106 *Mathnawī*, III: 3741.
107 *Mathnawī*, III: 3704.
108 *Mathnawī*, III: 3780–3.
109 *Mathnawī*, VI: 4367–68. One wonders whether or not Rūmī believed this likeness to Jesus occurred within the imagination of the Jews. Rūmī's story of the prince again reflects the Qur'ān version of the crucifixion, since *sūra* 4: 157 states that the Jews believed they had crucified Jesus when in fact someone else who had a likeness to him was presented to them (*shubbiha la-hum*) and crucified in his place.
110 See M. A. Razavi, *Suhrawardi and the School of Illumination* (Richmond: Curzon, 1997).
111 Najm al-Dīn Rāzī, *The Path of God's Bondsmen From Origin to Return*, trans. H. Algar (New York: Caravan Books, 1982), pp. 239, 289.
112 For Simnani see H. Corbin, *The Man of Light in Iranian Sufism*, trans. N. Pearson (New York: Omega Publications, 1994), pp. 121–44.
113 This *ḥadīth* has been cited by many mystics including 'Ayn al-Quḍāt, *Tamhīdāt,* ed. A. Osseiran (Tehran, 1373), p. 47, Najm al-Dīn Rāzī op. cit., p. 222, and 'Azīz Nasafī in *Maqṣad-i aqṣā*, appended to Jāmī, *Ashi"āt al-lama'āt*, ed. H. Rabbani (Tehran: 1973), p. 226.
114 *Mathnawī*, IV: 1555–60.
115 *Mathnawī*, VI: 1477–80.
116 *Dīwān-i Shams,* no. 2684, lines 28460–4.
117 Reference to *sūra* 3: 103, "And hold fast to God's cord all together, and be not divided."
118 *Dīwān-i Shams,* no. 2498, lines 26410–1.
119 *Ibid*., no. 364, line 3895. This verse, as Arberry, *Mystical Poems 1,* points out (p. 176) was composed by Sanā'ī.
120 *Sūra* 20: 122 states that having succumbed to Satan's temptation, Adam repented and "thereafter his Lord chose him, and turned again unto him, and He guided him." In 2: 38 God told Adam to leave the Garden but "whosoever follows My guidance, no fear shall be on them, neither shall they sorrow." Moreover, *sūra* 2: 140 states that each person is responsible for his or her own actions and that the sins of one generation are not passed on to the next.
121 H. Corbin, *Creative Imagination in the Sufism of Ibn 'Arabi*, trans. R. Manheim (Princeton University Press, 1969), p. 275.

6

The Esoteric Christianity of Islam: Interiorisation of Christian Imagery in Medieval Persian Sufi Poetry

Leonard Lewisohn

I. INTRODUCTION

"The spiritual adventure of mystics and saints," S. H. Nasr rightly suggests, "with its characteristic symbolic language and solutions proposed to specific problems should make possible a fundamental dialogue between Christians and Muslims."[1] However, when studied and viewed from its own proper perspective – mystical experience, and the interior life and experience of faith – one finds that the subject matter and terminology of this dialogue is quite subtle, since its theses are established on the ground of apophasis rather than the bases of logic. The subject-centricism of the mystics is a world apart from the categories of theologians and philosophers and the abstract moral hypotheses of priests and mullahs. Sufism's theosophy is more indebted to the persuasive certitudes of aesthetic consciousness than raciocinative arguments drawn from the sages of ancient Greece. Their dialogue operates on a higher level, where, as Michael Sells put it, "theological arguments are pushed to their extreme to reveal the essential irresolvability of the dilemma outside of mystical union."[2] Such a dialogue is engaged with the poetically ambiguous insights and the imaginal realities of spiritual perception within the heart. The central assumption of such a dialogue is that a "mystical opening" – as Roger Arnaldez has called it – does exist, which allows the adept access to the interior identities or metahistorical parallels between Christianity and Islam. There, where the *lingua franca* of One Holy Spirit is spoken, a common ground is found and a mystical dissolution of separative identities between the messages of Jesus and Muḥammad can be discerned.[3]

Regarding similarities in spiritual psychology and mystical terminology, Christian scholars of Islamic thought have long detected the presence of mutual common ground between the two faiths.[4] When Western scholars first seriously began to examine the historical development and study the psychology and metaphysics of Muslim mysticism in the beginning of the twentieth century,[5] there was a realisation (on the part of many of them at least – foremost of whom R. A. Nicholson, E. G. Browne, D. Miguel Asin Palacios, Louis Massignon and Duncan Macdonald may be mentioned) that the two faiths share far more in common than mere superficial similarities in technical terminologies.[6]

Attempting to sketch the contours of "The Unity of the Mystical Experience in Islam and Christianity," Duncan Macdonald pointed out as long ago as 1935 that, "it is evident that the course run by these followers of a common religious life in Islam and Christendom was the same. Like the origin of darwish fraternities we have in Europe the rise of the Franciscans, the Dominicans and others. The similarity extends to the existence in both cases, of both men and women Tertiaries, those not living the common life but connected with their Order by common duties and rituals. Thus when Saint Francis preached before the Fatimid Court in Cairo he was regarded as one of those 'near to' Allah, a walī, and was safe."[7] A decade later (in 1947), the Swedish orientalist Tor Andrae, in what still remains the foremost monograph on this topic, described the relationship between Muslim and Christian mysticism as resembling "rays separated from their source of light," and characterised the ascetico-mystical tendencies within Islam as being "in its spirit and essence … closer to the Gospel than any other non-Christian religion known to us."[8] By the middle of the century (1957 to be precise), apropos of Asin's studies of Ibn 'Arabī and Dante's *Divine Comedy*,[9] Louis Massignon drew attention to the "structural influence of the Scholastic presentation of Muslim theology on the formation of Latin Catholic Scholasticism, both Scotist and Thomist … found exactly formulated in a canon of the Lateran Council of 1209 on the Divine Essence."[10] Other scholars have taken up these threads and eventually a pattern underlying the study of comparative Christian-Muslim mysticism has begun to emerge.[11]

The polymath Iranologist Henry Corbin definitively highlighted the contribution of Sufism to the ongoing dialogue between the Christian and Islamic faiths in the introduction to his *Creative Imagination in the Sufism of Ibn 'Arabī*, where he pointed out that while neither Christianity nor Islam is an initiatory religion in its official historical form, "there is an initiatory version of these religions, a Christian as well as an Islamic gnosis."[12] The "presence of Sufism in Islam," and the consequent "Sufī interpretation of Islam," speculated Corbin, has "led to a situation which, though almost entirely disregarded in the West today, might radically change the conditions of dialogue between Islam and Christianity, provided the interlocutors were Spirituals." Corbin's many monumental tomes on Persian Islam, Sufism and editions of numerous philosophical treatises on Islamic esotericism and gnosis tend to substantiate this very point. His researches have today, in turn, prepared the way for the recent wave of Iranian and Western scholars who at last recognise and address the need for comparative cross-cultural studies, openly espousing a pluralistic perspective on religious diversity.

The long historical relationship of Persia with Christianity and the strong presence of Christian imagery in Persian poetry make the study of Christian-Muslim relations in Persian Sufi literature less daunting a task than it might appear. A considerable number of works touching on, sometimes directly treating, the topic of Christianity in Iranian Islam already exist, foremost among which may be mentioned G H. B. Dihqāni-Taftī's three-volume monograph on *Christ and Christianity Among the Persians*, the first volume of which explores historical relations between Persia and Christianity; the second volume, Persian classical poetry and Christianity; with a large third volume discussing the presence of Christian imagery and influence of Christian thought on contemporary Persian art and literature.[13] Qamar Āriyān's work on *The Image of Jesus in Persian Literature* likewise contains valuable insights on the same theme,[14] and more recently, the historical relationship of Iran with Christianity has been treated in a lengthy multi-author article in the *Encyclopedia Iranica*. Describing Christian elements in classical Persian literature in this article, the latter author notes that in Persian literature

> Many verse and prose works provide evidence of a long familiarity with Christianity in its oriental, mainly Nestorian, forms. They contain stories and references to Jesus (*'Īsā*) that appear to have been derived from the Gospels; the authors must have learned of them from written or oral sources connected with Christian circles.[15]

Christianity in Persia had a very ancient history, and as early as the second century A.D., the religion was well-established there. About twenty bishoprics were established about the third century, and the

Persian Church even sent missionaries of its own from Iran to distant countries of the Far East, such as China. In Islamic times, although Iran never faced any direct threat from the Crusades (48–690/1095–1291) "the conquest of the holy land by European Christians in 492/1099 was deeply resented."[16] The Sufi humanist Sa'dī tells the story in the *Gulīstān* (II, 31), probably apocryphal, of his capture by the Franks outside Jerusalem, where he was forced to work as a slave-labourer, and of course as expected, speaks with utter contempt of Christians in this passage. Here, he would seem to echo similar scornful remarks about the "Franks of Palestine" made by the poet Niẓāmī (d. 605/1140) in the *Sharaf-nāma*.[17] In another passage, reflecting on the ubiquitous nature of the divine *caritas*, Sa'dī comments that God's beneficence is so great that "both Magian and Christian enjoy the same repast from your invisible treasury. If this is the way you treat your foes, how should you ever exclude your friends (i.e. Muslims)." Sa'dī's remarks here are characteristic of what might be called the "tolerant exclusivism" which prevailed in much nomocentric Islamic theology, the outlook of which contemplated other religions as metaphysically disreputable, theologically erroneous,[18] inferior in piety,[19] but, albeit, necessary evils. This type of tolerant exclusivism continues today in the Islamo-Christian controversy which still continues to produce a considerable literature in Persian.[20]

But that is not the whole story. When, as one often reads, the Sufi masters acted intolerantly towards the Christian "infidel," their hagiographies are often honest enough to admit that the God of the Sufis appeared to rebuke those *awlīyā'* who, in their spiritual short-sightedness sported robes of wool yet viewed as anathema the souls of God's Christian sheep.[21] Among the eminent Sufis of the classical age, other mystics, intoxicated with the God of Abraham and Jesus – Ḥallāj, 'Ayn al-Quḍāt Hamadhānī and Abū Sa'īd ibn Abī'l-Khayr, for instance, come readily to mind – all had acted with Christ's command to "judge not lest you be judged" in mind, beware of the Gospel's call to mind the beam in one's own eye rather than the mote in one's brother's (Luke VI: 37, 42); these, the Sufi elect, behaved and spoke with tolerance towards Christians.[22]

However, during the latter half of the thirteenth century, as we will see below, a Muslim Sufi perspective on religious diversity developed which was often more inclusivistic and ecumenically minded. By medieval times in general and the Mongol period in particular in Persia (1256–1336), attitudes of contempt towards Christians (and Jews) were often gradually replaced, among the Sufis at least, by one of ecumenical tolerance. This change in attitude among the mystics seems to have been, partially at least, politically motivated. Most scholars concur that religious tolerance was a – if not the – central feature of Persian piety under the Mongol government in Persia.[23] The Mongols' amorphous Shamanistic faith was from the start far from exclusive; they were rather "known for their tolerance – even their indifference to – all religions."[24] As Michel M. Mazzaoui points out:

> the Mongol period was marked with tremendous religious controversies; but at the same time it was a period of co-existence of various Muslim religious views. This co-existence amounted almost to a freedom of religious beliefs and reciprocal toleration ... The Mongol Sulṭāns, by and large, seem to have been playing the part of innocent bystanders ... they showed interest in and appreciation of the lively controversies. But they remained essentially foreign to what was going on along the religious level.[25]

Insofar as the Mongols espoused a shamanistic brand of Buddhism and made it the official creed in the lands they ruled (at least from 1221–1295), Muslims were forced to tolerate differences of religious belief, leading among other factors, to the rise in the popularity of Sufism, for which tolerance is second-nature. There was also an openness to Christian evangelism of various denominations, demonstrated, among other things, by the presence of an estimated fourteen Franciscan convents in the Īl-Khānid Persian state.[26] No doubt the use of Christian imagery and symbolism on the part of poets such as Shabistarī – whose thought is the main focus of this study, see part III below – owed much to the large Christian presence and numerous churches in Tabriz in the early thirteenth century, as Marco Polo in his visit to Tabriz in 1295, had noted.[27] Although in England, it was not until 1526 that the Bible was translated from Latin into English – and even then its translator, William Tyndale, was persecuted and burned at the stake as a heretic, and as late as 1600, only 30 of the 6000 volumes in the Oxford University Library were in English – as early as the late thirteenth century, during the Īl-Khānid reign in Persia, the first Persian translation of the Gospels had already appeared. Indéed, after a succession of strictly "Islamic" dynasties ruling the land, it was only during the Mongol rule that the political climate of Persia was favourable enough for the translation of such a text.[28]

It is difficult to assess the effect of the Mongols on Persian society, particularly in the religious sphere. While in Iran proper Buddhism and Christianity often gained an upper hand in the Mongol administration, as, for instance, under Abāqā (for Christianity) and Arghūn (for Buddhism), the majority of the population clearly remained Muslim. Claude Cahen points out that all through this period "Asia Minor remained a Muslim country," and "that the reduction of Islam to the rank of one religion along with others, a situation which to some extent had characterised the early period of Mongol domination in Iran and Mesopotamia (*waqfs* in those countries being more or less integrated into the general economy and used for the benefit of the different creeds without distinction) occurred hardly at all under the protectorate of Asia Minor."[29] He also stresses the total domination of Anatolian society by the Muslim majority during the entire Mongol reign.[30] The same is also partially true in the Eastern Iranian Mongol kingdom "under Infidel Government" – as David Morgan calls the pre-Ghāzān Īl-Khānid era (663/1265 – 694/1295)[31] – where Islam certainly remained the most dominant current in the religious life of Persia. Nonetheless, as Trimingham notes, the most immediate consequence of the Mongol conquest was displacement of Islam as the state religion throughout the region, and this meant that "Islam now had to prove itself and accommodate itself to non-Muslim rulers, Shamanist, Buddhist, or crypto-Christian."[32] This epoch, being "an inextricable mélange des religions," as Jean-Paul Roux represents it,[33] contained a new spiritual dynamic which was, to use Trimingham's simile: "pregnant with possibilities."[34]

However, the most significant change which did occur during the Mongol period was *the establishment of Islam on a Sufi foundation.* The Mongol invasion in fact, indirectly prompted a great period of flowering of Sufism in Persia, as is demonstrated by the phenomenal rise of the Kubrawiyya, Nūrbakhshiyya, Naqshbandiyya and Ni'matu'llāhiyya Orders,[35] probably due to the economic advantages given to the *'ulamā'* and Sufi *fuqarā'* alike (exemptions from taxes, liberal endowments to their mosques and *khānaqāhs*, offers of *tarkhān* and grants of *soyūrghāls*, etc.).[36] The predilection of Mongol princes like Ghāzān Khān for Sufism, rather than for purely exoteric and legalistic religiosity, has been underlined by H. Landolt's monograph on the thirteenth-century Kubrāwī master Nūr al-Dīn Isfarāyinī.[37] The Sufi affiliations of the Mongol ruler Uljāytū Khān (reg. 1304–1316) are evident by his reconstruction of the tomb of Bāyazīd Basṭāmī and his naming of three sons after this Sufi saint: Basṭāmī, Bāyazīd, and Ṭayfūr.[38]

Insofar as the Mongols' reign in thirteenth century Persia constituted the golden epoch for Muslim re-evaluation of Christian ideas and symbolism, and the Sufis' particular mystical interpretation of Christianity, the above digression into Mongol history has been merited. In the wider Turco-Indo-Persian cultural sphere, modes of inter-religious understanding which developed during the Mongol period profoundly affected the interpretation of Christianity in Persianate *belles lettres* and theosophy down to the end of the seventeenth century – such that even today one still finds poets and writers who advocate the type of esoteric Christianity or interiorised Christianity in an Islamic Sufi garb which is discussed below (part III). The fact that the religious promiscuity of Persian society in thirteenth-fourteenth century Mongol Persia bears much similarity to the amorphous diversity of the multi-religious culture of today's post-modern society, also makes the views of the poets examined below of special relevance to the contemporary scope of the present volume.

However, before gazing through Islam's mystical opening into Christianity and exploring our main theme – interiorisation and exegesis of Christian symbols in Persian Sufi poetry – a brief examination of the hermeneutics of this interiorised vision and the theory of symbolism underlying Muslim mysticism, by way of some brief background illustration to the theme, is required. Since what is interiorised through poetic symbolism is based on the peculiar exegesis which the Christian symbol imparted to the Sufi poet, both these subjects – hermeneutics and interiorisation – are anyway interdependent.

II. THE "ESOTERIC HERMENEUTIC" WITHIN MUSLIM MYSTICISM

Echoes if not direct analogies of the traditional methods of hermeneutics of poetry advocated in the two other great Semitic faiths – Judaism and Christianity – are clearly found in Islam. Thus, just as there were held to be four hermeneutic degrees in biblical exegesis, so in Qur'ānic hermeneutics near-identical equivalencies have been drawn, as in *ẓāhir=historia*; *bāṭin=allegoria*; *ḥadd=tropologia*; *maṭla'=anagoge*,[39] a fourfold scheme ultimately derived from Aristotle's fourfold theory of causes which, translated into semantic terms, provides the following correspondence: literal – material; allegorical – formal; tropological – efficient; analogical – final.[40]

The significance of many such borrowings, whether of symbol and symbolic theory, in the history of the mysticisms of the two faiths was briefly examined by Louis Massignon who enumerated many of the key certain structural analogies, fertile hybridizations and syncretism which exist between Islamic Sufism and Christian mysticism.[41] Despite Massignon's conclusion that the Qur'ān is the main "source of Islamic mysticism,"[42] a thesis which few scholars can contest, it should be stressed that each of the two faiths, being "religions of the book," share virtually the same esoteric hermeneutic, as Henry Corbin[43] and Mircea Eliade[44] have conclusively shown. Hence, Corbin is quite right to draw our attention to the fact that

> There is a similarity in the way in which a Boehme or a Swedenborg understands Genesis, Exodus or Revelation, and the way in which the Shi'ites, Ismaili as well as Twelver, or else the Ṣūfī theosophers of the school of Ibn 'Arabī, understand the Quran and the corpus of the traditions explaining it. This similarity in perspective is one in which the universe is seen as possessing several levels, as consisting of a plurality of worlds that all symbolize with each other.[45]

Reviewing the hermeneutics of poetry in Persian Sufism of the Mongol period, the same theory of poetic symbolism based on scriptural (albeit Qur'ānic rather than biblical) references and an identical parabolic approach to the language of divine inspiration also appears. Sufis had strictly distinguished between the outward literal meaning (*'ibārat*) and the inner symbolic allusions (*ishāra*) concealed in words, natural objects, and the Qur'ān, and described themselves as members of an "Allusionist School" (*ahl al-ishāra*), professing that keys to their knowledge were to be found in symbology (*'ulūm al-ishāra*). In the earliest comprehensive manual of Sufi doctrine, *Al-Ta'arruf li-madhhab ahl al-taṣawwuf*, Abū Bakr Muḥammad Kalābadhī of Bukhārā (d. 380/990), elaborated the mystical theology underlying this symbolic theory. The science of allusion, he states, "is the science *par excellence* of the Sufis ... The term 'allusion' is given to this science for this reason: the contemplations enjoyed by the heart, and the revelations accorded to the conscience (*sirr*), cannot be expressed literally; they are learnt through actual experience of the mystical, and are known only to those who have experienced these mystical states and lived in these stations."[46] Kalābadhī describes these symbolic allusions as consisting of a "code" which can be apprehended by Sufis, but which "escaped any listener who had never dwelt in that station."[47] Paul Nywia points out that the sixth Shī-'ite Imām Ja'far al-Ṣādiq (d. 148/765), often celebrated by the Sufis as one of their own, had applied the exactly same theory of symbolism to the Qur'ān in his

Tafsīr.[48] The Qur'ān, according to al-Ṣādiq, contains both a "literal word" (*ibāra*) and an inner allusion (*ishāra*), the former befitting the common believers and the latter proper to the select few (*khawāṣṣ*), respectively corresponding to the outer literal sense (*ẓāhir*) and inner spiritual sense (*bāṭin*) of the Scripture; the interior allusion is discovered only by the heart of the mystic.[49]

The broadest theoretical elaboration of this perspective in later Sufis occurred in the philosophy of Muḥyī al-Dīn Ibn 'Arabī (d. 638/1240) whose writings represent an attempt to bridge the divine world of Reality and the temporal realm of Appearance by means of a metaphysics of imagination.[50] Since Ibn 'Arabī's theosophy was the major intellectual influence on all the Sufi poets of the Mongol period, which effectively created what I have called elsewhere its own "hermeneutic tradition,"[51] it will be useful to briefly introduce his views here. Superfluous as any discussion in detail would be here suffice it to say that Ibn 'Arabī believed that the key to understanding prophetic revelation lies in the creative imagination. Both prophetic revelation (*waḥy*) and poetic inspiration (*ilhām*) are understood as the a kind of disclosure *(kashf)* of archetypal meanings or ideas (*mā'nā*) which must pass through the level of Imagination before they reach the realm of the senses. Imagination's role in this process of descent of meanings is to give a sensory form to spiritual entities, which is what happens in dreams, poetry and prophecy. Ibn 'Arabī stated:

> Revelation is a meaning. When God wants meaning to descend to sense perception, it has to pass through the Presence of Imagination before it reaches sense perception. The reality of imagination demands that it give sensory form to everything that becomes actualised in it.[52]

As Qāsim Ghanī pointed out in the 1950s,[53] the foremost Persian poet to put Ibn 'Arabī's metaphysical theory of the imaginal origin of poetic imagery into practice through creating an exclusively the symbolic language for his poetry was Maghribī (d. 1408). In Maghribī's manifesto of Sufi symbolism in the prose introduction to his collected poems (*Dīwān*), he explains the "esoteric hermeneutic" underlying his verse in these lines:

> ... Then of down and beauty-spots should I speak,
> The eyebrow's bend and towering statures praise,
> Take note of cheeks and cheekbone,
> Impudent eyes, and teeth, lovely waists;
> Of faces and braids should I sing

Or else of cuff and fist insist you listen –
At such idioms be flustered not;
Of their object inquire.
Of long and short feet,
Of my phrases' morphology don't ask
If with symbolists you'd be confident,
Into hermeneutics an initiate.

Rectify your eye
You'll see straight.
Perfect your insight
You'll see right.
Reject the rind
The nut you'll find.

Unless the crust you reject
Howsoever will you become a Kabbalist?

O, within each and every phoneme of mine
  a live soul resides.
within every *lexis*, an *animus* there is,
  a soul alive within each word,
in every letter a cosmos concealed.

You should seek its spirit, its flesh reject,
  its noumenon pursue and Named-Essence adopt
its phenomenon do not claim.

Neglect no Minute Particular
If in the truths of the symbolists
You'd become adept.[54]

As I have noted elsewhere,[55] these verses give the most comprehensive summary in classical Persian literature of the "symbolist mentality" and the parabolic consciousness characteristic of the Persian Sufi poets who advocated the use of a hermeneutical approach to both poetic and Qur'ānic inspiration. Maghribī approaches poetic discourse as a means to recover the transcendent Truth, thought to be underlying – or rather, "over-flying" – its literal verbal expression. Thus, words only have "meaning" in the context of the apophatic discourse with the Divine which sustains them; their "meaning" only thrives in the brakes and wilds of "unsaying."[56]

III. THE INTERIORISATION OF CHRISTIAN SYMBOLS IN PERSIAN SUFI POETRY

The following analysis of the interiorisation of Christian symbols in medieval Persian poetry concentrates on one key work, the *Gulshan-i rāz* or *Garden of Mystery* of Maḥmūd Shabistarī (d. after 1339). Often characterised as a *summa theologica* of Sufi speculative mysticism (*ḥikmat-i naẓarī*),[57] this metaphysical essay-in-verse was composed in 1317 in rhyming couplets (the *mathnawī* metre of *baḥr-i hazaj*)[58] amounting to about one thousand distichs. Composed in a highly symbolic language, and drawing upon the lexicon of several centuries of Persian symbolic poetry, the *Garden of Mystery* sets forth the *dicta* of the Sufis on a variety of themes such as "Thought" (*fikr*), "the Soul" (*nafs*), Knowledge (*ma'rifat*), the Multiplicity and Unity of the Realms of Being, the Hierarchical Levels of Being, the Spiritual Voyage (*sayr*) and Methodical Progression on the Sufi Path (*sulūk*), nearness (*qurb*) and distance from God (*bu'd*), and the evolution of the soul.[59]

Shabistarī's insights are usually expressed in an abstract apophatic language, resembling mystical theologians such as Meister Eckhart, or Ibn 'Arabī (whose ideas he explicitly followed), yet his arguments are as carefully reasoned as any of the great Perso-Islamic theologians such as Naṣr al-Dīn Ṭūsī or Ghazālī. Ecstatic utterance is balanced by scriptural *dicta*, Qur'ān and *ḥadīth* texts are adduced, and the poet's admiration for the supreme Sufi Sunni theologian Abū Ḥāmid Ghazālī is evident everywhere.[60]

Soon after its composition, the *Garden of Mystery* soared in fame, and by the middle of the sixteenth century close to thirty commentaries had been written upon it by a number of Persian mystics, both renowned and obscure.[61] Among the Persian poets and mystics who devoted their talents to elucidating the arcana of the *Garden*, the greatest commentator on the poem was undoubtedly Muḥammad Lāhījī (d. 912/1507), a visionary theosopher of Shabistarī's own calibre,[62] whose voluminous exegesis of Shabistarī's masterpiece, entitled *Mafātīḥ al-i'jāz fī sharḥ-i Gulshan-i rāz*, is steeped in the poetry and theosophy of medieval Persian Sufism, being replete with quotations from Shabistarī's other works as well as ample references to the *Diwāns* of Rūmī, Maghribī, and 'Irāqī, all interspersed with the author's personal accounts of dreams, visions and mystical experiences. Springing from the same fount of inspiration (*mashrab*) that Shabistarī's own verse is drawn, two basic strands of theosophy wind through Lāhījī's *Sharḥ-i Gulshan-i rāz*: first, is the lyrical Sufism of Rūmī, and second is the theosophy of Ibn 'Arabī and his followers such as the gnostic poets 'Irāqī and Maghribī.[63] The broad scope of Lāhījī's mystical interests and erudition combined with Shabistarī's canonical position as the foremost Persian Sufi poet (with the possible exception of 'Irāqī) to introduce Ibn 'Arabī's ideas and terminology into Persian literature,[64] thus allows our examination of esoteric Christianity in Islam below to overcome the bias which an exclusive focus on a single work or author might otherwise present.

1 Esoteric Christology

At the outset, it will be useful to examine the first reference to the symbol of Jesus in the *Garden of Mystery*.[65] Shabistarī's Christology closely follows that of Ibn 'Arabī for whom, as Neal Robinson has pointed out, Jesus "is a trans-historical figure who continues to have an influence on certain types of saints, an honour which he shares with other eminent prophets."[66] Shabistarī's understanding of the *communio sanctorum* of the Sufi notion of saintship (*walāya*), conceived of in the Akbarian tradition as "an all-inclusive and universal function that never comes to an end,"[67] dogs Ibn 'Arabī's belief in the authentic spirituality, which, the latter believed, could still be found in certain "Christ-like saints." This conception lead the Shaykh al-Akbar "to depict *walāya* in a way which is far more inclusive than the definitions which confine it within the framework of a sociological Islam."[68] Shabistarī's Christology and attitude towards this trans-historical figure of Jesus, and his view of Christianity as representative of a kind of esoteric sainthood clearly reflects the liberal Akbarian perspective of his intellectual mentor.

In the Qur'ān, Jesus is given the epithet of being a "spirit from God" (4: 171), a reference which led many later Muslim writers and poets to describe Jesus as *Spiritus Dei* (*rūḥallāh*); elsewhere, he is described as having been fortified by the Holy Spirit in order to accomplish his mission (2: 254; 5: 110; 19: 30–33).[69] Drawing on this traditional Muslim epithet, the poet portrays Jesus (Spirit of God) as symbolic of the liberated human spirit in these verses:

Within the inner court of sacred Unity
  lies the soul's monastery,
perch of the Simurgh of subsistent Eternity,
  from the Spirit of God such labour sprang,
brought forth by the Holy Spirit.

A trace of sanctity lies manifest
in the God-bestowed soul before you.
If you acquit yourself of this passion-bound
soul of humanity, then step within
the inner court of sacred Divinity.
Whoever, like an angel, becomes detached,
liberated from matter's trappings,
ascends to the fourth heaven
like the Spirit of God.[70]

In a highly individualised and interiorised vision of the Sufis' esoteric Christianity, Jesus (as *spiritus dei*) is introduced here by the poet as the archetype of human spirituality. Shabistarī's understanding of – the trans-historical nature of – Jesus as representative of the divine name "Allāh" partially overcomes the problem which the Christian dogma of the Incarnation otherwise poses for the Muslim. Of course, Shabistarī's interiorised Christology, the understanding of Jesus as a symbol of the mystic's soul detached from the fetters of matter, implicitly rejects the (pseudo-) orthodox absolutist Christian dogma of the Incarnation as a decisive, unique historical event of salvic importance. Rather, he approaches the Augustinian perspective of the Logos (in Christ) as representative of the "true light" (John I: 9) within every man, that "the true religion, although formerly set forth and practiced under other names and with other symbolic rites than it now has … is one and the same in both periods."[71] His views provide the potential groundwork for a dialogue between Christians and Muslims, bearing comparison with the views of many modern protestant Christian theologians who have reinterpreted the Incarnation outside the categories of the Nicene-Chalcedonian creed ("only-begotten Son of God … " etc.), and maintained that the title of "Son of God" is largely "metaphorical and honourific,"[72] arguing that the doctrine of the Incarnation may be interpreted simply to mean that "it is supremely through Jesus that the self-giving love of God is most fully expressed and men can be brought up into the fullest response to him."[73]

Lāhījī's interpretation of these verses, from the perspective of the classical Sufi tradition, is as follows:

> The "labour" here implied is that of dispassion, detachment and emancipation from the bondage of multiplicity, conventionality and habit – all of which Christianity represents – and the consequent attainment of the spiritual level and monastery of the Divine Essence in

> its sacred Oneness, which was manifested by Jesus in his capacity as the "Spirit of God." No previous prophet, however graced with the virtues of perfection, ever quite attained his degree. Hence, the dictum of the Prophet Muḥammad: "Of all men I am most akin to Jesus, for no other prophet appeared between him and me."
>
> The archetypal form (*ta'yyun*) of Jesus pertains to the innermost dimension of the All-Comprehensive Oneness of the Divine Nature; hence, his appellation as the "Spirit of God" (*rūḥallāh*); for he is that Perfect Spirit which is a theophany (*maẓhar*) of the All-Comprehensive Name Allāh.
>
> Solely the Divine Name Allāh – no other divine name – by virtue of its Gabrielic form, is the animator-inspirer (*nāfakh*) of him [i.e. Jesus as divine Spirit]. Insofar as Jesus was a real devotee (*'abdu'llāh ḥaqīqī*) of God, he resurrected the dead, he created and brought birds to life, and cured the congenitally blind and healed lepers. All of these feats were "brought forth by the Holy Spirit (*rūḥ al-qudus*)." Yet, the truth of the matter is that the animator of the Gabrielic form was the All-Comprehensive name of God: Allāh, that was imaginalised in Jesus's form.[74]

Lāhījī's appraisal of Shabistarī's Christology in these lines may be summarised as follows:

1 Among world faiths, "Christianity" for the Sufi symbolises "detachment" from the false conventions, formalities and customs of purely nomocentric religion;
2 Jesus – understood in the purely spiritual, trans-historical sense – symbolises the most comprehensive divine Name (Allāh);
3 Jesus's miraculous powers ultimately stem from the Holy Spirit, whose power was "imaginalised" in him by virtue of his closeness to God.

Since, as Shabistarī/Lāhījī put it, Jesus is understood as the Spirit of God, or at least, as inspired by the Holy Spirit in whose capacity he acts as "a theophany (*maẓhar*) of the All Comprehensive Name Allāh," the origin of the great "labour" of human spirituality stems from him. *Ergo*, another very important basic conclusion which may be drawn from both the verses cited here and the exegesis which accompanies them is *that spirituality in Islam is as much a "Christian" as a "Muslim" experience*. In this context, I should add that in Islam, all prophets are, by the very nature of their Prophethood, saints as well, and thus, Jesus is regarded as a saint as well as a prophet. The famous passage in the Gospel of John (XVI: 16), where Jesus states

"I go to the Father," is therefore taken by the Sufis to imply that the saints are spiritual children of God. Shabistarī ventures to give a Sufi gloss on this verse from St. John in the following passage in the *Garden of Mystery*:

First the suckling infant,
bound to a cradle, is sustained on milk.
Then, when mature, becomes a wayfarer,
and if a man, he travels with his father.

The elements of nature for you
resemble an earthborn mother.
You are a son whose father
is a patriarch from on high.

So Jesus proclaimed upon ascension:
"I go to my Father above."
You too, O favourite of your father,
Set forth for your Father!

Your fellow-travellers went on; you too pass on!
If you wish to be a bird in flight,
Leave the world's carcass to vultures.[75]

Shabistarī's interiorised understanding of the spiritual role and character of Jesus in these lines, in which the Incarnation becomes a metaphor for the soul's descent into Nature and Matter, is of course in line with Muslim thought on this theological issue. "There is no denying the fact that serious Muslim thinkers cannot accept the penetration of *lāhūt* into *nāsūt* or the incarnation of God in any form unless incarnation be understood in a metaphysical or symbolic sense," S. H. Nasr pointed out.[76] However, as in the previously cited passage (vv. 927–32), Shabistarī's use of anthropomorphic imagery (the Persian *Pidar* translating the Christian *Abba*) has psycho-spiritual significance only. While the spiritual development of the Muslim Sufi, the poet propounds, must be "Christocentric" in following Jesus in his "detachment" from family, kinship ties[77] and the world, the epiphany of Christ is not so much a definitive historical event as a perpetual fact of the *eternal nunc aeternum*, for

Pre-eternity and post-eternity are here but one and the same:
The epiphany of Jesus occurred with the creation of Adam.[78]

2 Esoteric Christianity

Shabistarī's recognition of the symbolic value, and hence, inner religious truth within non-Islamic faiths is especially conspicuous in his treatment of "Christianity" as a religion. The last two sections of the *Garden of Mystery* contain seventy-seven verses (927–1004, some of which will be discussed below) consecrated to the Sufi understanding of Christianity, depicting an ideal inscape and a visionary topography of what one could term an Islamic esoteric Christianity. Aside from certain references in another contemporary poet's work, the *Jām-i jam* by Awḥādī of Marāgha (d. 738/1337–8),[79] these verses represent the first serious excursion into comparative mysticism in the history of Persian poetry of the Mongol period.

In Shabistarī's Sufi hermeneutic, the religion of Christianity (*tarsā'ī*) symbolises the state of detachment (*tajrīd*) both from the world and the hereafter, as well as from any desire for compensation or reward, involving single-minded concentration on God in acts of devotion. Thus, he wrote:

> Non-attachment and detachment –
> Freedom from the fetters of imitation,
> are the pith and whole design
> I see in Christianity.[80]

Closely related to the symbolism of Jesus and Christianity in the poetry of Shabistarī is his conception and interpretation of the term "Christian" (*tarsā*) and Christian "monk."

3 The "Christian" and "Monk"

The meaning of the word *Tarsā* (=Christian) in Persian Sufi poetry has been explained by numerous Sufi poets and masters as symbolising the highest level of the human spirit. Thus, the great encyclopedist of philosophical and mystical terminology Tahānawī (d. 1745) notes that in Sufi poetry the poetic symbol of the "Christian" represents "the spiritual person, whose blameworthy qualities (*nafs-i ammarā*) has been converted into praiseworthy ones." He also adds that "the 'Christian' may also symbolise the man who adheres to Divine Unity (*mard-i muwaḥḥid*)."[81]

In the writings of Sufis of the Mongol period this accentuation on the poetic symbol of the "Christian" as representing the highest degree of spirituality was reaffirmed. Abū 'l-Mufākhir Yaḥyā Bākharzī

(d. 736/1335–6), a Sufi master contemporary with Shabistarī who was a major leader of the Kubrāwī order, in his celebrated manual of Sufism, the *Awrād al-aḥbāb*, thus wrote:

> By the term "Christian" (*tarsā)* in the technical terminology of the Sufis is meant the "spiritual man" (*mard-i rūḥānī*) who is detached from his passional nature and corporeality, and who has attained the level of the Spirit. Hence the Christian is one liberated from the bonds of normative religious customs, rites, formalities and free from the literal letter of religion. He sees everything in [the light of] God and through [the light of] God. The religion of Jesus is his very Spirit and the Messiah is his very soul. He is liberated from the constraints of his individual passional selfhood and reason, and rests in joy in the expanse of the unveiling of spiritual realities (*kashf al-ḥaqā'iq*) and gnosis (*ma'rifat*).[82]

Demonstrating the ecumenical nature of Sufi teachings on Christianity, in Bākharzī's definition above, the symbolic image of "the Christian" is used to denote the ideal Muslim unitarian.

The symbol of the "Christian monk" (*rāhib*) has a similar esoteric significance and carries the same ecumenical connotations as the "Christian," the "monk" representing the true Sufi who seeks the interior reality within various religions and overlooks illusory formal differences while regarding their unifying spirit. Shabistarī states:

> Detach yourself, be *ḥanīfī*,
> And from all faiths' fetters free;
> So come, like a monk, step up
> into religion's abbey.[83]

As a follower of Ibn 'Arabī, Shabistarī was no doubt aware of the Shaykh al-Akbar's doctrine that living "executors" (*awṣiyā*) of past prophets who are also numbered among the Sufi *awliyā'*[84] always exist (and that is one reason why the Prophet forbade the killing of monks [*ruhbān*], ordering that they should be left alone to pursue their devotions).[85] Lāhījī's commentary on the above line is most illuminating and reveals the profundity of Shabistarī's attitude to religious freedom:

> Be detached and free and pure from contamination by the restrictions of imitative devotion, customs and habit. Be like the true monk and "step up into religion's abbey," which means to come into mosques and other places of worship, girding yourself with the cincture of service, acting as the monk whose very vocation is detachment, being liberated and disengaged from all formal and spiritual interests or obstructions.

> Do not be inhibited by the fetters of "infidelity" (*kufr*) and Islam, for whatever is in essence good, and is a cause of human perfection, is, of course, praiseworthy.
>
> Leave every religion and people to their own rites and observances, since to be bound by mere words and expressions generally employed in other religions – such as "Idol" (*but*), "Cincture" (*zunnār*), "Monastery" (*dayr*), "Christian" and "Ḥanīfa" – is itself just another type of infidelity (*kufr*). Endorsing such conceptual restrictions is contrary to the way and method of the Sufi gnostics.[86]

4 The "Christian Child"

Even more fascinating than the image of the "Christian" and "monk" in Persian Sufism is the related symbol of the "Christian child" (*tarsā-bacha*), who denotes the highest spiritual adept among the Sufis. Abū 'l-Mufākhir Yaḥyā Bākharzī thus notes that the Sufis' technical term for

> a spiritual messenger is the "Christian child," that is to say, an infusion (*wārid*) from the spiritual realm which overwhelms the heart, reason and psyche of the mystic through divine grace and so totally occupies him that he is unconscious of all else, utterly concentrating his soul.[87]

Shabistarī devoted a long section of his conclusion to the *Garden of Mystery* to interpretation of the symbolic meaning of the Christian child, who in his lexicon of Sufi symbolism is the personification of the spiritual master (*pīr*). He mentions the disturbing effect which the presence of this "Christian child" – apparently an ideal embodiment of Shabistarī's own spiritual master – has upon the complacent and tepid mystics who passed their lives in the Muslim mystics' secluded cloister or *khānaqāh*. He describes his master's visage, the "Christian child," as having conveyed him, figuratively speaking, into a sacred garden, where he was to pluck the bouquet which later became the entire Garden of Mystery.

> The Christian child, that "idol" is but a symbol
> of light that's pure and manifest from the faces
> of idols: iconic forms of his theophany.
> All hearts he welds together, conjunct:
> sometimes, the lutanist, he sweeps the strings;
> sometimes, the Saki, he purveys the wine.

What a bard – whose key of grace chimes
such measure, it sets aflame the coffers
of a hundred pietists, a myriad pharisees …!
And what a Saki – whose beaker's brew
bereaves of self and stirs to ecstasy
two hundred men of over seventy.
Drunken in a stupor, if he comes at dusk
to the *khānaqāh,* he shows the Sufi's piety
to be but cant – all spells and conjury.
If at dawn, for matins he goes
into a Mosque, no man therein he leaves
in sober sense, of self cognisant.
Like a drunk in masquerade, he goes in the Madrasa –
the judges and the jurists there, he leaves in dire straits.
Not just the judges does he befuddle,
the puritans, from love of him are shorn
of kith and kin, of house and home.
One man from him becomes an "infidel,"
Another – pure and "faithful." It's he who fills
the world with such mêlée and misery,
from him come all these woes and ills.
The Tavern of Ruin blooms
with life and health from his lips;
his visage beams light and lustre
upon the mosque. Thus, everything for me
by him seems now easy: because I see
through him the possibility of liberty
from this egocentric heresy: my soul-of-infidelity.[88]

In his commentary on the first couplet cited above, Lāhījī explains that by the "Christian child" is meant the perfect Sufi master who the Lord of his Age (*murshid-i kāmil ṣāḥib zamān*). The "idol" which he, in particular, adores is the all-inclusive Unity of the divine Essence. He is the genetrix and source of all perfections in Existence, and the degree of the Major Poleship (*quṭbiyyat kubrā*) is his.[89] Thus, in the course of commenting on this above-cited verse:

One man from him becomes an "infidel,"
Another – pure and "faithful."
It's he who fills the world with such mêlée and misery,
from him come all these woes and ills.

Lāhījī explains that the salvation of everyone, no matter what their religious affiliation may be, depends on recognition of the living saints. Just as the Qur'ān (2: 213) declares that "Mankind was one community, and God sent (unto them prophets as bearers of good tidings and as warners" – so in every age, a Perfect Man exists among them. "The distinction which exists between the believer and the infidel, the ascetic and the profligate, the righteous devotee and the sinner, and all the discussions and debates which are carried on in order to clarify the difference between the two, are all due to the [effect of] the agency and mediation of this Supreme Adept." The difference between salvation and damnation hinges on an individual's recognition of and devotion to this Supreme Adept. "Those who accept him attain to the level of spiritual perfection, realizing the states of union with God, while those who reject him remain veiled in the veil of divine majesty, never finding a way to certain gnosis, and in truth, "infidelity" (*kufr*) is that very veil."[90]

Now, the true "Christian child," who represents the iconic reality underlying the idol's appearance, is this supreme adept.[91] Commenting on the verse,

> Drunken in a stupor, if he comes at dusk
> to the *khānaqāh*, he shows the Sufi's piety
> to be but cant – all spells and conjury.

Lāhījī remarked:

> The Perfect Man's being in comparison with ordinary novices on the Path to God, is like an ocean before a drop of water. When such a mystic enters the *Khānaqāh*, which is the house of wayfarers travelling the Way of the *Ṭarīqat*, he enters as one drunk on the nocturnal wine of contemplation of the Absolute Divine Beauty, a beverage which is imbibed in the symposium of the Divine Selfhood held in the non-manifest or supraformal realm. The reason why he said "at dusk" is that perception and intellectual discrimination cannot penetrate into the non-manifest side of the Divine Selfhood. So alas, he makes the "mystical states" of the Sufis who pass their time in *khānaqāhs* seem but idle flights of fancy, or as he says, "cant, spells and conjury." That is because the mystical states of the Sufis who are undergoing the station of the "journey to God and with God" (*sayr ilā Allāh wa ma'a Allāh*), which is a station of fluctuation wherein one is merely endowed with realisation of the variegated divine illuminations, levels and theophanies of the God's Acts, in relation to the spiritual plenitude of the Perfect Man …

> are completely vainglorious. His entry [into the *khānaqāh*] reveals to them the worthless hallucinatory nature of their spiritual experiences.[92]

As Lāhījī emphasises in this passage, to the Perfect Man who has attained to the sublime heights of Reality (*ḥaqīqat*) the Path (*ṭarīqat*) itself appears as mere chimera; its rites and regula mere flights of fancy suitable only for dull pedestrians.

However, more important for the purposes of the present study, is the pluralist vision which underlies the theosophical doctrines and poetic symbolism of these lines. *Albeit in their symbolic sense, the cognitive significance which the images of the "Christian child," "monk" and the "Christian monastery" evoke to the Sufis take precedence over corresponding traditional Muslim religious terms, such as "believer," "ascetic," "mosque," etc. For the Sufi mystic in the realm of the spirit, in symbol but not in fact, the esoteric "Christian" is preferable to the exoteric "Muslim".*[93]

Shabistarī/Lāhījī's exposition of the doctrine of the "Christian child" in this passage of his *Garden of Mystery* treats us to a unique philosophical articulation of religious inclusivism, but an inclusivism which – unlike the inclusivistic "religious pluralism"[94] of contemporary scholars of religious mythology such as Mircea Eliade or of historians of religions such as Joseph Campbell – is founded on an entirely theocentric metaphysics wherein "Existence" implies God's Existence and is thus, the ultimate ontological fact.[95] His exposition of this metaphysical relativism of beliefs[96] however, is not simple to grasp, as Lāhījī's monumental commentary (603 printed pages of single-spaced small Persian type) on the Garden of Mystery illustrates.

5 Beyond Faith and Infidelity: The "Christian" Sufi "Muslim"

With the possible exception of the last-quoted lines, Shabistarī's pluralist views on faith and infidelity – his disdain and disregard for what Lāhījī calls "the fetters of infidelity and Islam" and advocation of the faith of "real infidelity" versus the faith of "false Islam" – are most clearly expressed in eleven couplets found in the last quarter of the Garden of Mystery.

957 The Mosque in which you step to pray
    is just a pagan temple
as long as you're engrossed in else than Truth,
958 but when that alien raiment is taken off
the temple's form becomes for you a Mosque.

959 I do not know ... but still, whatever state you possess,
combat the Infidel Selfhood: you'll then be free.
960 The "Christian creed," the "cincture," "idol," "churchbell"
are symbols for the loss of face, forgoing of fair name.
961 If you would be a servant known for high degree,
a chosen bondsman, prepare to render pure devotion,
inure yourself to truthfulness.
962 Go – take this "self" which bars the path;
each moment engage yourself in Faith anew.
963 Inside us all the lower soul's an infidel:
Rest not content with this Islam of outer form.
964 Each instant at heart regain your faith afresh.
Be Muslim, Muslim, Muslim, Muslim!
965 How many a faith there is – born of infidelity;
what strengthens faith is not infidelity.
966 Be free of shame and name – hypocrisy and notoriety –
Cast off the dervish frock, tie on the cincture
967 and like our master, be inimitable in Infidelity
if man you be: unto a Man commit your heart entirely.
968 Give up your heart to the Christian child;
Free yourself of all denial and affirmation.[97]

Space does not permit any in-depth examination of the theosophical doctrines contained in these verses.[98] However, in order to reveal the presence of what I have termed an "esoteric Christianity" in Sufism, a few comments on select lines (960, 964, 965 and 968) are in order.

Beginning with couplet 960, in accordance with the ancient Sufi *malāmatī* teachings which stressed that the only real way to realise sincerity (*ṣidq*) in spiritual practice and to behold the heart-truth (*taṣdīq*), otherwise veiled by a piety which is put out on public display, is by conscious and public repudiation of all one's external acts of piety, Lāhījī explains:

> Those Perfect Masters who discourse on idolatry, the tying on of the cincture, the practice of Christianity and ringing the church-bell, symbolically allude by usage of these images to the abandonment of personal name and honour. According to them, all decadence and error in religious belief stems from the wish to preserve one's personal "fair name," "honour" and "reputation." The thickest veil which beclouds people of high social position and status is their "honour" and "reputation" – for such folk it is easier to abandon the world than to lose their reputation.[99]

The broadminded tolerance of the Sufi vision of faith is evident in Lāhījī's exegesis on couplets 964 and 965, from the following passage is translated:

> As we have explained in the above passages,[100] faith is increased by such objects as the "idol," "cincture" and the "Christian faith." In this sense, one of the principles of real divine unity (*tawḥīd-i ḥaqīqī*) is that the idol is a theophanic manifestation of divine unity. According to the same doctrine, the cincture refers to the contract of service, obedience and divine worship which one [as a true Sufi] vows to observe, while the "Christian faith" is symbolic of divesting oneself of materiality (*tajrīd*), severing one's attachments, and becoming liberated from the restraints, conventions, customs and imitative forms of religious devotion. Insofar as from these things [i.e. "idol," "cincture" and the "Christian faith"] true faith is born – *God forbid that this "infidelity," which stimulates an increase of faith, should be conceived of as heresy or infidelity per se! On the contrary, it is the most perfect form of Islam, although it appear in the guise of infidelity.*[101]

Referring to the last couplet (968),

> Give up your heart to the Christian child;
> Free yourself of all denial and affirmation.

Lāhījī explains that Sufi teaching is based on religious inclusivism. Freeing oneself of "all denial and affirmation" hence implies that

> One must totally and absolutely detach and liberate oneself from all manner of denial and affirmation (*ankār wa iqrār*) regarding all people – whosoever they may be – in the world of outer appearances (*ṣūrat*). One should not judge or weigh their morality or behaviour on one's scales of one's own self, nor let your own individual being interfere in this. Rather, consider yourself ignorant and unaware, and give up your heart at once to the "Christian child" who is the Perfect [Sufi] Master.[102]

This interiorisation of Christian symbols in Sufism, whereupon each Christian symbol, doctrine and custom assumes a spiritual sense, expresses a particular sort of esoteric Christianity, which, assert the Sufis, makes pietistic formalism, whatever its religious brand-name, the *de facto* heresy. Shabistarī's esoteric Christianity represents a radical, Sufi reappraisal of Islamic religious customs, dogma and tradition, based on reinterpretation of the inward sense of Gospel references and an allegorical reading of Christian symbols from within the Islamic tradition.

6 The Christian "Monastery" or "Cloister"

Shabistarī's tolerant outlook on other religions is most apparent in his doctrine of the "Law of Contraries," which espouses the relativity of heresy and true faith and dictates the necessity for the existence of other faiths.[103] Faith is only sincere when performed in the spirit; the mere rite or form, the letter or the ritual act are themselves valueless. In fact, states Shabistarī, they constitute a type of secret idolatry insofar as "any type of devotion which is performed out of habit and by rote is merely food for passion. The only remedy [from hypocrisy] for a person of religious sensibility is to be found in the form of contraries (*ṣūrat-i aḍdād*). That is to say, it is more virtuous for you to frequent a Christian cloister (*dayr*) than to attend a mosque while imagining yourself superior to others."[104]

This perspective leads us to consider Shabistarī's understanding and interiorisation of another Christian symbols: the Christian monastery or cloister. Just as the poetic symbol of the "Christian" indicates the perfect Sufi who sees all faith in the light of God, so the term "monastery" or "cloister" (*dayr*) in Sufi terminology is interpreted as symbolic of the supra-formal, interior level of religious understanding. Abū 'l-Mufākhir Yaḥyā Bākharzī in this context in his *Awrād al-aḥbāb* writes:

> The term church (*kalīsā*) and monastery (*dayr*) symbolise the realm of divine infinity (*'ālam-i iṭlāq*) which is the world of Essential Unity (*waḥdat-i dhāt*), being the spiritual realm in which all the divine Attributes are one and same vis-a-vis the divine Essence. Thus, before Him: wrath and grace, mercy and rigor, contraction and expansion, and even sin and obedience and death and life are one and the same. Such differentiations and distinctions are only found in [the level of] the divine Names, Attributes and Commands, which display him through laws, decrees and the pleasures [of paradise] and the fire of hell.[105]

At this level, Lāhījī points out, the distinctions between "sin and obedience, and death and life" dissolve, for before the divine Essence, such matters become marginal. In his commentary on one of the first passages cited above:

> Within the inner court of holy Oneness
> Lies the soul's monastery,
> Perch of the Simurgh of Subsistence.

Lāhījī explains that "the inner court or sanctum of the holy Oneness (*waḥdat-i dhāt*) of the Divine Essence, which transcends and is hallowed from all blemish of multiplicity (*kathrat*), is the soul's monastery (*dayr-i jān*)."[106] In order to explain the reason for this apparent inversion of religious values – where the highest realm of contemplation is symbolised by the Christian monastery, Muslim "faith" being arrayed in "infidelity's" attire, Lāhījī notes that while

> the monastery (*dayr*) is the house of worship (*ma'bad*) of the Christians who belong to the community of the prophet Jesus. But [on the psychologically interiorised level of the] holy monastery of Divine Unity [one discovers] the house of worship for the soul, the human spirit (*rūḥ-i insānī*) whose origin of which is in the Supraformal Realm (*'ālam-i tajarrud*).

Thus, according to the interiorised vision of religion maintained by the Sufis, the level of the Christian monastery symbolises the supraformal reality of all religion. It is indeed a testimony to the lack of sectarian bias, and a tribute to the cosmopolitan reach of the ecumenical imagination of the fourteenth-century Persian Sufis that a Christian monastery, the house of worship of an alien faith, should serve as a supreme symbol of the human spirit's divine homeland.

NOTES

1 S. H. Nasr, "The Islamic View of Christianity," in Paul J. Griffiths (ed.), *Christianity through Non-Christian Eyes* (Maryknoll, New York: Orbis Books, 1990), pp. 100–111.
2 Michael Sells, *Mystical Languages of Unsaying* (Chicago: University of Chicago Press, 1994), p. 102.
3 Roger Arnaldez, *Three Messengers for One God,* trans. G. W. Schlabach et al., (Indiana/London: University of Notra Dame Press, 1994), pp. 16–17; 47–51; 56–153.
4 William James made some preliminary remarks concerning the similarities of both faiths in *The Variety of Religious Experience* (New York: Penguin Books, 1985), pp. 402–06, 420, and his viewpoint was expounded with great rigor and detail by Evelyn Underhill in her classical work on *Mysticism*, first published in 1911.
5 See A. J. Arberry, "The Beginning of Ṣūfī Studies in Europe," in his *An Introduction to the History of Sufism* (Hyderabad: Orient Longman, 1992), pp. 1–26.
6 See L. Massignon, "Muslim and Christian Mysticism in the Middle Ages," in H. Mason (ed.), *Testimonies and Reflections: Essays of Louis Massignon* (Indiana: University of Notra Dame, 1989).
7 D. Macdonald, "The Unity of the Mystical Experience in Islam and Christianity," *The Moslem World*, XXV/4 (1935), p. 332. Cf Massignon's remarks on St. Francis in *ibid.*, pp. 130–32.

8 *In the Garden of Myrtles*, trans. B. Sharpe (Albany: SUNY Press, 1987), p. 124.
9 D. Miguel Asin Palacios, *Islam and the Divine Comedy,* trans., and abridged H. Sutherland (London: Frank Cass, 1968).
10 L. Massignon, *op. cit.*, p. 130.
11 N. Robinson, *Christ in Islam and Christianity* (Albany: SUNY Press, 1991), chapters 7, 17; Arnaldez, *op. cit., passim.*
12 H. Corbin, *Creative Imagination in the Ṣūfism of Ibn 'Arabī*, trans. R. Manheim (Princeton, N. J.: Princeton University Press, 1969).
13 *Masīḥ wa Masīḥiyyat nazd-i Īrāniyān, I: Sayr-i ijmālī dar tārīkh; II: Dar Shi'r-i fārsī dawrān-i sabk-i kuhan; III: Dar nazm wa nathr wa hunar-i mu'āsīr* (London: Suhrāb, 1992–94).
14 *Chihrah-yi masīḥ dar adabiyāt-i fārsī* (Tehran: Intishārāt-i mu'īn 1990).
15 Qamar Āryān, "Christian Influences in Persian Poetry," s.v. "Christianity" in *Encyclopedia Iranica*, V. p. 540.
16 *Ibid.*, p. 539.
17 *Ibid.*
18 Cf. Shiblī's refusal to accept medical aid from a Christian physician and his characterisation of Christians as "foes"; 'Aṭṭār, *Tadhkirat al-awliyā'*, ed. M. Isti'lāmī (Tehran: Zawwār, 1372/1993), p. 626.
19 Cf. Rūmī's debate with a Christian over the character of Christ, in Rumi, *Signs of the Unseen: The Discourses of Rumi*, trans. W. Thackston (Vermont: Threshold, 1994), pp. 30 ff.
20 See Edward Browne, *A Literary History of Persia* (Cambridge: Cambridge University Press, 1924), IV, p. 421.
21 As 'Aṭṭār relates of Shiblī, for instance: *Tadhkirat al-awliyā'*, p. 624.
22 See the articles by L. Lewisohn, J. Nurbakhsh and T. Graham in L. Lewisohn (ed.), *The Heritage of Sufism* (Oxford: Oneworld, 1999), vol I.
23 Noting that "there was a very considerable degree of tolerance within the Mongol Empire," Thomas Haining cites this article from Genghis Khān's Yāsa: "It is ordered that there is only one God, Creator of Heaven and earth, Who alone gives life and death, riches and poverty as pleases Him, and Who has over everything an absolute power ... Leaders of a religion, preachers, monks, persons who are to be freed from all public charges." – "The Mongols and Religion," *Asian Affairs*, XVII/I (1986), p. 26. Also see M. Murtaḍawī's lengthy discussion of the Mongol's lack of ereligious prejudice: *Masā'īl-i 'aṣr-i Īlkhānān*, pp. 350–68; and Jean-Paul Roux, "La Tolérance Religieuse dans les Empires Turco-Mongols," *Revue de l'Histoire des Religions*, CCIII–2/ 1986, pp. 131–68.
24 D. Morgan, *Medieval Persia 1047–1797* (London: Longman, 1988), p. 53.
25 M. M. Mazzaoui, *The Origins of the Ṣafawids* (Wiesbaden: Franz Steiner, 1972), p. 38.
26 Jean-Paul Roux, p. 137, and Qamar Āriyān, p. 87.
27 Cf. Sa'īd Nafīsī (ed.), *Dīwān-i Awḥādī Maraghī* (Tehran: Amīr Kabīr, 1340/1961), p. 57.
28 Qamar Āriyān, *Chihra-yi Masīḥ*, p. 87.
29 C. Cahen, *Pre-Ottoman Turkey*, trans. J. Jones-Williams (London: Sidgwick & Jackson, 1972), p. 348.

30 "Christians had nowhere really regained the upper hand, the Muslims being so much in a majority and so dominant socially that, even at a time when they had not been converted, the Mongols could not but recruit the bulk of their administrative personnel, including the viziers, from among them. And this situation was only accentuated when the Mongols were converted to Islam. In its institutions Asia Minor had remained Muslim, the whole administrative personnel was Muslim, and the Muslim viziers of the Ilkhāns themselves were anxious to figure as Muslim patrons, sometimes even more than in their own country." *Ibid.*
31 D. Morgan, chapter 7.
32 J. S. Trimingham, *The Sufi Orders in Islam* (Oxford: Oxford University Press, 1973), p. 90.
33 Jean-Paul Roux, p. 132.
34 J. S. Trimingham, p. 90.
35 Cf. S. H. Nasr, "Sufism and Spirituality in Persia," in S. H. Nasr (ed.), *Islamic Spirituality II* (New York: Crossroads, 1991), p. 210.
36 For a good discussion of which, see Jean-Paul Roux, pp. 159–63; M. Murtaḍawī, *Masā'il-i asr-i Īlkhānān* (Tehran: 1991), pp. 311–50; Jean Aubin, "Le Patronage Culturel en Iran sous les Ilkhans," *Le Monde Iranien et l'Islam*, III (1975), pp. 107–18; A. K. S. Lambton, "Mongol Fiscal Administration in Persia," *Studia Islamica* LXIV (1986), Part 1, p. 89; also some of Maria Eva Subtelny's observations in her "Socioeconomic Bases of Cultural Patronage under the Later Timurids," *IJMES* 20 (1988), pp. 480–82, are relevant to the Mongol period. Of course, such explanations ignore the movements of that spiritual *Zeitgeist*, which itself is both cause and effect. As Schimmel put it: "Strangely enough this [Mongol] period of the most terrible political disaster was, at the same time, a period of highest religious and mystical activity. It seems as though the complete darkness on the worldly plane was counteracted by a hitherto unknown brightness on the spiritual plane," *The Triumphal Sun* (London: Fine Books, 1978), p. 9.
37 See "Le milieu baghdādien: politique et religion," in *Nuruddin Isfarayini,* (ed.), H. Landolt (Paris: Éditions Verdier, 1986), pp. 31–6.
38 See P. Soucek, "Iranian Architecture," in E. Yarshater & R. Ettinghausen, *Highlights of Persian Art* (Boulder: Westview Press, 1979), p. 148.
39 See J. Wansbrough, *Qoranic Studies* (London: 1980), pp. 242–3. According to 'Alī, the fourth Sunni Caliph, first Shī'-ite Imām, there is no Qur'ānic verse which does not have these four senses.
40 A. Fletcher, *Allegory: The Theory of a Symbolic Mode* (Ithaca: Cornell University Press, 1964), p. 313.
41 *Essai sur les origines du lexique technique de la mystique musulmane* (Paris: J. Vrin 1954), pp. 69–81.
42 *Ibid.*, p. 104.
43 H. Corbin, *Histoire de la Philosophie Islamique*, p. 30. Corbin's most profound exploration of this esoteric aspect of Islam-Christian studies was his essay on "Comparative Spiritual Hermeneutics," in his *Swedenborg and Esoteric Islam*, trans. L. Fox (West Chester, Penn.: Swedenborg Foundation, 1995), pp. 35–149.
44 M. Eliade, *A History of Religious Ideas*, III (Chicago: University of Chicago Press, 1985), pp. 116–19.

45 H. Corbin, *Histoire de la Philosophue Islamique*, p. 24.
46 Kalābādhī, *Al-Ta'arruf li-madhhab ahl al-taṣawwuf*, trans. Arberry, *The Doctrine of the Sufis* (Cambridge: Cambridge University Press, 1989), p. 76.
47 *Ibid.*, p. 77.
48 *Exègése Coranique et Langage Mystique* (Beirut: 1970), p. 167.
49 P. Nywia, "Ishāra," EI^2, p. 114.
50 See W. C. Chittick, *The Sufi Path of Knowledge* (Albany: SUNY Press, 1989).
51 L. Lewisohn, *Beyond Faith and Infidelity* (London: Curzon, 1995), p. 204ff.
52 Cited by W. Chittick, *Imaginal Worlds* (Albany: SUNY Press, 1994), p. 75.
53 Q. Ghanī, *Baḥth dar āthār wa afkār wa aḥwāl-i Ḥāfiẓ* (Tehran: 1977, 3rd ed.), pp. 562–63.
54 L. Lewisohn (ed.), *Diwān-i Muḥammad Shīrīn Maghribī*. Persian text edited with notes, introduction, and index. (Wisdom of Persia Series XLIII. Tehran: McGill Institute of Islamic Studies, Tehran Branch; London: SOAS, 1994), pp. 6–8.
55 *Beyond Faith and Infidelity,* p. 205.
56 Cf. Sells, *op. cit.*, p. 3
57 'Abd al-Ḥusayn Zarrīnkūb, *Justujū dar taṣawwuf-i Irān* (Tehran: Amīr Kabīr, 1978), p. 327.
58 A metre popular among the Sufi poets. See Finn Theisen's *A Manual of Classical Persian Prosody* (Weisbaden: Otto Harrassowtz, 1982), p. 125.
59 Also, cf. the analysis by Zarrīnkūb, *Justujū*, p. 313.
60 L. Lewisohn, *Beyond Faith and Infidelity*, pp. 33–40.
61 For summaries of these commentaries, see (in French) H. Corbin, *Trilogie Ismaelienne* (Tehran/Paris 1961), pp. 21–23; and (in Persian) 'Azīz Dawlatābādī (ed.), *Sukhanwarān-i Adharbāyjān* I (Tabriz: Intishārāt-i Mu'asasa-yi Tārīkh wa Farhang-i Īrān, 1355/1976), pp. 162–73, who cites 49 different commentaries.
62 On Lāhījī, see M. Glünz, "Sufism and Poetry in Fifteenth-Century Iran," in L. Golombek and M. Subtelny (eds.), *Timurid Art and Culture* (Leiden: Brill, 1992), pp. 195–200; B. Zanjānī (ed.), *Dīwān-i ash'ār wa rasā'īl-i Asīrī Lāhījī* (Tehran: McGill University Istitute of Islamic Studies, 1978), N. Anṣārī's introduction.
63 L. Lewisohn, *Beyond Faith and Infidelity*, chapter 6.
64 *Ibid.*, p. 143.
65 Ṣ. Muwaḥḥid (ed.), *Majmū'a-yi āthār-i Shaykh Maḥmūd Shabistarī* (Tehran: Kitābkhāna-yi Ṭahūrī, 1365/1986), p. 80, v. 335.
66 N. Robinson, *op. cit.*, p. 58.
67 As Ibn 'Arabī in the chapter on Ezra in the *Fuṣūṣ al-ḥikām* explained; see R. J. W. Austin (trans.) *Ibn al-'Arabī: The Bezels of Wisdom* (New York: Paulist Press), p. 168.
68 M. Chodkiewicz, *Seal of the Saints: Prophethood and Sainthood in the Doctrine of Ibn 'Arabī*, trans. L. Sherrard (Cambridge: Islamic Texts Society, 19993), p. 79. On Ibn 'Arabī's tolerant outlook on non-Islamic faith, see W. Chittick, *Imaginal Worlds*.
69 G. Parrinder, *Jesus in the Qur'ān* (Oxford: Oneworld, 1996), pp. 48–51.
70 *Gulshan-i rāz*, in *Majmū'a-yi āthār,* p. 105, vv. 927–32.

71 Epistles 102: 12; cited by John Hick, "Trinity and Incarnation in the Light of Religious Pluralism," in John Hick and Edmund Meltzer (eds.), *Three Faiths–One God* (Albany: SUNY Press, 1989), p. 198.
72 John Hick, "Jesus and the World Religions," in John Hick (ed.), *The Myth of God Incarnate* (London: SCM, 1993, second edition), p. 175.
73 Maurice Wiles, "Christianity without Incarnation?" in John Hick (ed.), *The Myth of God Incarnate,* p. 8. See also, John Hick, *The Metaphor of God Incarnate* (London: SCM, 1993).
74 *Mafātīḥ al-i'jāz*, ed. Khāliqī & Karbāsī, p. 565.
75 *Gulshan-i rāz*, pp. 105–6, vv. 932–38.
76 S. H. Nasr, "Comments on a Few Theological Issues in the Islamic-Christian Dialogue," in Y. Y. Haddad & W. Z. Haddad (eds.), *Christian-Muslim Encounters* (Gainesville: University of Florida Press, 1995), p. 458.
77 Verses 940–51 immediately following those cited here actually concern the "Christian" mode of detachment the poet propounds, for a translation of which see Lewisohn, *Beyond Faith and Infidelity*, pp. 2–3.
78 *Gulshan-i rāz*, v. 155.
79 See S. Nafīsī (ed.), *Diwān-i Awḥadī Maraghī*, pp. 626, 656, 660.
80 *Gulshan-i rāz*, v. 927.
81 *Kashshāf iṣṭilāḥāt al-funūn (A Dictionary of the Technical Terms Used in the Sciences of the Musalmans)*, ed. M. Wajih, 'Abd al-Ḥaqq & Gh. Kadir, under the superintendence of A. Sprengler & W. Nassua Lees. (Calcutta: 1862), I. p. 1555. Cited in *Farhang-i Nūrbakhsh*, III, p. 186.
82 *Awrād al-aḥbāb wa fuṣūṣ al-ādāb*, 2nd vol., ed. Ī. Afshār (Tehran: 1345/1966), p. 245. Cited in *Farhang-i Nūrbakhsh*, III, p. 187.
83 *Gulshan-i rāz,* p. 106, v. 956.
84 M. Chodkiewicz, *Seal of the Saints*, p. 78–9.
85 Bukhārī, *anbiyā'*, 45; Muslim, *tawba*, 46–7: *zuhd,* 73.
86 *Mafātīḥ al-i'jāz*, p. 577.
87 *Awrād al-aḥbāb*, p. 245; cited in *Farhang-i Nūrbakhsh*, III, p. 188.
88 *Gulshan-i rāz*, vv. 969–79.
89 *Mafātīḥ al-i'jāz*, p. 588.
90 *Ibid*., p. 592.
91 Cf. Rūmī, *Mathnawī*, II: 3325.
92 *Mafātīḥ al-i'jāz*, p. 588.
93 Cf. my discussion of *kufr-i ḥaqīqī* in *Beyond Faith and Infidelity,* p. 288ff.
94 Cf. J. Hick, s. v. "Religious Pluralism," in M. Eliade (ed.), *Encyclopedia of Religion*; W. C. Smith, *Religious Diversity* (New York: 1976) and H. Coward, *Pluralism* (New York: 1985); I. Hamnett *Religious Pluralism and Unbelief* (London: Routledge, 1990); M. Eliade, "Methodological Remarks on the study of Religious Symbolism," in M. Eliade and J. Kitagawa (eds.), *The History of Religions* (Chicago: Chicago University Press, 1959), p. 91.
95 For a study of Ibn 'Arabī's views of non-Islamic religions which were the dominant influence on Shabistarī's dostrine in the passages cited immediately above and below, see W. Chittick, "Belief and Transformation," *The American Theosophist* 74/5 (1986), pp. 181–92; *idem.*, *Imaginal Worlds*, chapters 8–10; D. S. Houédard, "Ibn 'Arabī's Contribution to the Wider Ecumenism," in S. Hirtenstein & M. Tiernan (eds.), *Muhyiddin Ibn 'Arabī*, pp. 291–306.

96 For a good exposition of this Akbarian doctrine, see Chittick, "Transcending the Gods of Belief," *The Sufi Path of Knowledge*, pp. 335–56; Sells, "Gods of Belief" in *op. cit.*, p. 97–100.
97 *Gulshan-i rāz,* p. 103, vv. 863–81
98 For further study, see Lewisohn, *Beyond Faith and Infidelity*, chapter 8, where some ten pages are devoted to their exegesis.
99 *Mafātīḥ al-iʿjāz,* p. 579.
100 Lāhījī's reference is to his previous exegesis of certain verses in the *Garden of Mystery* concerning the symbolic meanings of these esoteric expressions. "The Transcendental Unity of Polytheism and Monotheism in the Sufism of Shabistarī," in *idem*. (ed.), *The Legacy of Medieval Persian Sufism*, pp. 379–406.
101 *Mafātīḥ al-iʿjāz,* p. 582.
102 *Ibid.*, p. 584.
103 On this doctrine see L. Lewisohn, "The Transcendental Unity," p. 392–3.
104 *Saʿādat-nāma*, in *Majmūʿa-yi āthār,* p. 232, vv 1384–86. A reference to the Qur'ān, *sūra* 28: 76, "Iblis said: 'I am better than him. You created me of fire, but you created him of clay.'"
105 *Awrād al-aḥbāb,* p. 245; cited in *Farhang-i Nūrbakhsh*, III, p. 190.
106 *Mafātīḥ al-iʿjāz*, p. 565.

Part II

The Modern Period

7

Sayyid Quṭb's Attitude Towards Christianity: Sūra 9.29–35 in *Fī Ẓilāl Al-Qur'ān*[1]

Neal Robinson

Sayyid Quṭb, who was executed by President Nasser in 1966, was the leading ideologue of the Muslim Brotherhood in the nineteen fifties and early sixties.[2] This paper will deal with Quṭb's attitude to Christians in his major Qur'ānic commentary, *Fī Ẓilāl al-Qur'ān* ("In the Shade of the Qur'ān" or "Under the Aegis of the Qur'ān").[3] It will focus primarily on his treatment of *sūra* 9.29–35. This particular passage has been chosen not only because of its intrinsic interest but also because of the importance which Quṭb evidently ascribed to it. In his commentary, Quṭb allotted a disproportionately large amount of space to *sūras* 4, 5, 6, 8, 9, 33, and 49 – *sūras* which focus on the structure of the Muslim community, relations with non-Muslims, the conduct of war, and the struggle for social justice, all of which are key issues for the Islamic movement.[4] Moreover, of the 180 pages which he devoted to *sūra* 9, no less than thirty concern this sequence of six *āyas*. I propose to summarise them and then offer a brief critique. Before doing this, however, I shall try to convey to the reader something of the extent and complexity of the Qur'ānic material about Christians.

I. QUR'ĀNIC REFERENCES TO JESUS AND CHRISTIANS

According to the Qur'ān, Jesus was a prophet sent by God who received a divine revelation, the Gospel. He was conceived by his mother Mary when she was a virgin and he performed miracles by divine leave. Nevertheless, he was not the Son of God and did not instruct his followers to regard him as divine. On the contrary, like all the prophets and messengers who preceded him, he was a humble servant of God who preached monotheism.[5]

The Qur'ān contains fourteen references to *naṣārā*, "Nazarenes." This is apparently a generic name for Christians, no distinction being made between those who subscribed to the Council of Chalcedon in 451, and so-called "heretics" such as Nestorians, Monophysites, Arians, Elkasaites and Gnostics, who may well have been operative in seventh-century Arabia.[6] It also refers once to *ahl al-injīl*, "the People of the Gospel" (5: 47), and once to those who follow Jesus (57: 27). In addition, there are a number of *āyas* which mention those who hold what, from the Qur'ānic perspective, are erroneous beliefs about Jesus. Finally, there are forty-one passages which refer to Banū Isrā'īl, "the Children of Israel"; thirty-one which refer to *ahl al-kitāb*, "the People of Scripture" or to "those to whom We gave the Scripture"; and two which refer to *ahl al-dhikr*, "the People of Remembrance." All of these expressions seem to be umbrella terms for the Jews and Christians of Arabia.

Within this mass of material, we may distinguish what appear at first sight to be four different assessments of Christians:

1 There are a number of passages, mostly from the Meccan period, which imply that the Jews and Christians alike are at heart Muslims, and that they immediately acknowledge the truth of Islam when they are presented with the Qur'ānic message:

> Those to whom We gave the Scripture before this believe in it [i.e. the Qur'ān], and when it is recited to them they say, "We believe in it. Surely it is the truth from our Lord. Indeed even before it, we were of those who submit themselves (*muslimīn*)." (28: 52)

2 There are two Medinan *āyas* which seem to imply that Judaism and Christianity are valid religions whose adherents will be judged on the basis of their works:

> Truly those who believe and those who are Jews, the Nazarenes and the Sabaeans, whoever believes in God and the Last Day and does right, for them is their reward near their Lord; they will have no fear, neither will they grieve. (2: 26, cp 5: 69)

3 There is a Medinan *āya* which condemns the Jews as being no better than the Arab pagans, but which is nonetheless highly appreciative of the Christians:

> Thou wilt surely find that the most hostile of men to the believers are Jews and those who associate [other divinities with God]. And thou wilt surely find the nearest of them in love to the believers are those who say, "We are Nazarenes." That is because some of the latter are priests and monks, and they are not arrogant. (5: 82)

4 There are late Medinan passages which stigmatise Christians as unbelievers because of their erroneous beliefs and practices. The most forthright of these is 9: 29–35, which is antagonistic towards Jews and Christians alike. It orders the Muslims to fight them until they pay the *jizya*; it classes both groups as unbelievers along with the pagans; and it castigates rabbis and monks for the deceitful way in which they amass wealth.[7]

A non-Muslim scholar, working on the assumption that the Qur'ān reflects Muḥammad's own views, might infer that these *āyas* represent his attitude to Christians in four successive phases of his career. During the Meccan period, when his day to day contacts were primarily with hostile Arab pagans, the distinction between Jews and Christians would have been relatively unimportant to him. The warm reception which some of his followers received from Christians in Abyssinia probably led him to suppose that all the People of the Scripture were potential converts who would recognise the truth of Islam. Soon after arriving in Medina, however, he came to realise that the Jews and Christians were not going to convert *en masse*, but he nonetheless looked on them as potential allies who believed much the same as him, and whom God would reward for their good works. Before long, however, he learned from experience that the Jews of Medina were not at all like the Christians of Abyssinia. Indeed, he found them as hostile to Islam as the Meccan pagans had been, although at this stage he still held out hopes of amicable relations with the Arab Christians. Finally, when his adopted son Zayd was killed in a skirmish with Byzantine troops at Mu'ta, and the Emperor Heraclius restored the true cross to Jerusalem, he realised the need to impose his authority on the Arab Christians. He marched northwards to Tabūk, in a massive show of strength, castigating Jews and Christians as unbelievers and imposing the *jizya*. Most non-Muslims who seek to elucidate the Qur'ānic reference to Christians argue along these lines. Needless to say, Sayyid Quṭb's approach is very different.

II. QUṬB'S COMMENTARY ON 9: 29–35[8]

The Introduction to the Section

Quṭb begins by stating that this is the second section of the *sūra* and that its purpose is to establish definitive regulations for relations between the Muslim society and the People of the Scripture (the Jews and Christians), just as the purpose of the first section was to establish definitive regulations for relations between this society and the associators (the polytheists who associate other deities with God). However, whereas the first section speaks about the associators in the Arab Peninsula, the second applies to all the People of the Scripture, those inside the Peninsula and those outside it. The definitive regulations in this section comprise fundamental changes to the principles on which the relations between the Muslim society and the People of the Scripture are based. The most conspicuous change is the command to fight against them until they pay the *jizya*. From now on, there are to be no pacts or truces with them except on this basis. Nevertheless, the principle that there should be no compulsion in religion[9] still holds good. If they pay the *jizya*, they are to be given protected status and allowed to practice their religion in peace. Alternatively, if they are convinced of the truth of Islam, they may become Muslims and gain exemption from payment.

Quṭb states that coexistence would be impossible without these regulations. This is because of the incompatibility of God's programme and the programme of the *jāhiliyya* – a term which originally denoted the "state of ignorance" that prevailed in pre-Islamic Arabia, but which he applied to modern society in general, including Nasser's Egypt. God's programme is, he says, to liberate human beings from bondage to each other so that they serve him alone. The *jāhiliyya*, on the other hand, seeks to wipe out the Islamic movement, which has burst forth with God's programme.

Next, he points out that according to these *āyas* the People of the Scripture are characterised by *shirk* (associating other deities with God), *kufr* (unbelief) and *bāṭil* (falsehood). He realises that this may seem surprising in view of the more positive things said about the People of Scripture elsewhere in the Qur'ān. He is also aware that Orientalists and Christian missionaries have alleged that this text reflects a radical change in Muḥammad's attitude. He is therefore at pains to stress that the Qur'ānic assessment of Jews and Christians is God's assessment of them, not Muḥammad's, and that it remains constant through the Meccan and Medinan periods. In his view, the only thing which changes is the divinely-prescribed basis for relations between the Muslim community, and the Jews and Christians.

To prove his point, he reviews the Qur'ānic references to Jews and Christians at considerable length. The linchpin of his argument is the existence of Qur'ānic passages from the Meccan period which trace the rebelliousness and unbelief of the majority of People of the

Scripture back to the time of Moses and Jesus. Concerning Moses' contemporaries the Qur'ān says;

> And [remember] when it was said to them, "Dwell in this town and eat therein whatever you will, and say 'Repentance' and enter the gate prostrating. We will forgive you your transgressions; We will increase [the reward of] those who do good." Then those of them who did wrong changed the word that had been told them. So We sent upon them wrath from heaven for their wrongdoing. (7: 161f)

Regarding Jesus' contemporaries, it says

> When Jesus came with clear signs he said, "I have come to you with wisdom and in order to make clear to you some of what you disagree about. So fear God and obey me. God, He is your Lord and my Lord so serve him. This is a straight path." But the sects among them disagreed. So woe to the wrongdoers because of the punishment of a grievous day! (43: 63)

From these passages and Medinan revelations which resemble them, Quṭb infers that it was always the case that the majority of the Jews and Christians were unbelievers. However, he states that there were no colonies of Jews and Christians in Mecca, only isolated individuals; and he contends that those individuals were in fact strict monotheists and genuine believers. They therefore received the call to Islam with joy and testified that the Qur'ān confirmed what they knew to be true. In Medina, on the other hand, the situation was very different. A substantial proportion of the population were Jews and they regarded Islam as a threat. Hence, they were hostile to the Muslims and denied that the Jewish scriptures prophesied the coming of Muḥammad. Nevertheless, even in Medina, a few individuals from the People of the Scripture responded to the call to Islam, although these individuals tended to be Christians rather than Jews. The vast majority of the People of the Scripture in the Arabian Peninsula were not, however, like this. They were vehement opponents of Islam which is why, the Medinan revelations tend to stress their wickedness and falsehood.

Quṭb maintains that history bears witness to the ongoing desire of the People of the Scripture to extinguish God's light. During the Prophet's lifetime, the Jews of Medina colluded with the pagan confederates who besieged the city. Later, Jews played a key part in the rebellion in which 'Uthmān, the third caliph was killed; they were also involved in the civil war between 'Alī and Mu'āwiya, in the Mongol sacking of Baghdad, and in the destruction of the caliphate. In the modern era, he says,

> they have been behind every disaster which has befallen Muslims in every place on the face of earth, and they are behind every attempt to crush the beginnings of the Islamic revival.[10]

As for the other branch of the People of the Scripture, he alleges that it has been no less persistent in its hostility. When Islam, the true religion, appeared in the Arabian Peninsula, the Church perceived it as a threat to what she had created with her own hands and had named "Christianity" (*masīḥiyya*), but which was in fact

> a pile of ancient idolatries and ecclesiastical errors clad in the vestiges of the words of Christ, peace be upon him![11]

Therefore, the Byzantine and Persian empires, which had been at war for centuries, forgot their differences in order to confront the new religion. Quṭb catalogues the Church's attacks on Islam, beginning in the Prophet's lifetime with Christian collaboration with the Persians in Southern Arabia and the Byzantine routing of the Muslims at Mu'ta; continuing with the atrocities committed during the reconquest of Spain and the crusades; and culminating in modern times with comparable atrocities in Zanzibar, Cyprus, Eritrea and Southern Sudan.

His Comments on 9: 29

> Fight against those who believe neither in God nor the Last Day, nor forbid what God and His Messenger have forbidden, nor practice the religion of truth, despite having been given the Scripture, until they pay the *jizya* with willing submission and feel themselves subdued.

Quṭb states that this *āya* and those which follow it were revealed in preparation for the campaign of Tabūk, and envisage the Byzantine and their Arab Christian clients the Ghassanids. They thus mention the characteristics of the people against whom the campaign was directed, as a justification and incentive for fighting them. Whereas 9: 29 states that these people did not believe in God and the Last Day; did not forbid what God and his Messenger forbade; and did not practice the religion of truth, 9: 30–32 and 9: 34 provide evidence that this was indeed the case. However, everything said in these *āyas* about the Christians of Syria and Byzantium, also holds true of the majority of Christians throughout history, right down to the present day. In particular, Quṭb stresses that "the hallowed compilations" (his term for the Christian scriptures and creeds) perverted the religion of Christ by speaking of him as Son of God and defining God as a Trinity of Divine persons. This *āya* is therefore a universal command. It establishes an absolute principle for dealing with the People of the Scripture to whom these characteristics, which were conspicuous in the Arab and Byzantine Christians apply.

Nevertheless, the Prophet forbade Muslims from fighting against non-combatants including children, women, the elderly, and monks who remained in their monasteries. There are no grounds, however, for holding that this *āya* only requires Muslims to fight against actual aggressors, as some Muslim scholars allege. Aggression exists in the beginning: aggression against the deity of God, and aggression against worshippers by enslaving them to other than God. Islam's struggle to defend the deity of God and human dignity therefore entails waging war against the nature of things.

In the course of his comments on the words "who believe neither in God nor the Last Day," Quṭb says

> It cannot be said of anyone who treats Ezra or Christ as Son of God that he believes in God. Likewise anyone who says, "God is Christ the son of Mary"[12] or "God is the third of three"[13] or "God became incarnate in Christ," and so forth of the ecclesiastical imaginings which the revered compilations have made up ... and those who say that they will not enter hell-fire except for a number of days[14] no matter how much they sin, because they are sons of God and his beloved ones,[15] and the chosen people of God, and those who say every disobedience will be forgiven through union with Christ and participation in the holy supper and that there is no forgiveness except by this way ... it cannot be said that they believe in the Last Day.[16]

As regards not forbidding "what God and His Messenger have forbidden," he argues that it is explained in 9: 34 as devouring people's goods deceitfully. The clearest example of this, he says, is usury, although he mentions others as we shall see when we examine his comments on that *āya*. As for their not practising the religion of truth, this is, he maintains, clear from what has been said previously.

Quṭb notes that there is no question of the fighting continuing until they become Muslims – for "There is no compulsion in religion."[17] Fighting is to cease when "they pay the *jizya* with willing submission and feel themselves subdued." Islam, as the sole true religion, sets out to remove obstacles from its path and to liberate human beings. Nevertheless it leaves every individual with freedom of choice.

The means for ensuring the simultaneous removal of obstacles to embracing Islam and compulsion to embrace it is the smashing of the might of the sovereign powers based upon other than the religion of the truth, so that they surrender and prove that they have done so by paying the *jizya*. When this happens, every individual will be free to choose the religion of truth out of conviction or, if he remains unconvinced, to pay the *jizya*. By paying the *jizya*, he will:

1 announce his surrender and the absence of his physical resistance to the summons to the true religion of God;
2 contribute to the expenses of the defences of himself, his wealth, his merchandise and his womenfolk, which Islam guarantees to the people with protected status;
3 contribute to the Muslim treasury which guarantees protection and sustenance to everyone incapable of work, Muslims and non-Muslims alike.

Quṭb refuses to discuss who should pay the *jizya*, the rates of payment, and the ways of fixing them. His reason for doing so is that at the time of writing these were purely theoretical issues, because no genuinely Muslim society ruled by God's law existed. In his view, the Islamic programme is a realistic one which refuses to become entangled in legal debates about things of no immediate practical importance. He dismisses Muslims who waste time on such matters as *ara'ayta'ūn*, or "have-you-considered-ers." He holds that the starting point for the Islamic movement today is the same as it was at the time of the rise of Islam. There must be a place on earth where people subscribe to the religion of the truth, testifying that there is no deity but God and that Muḥammad is the messenger of God, and hence ascribing dominion, power and the right to legislate, to God alone, and applying this is real life. Then, these people must attempt to burst forth into the world with this universal announcement for the liberation of mankind. When that happens, and only then, it will be necessary to codify the laws governing relations between the Muslim society and non-Muslims.

His Comments on 9: 30

> The Jews say that Ezra is the Son of God and the Christians say that Christ is the Son of God. That is the utterances of their mouths. They imitate the utterance of those who disbelieve of old. May God fight against them! How they are perverted.

Quṭb notes that whereas Christians still claim that Christ is the Son of God, the Jews do not nowadays say the same of Ezra. He has no fresh light to shed on this problem but quotes Riḍā's treatment of it in the *Manār* Commentary.[18] Riḍā stressed that Jews believe that God revealed the Law of Moses to Ezra after it had been lost, and that consequently for them Ezra is closely associated with God's word. In view of the fact that the Jewish philosopher Philo of Alexandria said that "God has a Son; he is His word by whom He created things," Riḍā thought it likely that some of the Jews of Arabia did in fact refer to Ezra as the Son of God.

As for the Christians' erroneous belief that Christ is the Son of God, Quṭb states that it originated with Paul, who falsified Christ's message – Christ himself having taught the unity of God. He then quotes Riḍā's excursus on the Trinity.[19] Riḍā explains that Christians believe that the Godhead comprises three persons – Father, Son and Holy Spirit – and that this is the teaching of the Catholic Church, the Eastern Church, and most Protestants. He says that those who hold to this doctrine think that it is in conformity with the Bible because they interpret the Bible in the light of the writings of the Church fathers and councils. The Old Testament texts which they cite are open to different interpretations. The New Testament does, however, contain two groups of texts which they allege as proofs: those which refer to Father, Son and Holy Spirit together, and those which mention them separately but imply their interrelationship. Riḍā states that the dispute about the persons of the Godhead began in Apostolic times under the influence of Hellenistic and Gnostic philosophies; that Bishop Theophilus of Antioch was the first Christian writer to use the Greek word *trias* to denote a divine triad; and that Tertullian coined the Latin term *trinitas*. After this, he gives a brief account of early heresies; the decisions of the Council of Nicea in 325 and Constantinople in 381; and the ongoing dispute between the Greeks and Latins about the *filioque* which was promulgated by the Council of Toledo in 589. He then mentions recent German Lutheran theologians including those who hold that the three persons only denote three basic attributes of the Godhead such as power, wisdom and love, or three activities such as creating, preserving and controlling.

On the basis of Riḍā's survey, Quṭb concludes that it is clear that none of the denominations or schools of thought in the Christian Church follow God's true religion. Nor does he have any sympathy for the Arian heresy, because the Arians still spoke of God as "Father" and Christ as "Son" despite holding that the Son was a creature.

The Qur'ān's assertion that the Christians were merely imitating what unbelievers had said before them leads Quṭb to mention various pagan parallels. He asserts that earlier commentators were correct in pointing to the Arabs' belief that the angels were God's daughters, but in his view the Qur'ān also envisages other pagan beliefs held further afield. He refers to the divine triad Osiris, Isis and Horus in Pharaonic Egypt; Alexandrine Jewish speculations about the word as a "second god"; Assyrian references to Marduk as God's Word; Hindu belief in Brahma, Vishnu and Shiva; and the Greeks' practice of censing and aspersing their sacrifices three times.

His Comments on 9: 31

> They have taken their rabbis and monks – as well as Christ, the son of Mary – as lords beside God. Yet they were commanded to worship but One God. There is no god but He! Glory be to Him above those whom they associate with Him.

Quṭb observes that, whereas the previous *ayas* mentioned the erroneous utterances and beliefs of the People of the Scripture, this *āya* directs our attention to one of their practices which was based on corrupt belief: It is further evidence that they are not followers of the religion of truth. He cites *ḥadīth* in which the Prophet explains that the Jews and Christians did not literally worship their rabbis and monks, but they took them as lords in the sense of accepting their rulings concerning what is forbidden and what is permitted.

On the basis of these *ḥadīth* and the opinions of ancient and recent Qur'ānic commentators, Quṭb concludes that merely ascribing the right of legislation to someone other than God, even if this is not accompanied by belief in that person's divinity, or acts of worship directed towards him, constitutes *shirk*; and that the Qur'ānic text regards the Jews, who accepted legislation from the rabbis and obeyed it, and the Christians, who worshipped Christians as divine, as equally guilty of *shirk*, and therefore deems both groups to be unbelievers.

Quṭb concedes that the sequence's original purpose was to confront the Muslims' reluctance to wage war against the Byzantines, and to dispel the illusion that the latter were believers in God because they were People of the Scripture. Nevertheless, it sets forth absolute truths concerning religion. The only true religion in God's eye is Islam. It entails believing that he is the sole deity, and worshipping him alone. In addition, it entails following only his law. If human beings obey man-made laws, without contesting them and making clear that they do so only under compulsion, they are associators like the Jews and Christians, and like them they are unbelievers regardless of their alleged beliefs. Quṭb laments that the word religion (*dīn*) has lost its significance for human beings and that they have reached the point where they consider it merely to mean inner belief and outward rites, rather than subjection, submission and obedience. Hence, many so-called Muslims willingly obey laws other than those instituted by God. He considers that this dilution of the meaning of religion is the greatest danger facing Islam and the most deadly weapon with which its enemies wage war against it. These enemies of the true religion attempt to attach the label "Islam" to man-made statutes and human institutions. It is therefore the duty of its defenders to remove this misleading label, and to disclose what lies beneath it, namely: *shirk*, *kufr* and the taking of lords beside God.

His Comments on 9: 32–3

> They want to extinguish God's light with their mouths but God refuses [to let them, for He wishes] only to perfect His light, however hateful this may be to the unbelievers!
>
> It is He who has sent His Messenger with guidance and the religion of truth in order to make it prevail over every religion, however hateful this may be to the associators.

According to Quṭb, in these two *āyas* the Qur'ānic sequence takes a further step in spurring the believers on to fight. The People of the Scripture do not stop at deviating from the religion of truth, they actually declare war on it, and want to extinguish God's light, which is present in it and in its programme for moulding the life of human beings. They do this by uttering lies; by hatching plots; by persecuting Muslims; and by employing various means to block its progress including literally waging war. This was the state of affairs when these *āyas* were revealed, and it has been the same throughout the course of history.

Faced with the perennial opposition of the People of Scripture, God promises that he will perfect his light and cause the true religion to prevail. This brings reassurance to the hearts of the believers and impels them to proceed despite hardship and severe distress. At the same time it implies a threat to the unbelievers. Quṭb remarks that the element of repetition in the second of these two *āyas* serves to reinforce both promise and threat. It becomes clear in this part of the sequence that "the religion of the truth" is the religion with which God sent his final Messenger, Muḥammad, and that those who do not profess this religion are the ones envisaged in the command to fight. God will cause the true religion to prevail over every other religion in the comprehensive sense of every programme, every school of thought, and every organisation to which human beings subscribe obedience. This proved true once through the agency of Muḥammad and his caliphs, and those who came after them for a long period of time. In those days, the religion of truth prevailed, and other religions, which were not devoted exclusively to God, used to fear and tremble! Later, however, the adherents of the religion of truth left it step by step because of internal factors in the composition of Islamic societies, and because of the People of the Scripture's long drawn-out war against it. In Quṭb's view, however, this is not the end of the matter. God's promise stands. He awaits the Muslim federation which will bear the banner and advance, beginning from the initial position from which the Messenger of God began when he supported the religion of truth.

His Comments on 9: 34–5

> O you who believe! Many of the rabbis and monks do indeed devour people's goods deceitfully and bar from the way of God. As for those who treasure up gold and silver and do not expend it on God's cause, give them tidings of a painful punishment on the Day when it will be heated in the fire of Hell, and their foreheads, sides and backs branded with it! [Then they will be told] "This is what you have treasured up for yourselves! So taste what you have treasured up!"

Quṭb notes that this final part of the sequence addresses the believers directly and discloses to them the truth about the People of the Scripture. In the first of these two *āyas* there is a digression concerning the role of the rabbis and monks whom the Jews and Christians take as lords besides God. They are said to devour people's goods deceitfully. Quṭb states that this took various forms and still does. It includes charging fees for declaring lawful what is forbidden, and forbidden what is lawful, in the interest of the rich and powerful; receiving remuneration for hearing confessions and granting absolution; and usury, which is the most widespread and offensive method. He then launches into a diatribe against those who make concessions for combating the religion of truth. He states that the priests, bishops, cardinals and popes collected vast fortunes to finance the Crusades, and that they have continued to collect them for missionary activity and Oriental studies to hinder from the way of God. He notes, however, that the Qur'ān subtly refers to "*many* of the rabbis and monks" thus withdrawing judgement from the few who have abstained from this sin. There are, he says, individuals in every human society in whom there is a vestige of good. God will not wrong any of them.

He goes on, however, to assert that most rabbis and monks treasure up the goods which they devour deceitfully, and that history bears witness to the enormous wealth which ended up in the hands of the men of religion and passed to the churches and monasteries. There came a time, he says, when they were more wealthy than the ruling monarchs and sybaritic despots. He notes that the Qur'ānic sequence depicts their punishment in the hereafter with what they treasured up, and the punishment of everyone else who treasures up gold and silver and does not expend it God's way. It does so graphically in a manner which is both awesome and frightening. The step-by-step presentation of the spectacle serves to prolong it in the reader's imagination. This, he says, is intentional, as is the way in which the first of the two *āyas* ends with a summary reference to the punishment, which is taken up and spelled out in detail in the *āya* which follows.

Quṭb's Additional Reflections

After commenting on the whole of 9: 29–35, Quṭb pauses to offer some additional reflections on the contemporary situation. He maintains that Muslims only manifest their opposition to the *jāhiliyya* when it shows its true colours. Hence, in his view, it is extremely important to expose the speciousness of the People of the Scripture's claim to follow God's religion – a claim which is, he notes, accepted by most so-called Muslims. Indeed, he argues that exposing the People of the Scripture is even more important than criticising the polytheists, because the latter bear witness against themselves by their conspicuous pagan doctrines and practices.

He regards the label "People of the Scripture" as a misleading label with no substance to it. He also warns his readers against the modern alliance between People of the Scripture and the opponents of Islamic revival. They are alike extremely eager to attach an Islamic label to conventions, movements, tendencies, values, customs, and ideas which are in fact hostile towards Islam. The most pernicious enemy of Islam is the Atatürk movement in Turkey, which Quṭb describes as *al-ḥarakatu 'l-islāmiyyatu 'l-kāfira* – "the unbelieving Islamic movement." Atatürk even abolished the caliphate despite the fact that the Prophet had said, "This religion will be destroyed by two handles. The first is government and the second prayer." Quṭb concludes by taking a parting shot at a distinguished Christian Islamicist, the Canadian scholar Wilfred Cantwell Smith. He describes him as a deeply wicked and extremely cunning Crusader writer, and points out that in a book published in 1957, he had the effrontery to call the Atatürk movement the most significant and authentic movement of Islamic revival in modern history.

III. DISCUSSION

It is beyond the scope of this paper to attempt a detailed explanation of the Qur'ān's multifaceted representation of Christians. Suffice it to note that the non-Muslim approach and Sayyid Quṭb's approach are both problematic. Non-Muslim scholars generally assume that the Qur'ān reflects Muḥammad's views and that these changed with time. However, they run into difficulties with *sūra* five, an indubitably late Medinan *sūra* which contains both positive and negative statements about Christians.[20] Richard Bell declares that the positive statement in 5: 69 must be a fragment of an earlier revelation which dates from a time when there was still hope for an amicable understanding with previous monotheists.[21] He offers no evidence for this other than the fact that the *āya* in question resembles 2: 62, which is early Medinan, but this argument carries little weight because the Qur'ān contains numerous doublets and there is no reason why a late revelation should not echo or repeat an earlier one. Quṭb, on the other hand, assumes that the Qur'ān expresses God's views which are eternal and unchanging. His discussion has the merit of attempting to make sense of the Qur'ānic data without resorting to specious arguments about the date of individual *āyas*. However, his interpretation is open to criticism on the grounds that it is historically implausible. Admittedly, there are grounds for thinking that the original followers of Jesus were strict monotheists who did not hold that he was divine. Moreover, Muḥammad probably encountered individual Jewish Christians who were their spiritual heirs. Nevertheless, these were not the only Christians with whom he and his companions had amicable relations. The Christians of Abyssinia, who sheltered Muslim refugees from Mecca, were Monophysites, who believed that after the incarnation Christ had a single divine nature, as were the Christians of Najrān, whose martyrs the Qur'ān probably commemorates in *sūra* 85. It seems likely that some of the Qur'ānic *āyas* which view Christians in a positive light refer to these Monophysite Christians, even though their theology was defective from the standpoint of Qur'ānic monotheism.

Quṭb's claim that the Qur'ān's positive statements about Christians refer to a righteous remnant, who adhered to Christ's monotheistic teaching and rallied to Islam, accord with how these *āyas* were understood by the principal classical commentators.[22] Similarly, his contention that Paul was responsible for corrupting Jesus' teaching, by hailing him as the Son of God, is a stock-in-trade of traditional Muslim anti-Christian polemic,[23] as is his allegation that the Christian scriptures differ from the Gospel which God revealed to Jesus.[24] Nevertheless in other respects Quṭb's views represent a radical break with traditional Sunni Islam. God's promise to make the religion of truth prevail over every religion was traditionally understood by most commentators in one of two ways. Some thought it applied exclusively to the Arabian Peninsula, and was hence fulfilled in the Prophet's lifetime. Others held that it had universal application but would be fulfilled only when Christ returned and the people of every religion followed him. There were other minority interpretations but I am unaware of anyone having taken this *āya* as an incentive to global warfare against non-Muslims.[25] Moreover, the stark contrast which Quṭb draws between God's law and man-made laws runs counter to the teaching of all four law schools. The latter recognise that the Prophet deliberately adopted or tacitly approved of many customs which were prevalent in his lifetime. They therefore recognise that *'urf*, or custom, is a valid subsidiary source of law.[26] Even more serious is Quṭb's claim that all so-called Muslim countries are part of the *jāhiliyya*, and that Muslims who do not oppose their governments are apostates. This flatly contradicts the traditional belief that anyone who testifies that there is no deity but God and Muḥammad is the Messenger of God should be considered a Muslim. Finally, it is arguable that Quṭb is skating on dangerously thin ice when he describes the expression "People of the Scripture" as misleading. If as he alleges, Jews and Christians today are much as they were in the time of the Prophet, how can he question the appropriateness of the label which God gives them in the Qur'ān?

It would be unfair to assess Quṭb's merits as a commentator on the basis of the brief section of his commentary under discussion. Nevertheless, a few provisional remarks are in order. On the positive side, his exposition is clear and analytical; he shows how the *ayas* form a coherent sequence; and he is sensitive to the Qur'ānic rhetoric. Against this must be set his manner of imposing a highly questionable interpretative grid on the text. The word *jāhiliyya* is found only four times in the Qur'ān.[27] It does not occur in 9: 29–35 or for that matter anywhere else in *sūra* nine. Yet Quṭb's repeated use of it leads the uncritical reader to assume that it is an appropriate term to describe not only pre-Islamic Arabia but also the whole of contemporary society including so-called Muslim countries. The word *minhāj* occurs only at 5: 48, where God says that he gave each of the religious communities "a way to a watering place (*shir'a*) and an open path (*minhāj*)." Despite this, Quṭb employs it repeatedly in the sense of a procedure, method or programme, in contexts where he wishes to contrast God's programme with the programme of the *jāhiliyya*. As for *al-ḥarakat al-islāmiyya* – "the Islamic movement" – the expression is not Qur'ānic. Moreover, *pace* Quṭb, the first Muslims did not belong to a rigidly hierarchical movement like the Muslim Brotherhood and burst forth on the world with a programmatic blueprint for society. In addition to Quṭb's interpretative grid, his work is marred by a polemical reading of history. He supposes that Christians have always been power-hungry empire builders and inveterate enemies of true religion, whereas Muslim armies invariably serve simply to liberate subject peoples so that they are free to choose to serve God. I would argue, on the contrary, that Christians and Muslims alike must face up to the painful truth that at a relatively early stage both religions were hijacked by individuals and interest groups who were more concerned with extending their own power than in the spreading the ideals of their founders.

This last point leads me to two much more controversial issues both of which are hotly debated by contemporary Muslim intellectuals. The first of these is whether there is such a thing as an Islamic system of government. In 1925, 'Alī 'Abd al-Rāziq, an Egyptian judge, published a seminal work on Islam and the basis of political authority, in which he argued that it was not part of Muḥammad's divinely-given mission to found an Islamic state, and that the caliphate, far from being necessary, had actually been a source of evil and corruption.[28] The second issue is closely related to the first, and concerns the status of the Qur'ānic regulations. Within a century of the Prophet's death, Islam had become the ideology of a vast empire. In those circumstances, the Qur'ānic regulations inevitably came to be regarded as the first and most authoritative source of Islamic law. However, with the demise of the Ottoman Empire, the abolition of the caliphate, and the increasing importance of Muslim minorities in non-Muslim countries, Islam is beginning to rediscover its vocation to be a message inviting a response rather than an order which imposes itself. From this perspective, the Qur'ān's theological and ethical principles, many of which are shared by Jews and Christians because they are also found in the Bible, seem far more important that the Qur'ānic regulations. Some would go so far as to argue that the Qur'ān contains no fixed legislation, but rather *ad hoc* guidelines which need to be seen in their historical context. In any case, only 228 of the Qur'ān's 6,236 *āyas* have traditionally been regarded as containing legal prescriptions – far fewer than one might imagine from Quṭb's repeated references to God's law.

Quṭb's brand of political Islam and his hostility to Jews and Christians are intimately related to his troubled life. In 1949–50 he studied in the USA and became deeply disillusioned with Western civilisation. Among other things, he saw at first hand the unquestioning American support for the newly-created state of Israel despite the suffering that this was causing to the Palestinian Arabs. He also witnessed the decadence of American Protestantism and describes a church lit with coloured lights where couples danced to sexually arousing music.[29] In 1952, the Egyptian revolution was supported by the Muslim Brotherhood. When the Free Officers assumed power they sent for Quṭb who served six months as a consultant. To his chagrin, however, they did not adopt his ideas of establishing an Islamic state and appointing members of the Brotherhood to key leadership roles. In 1954, he was arrested along with other activists and sentenced to fifteen years hard labour for conspiring to assassinate Nasser. Despite the harsh prison regime and repeated torture, he found the time and energy to revise the first thirteen parts of his commentary, including the section of the tenth part which was examined in this paper. After serving ten years of his sentence, he was released thanks to the personal intercession of the President of Iraq. He was, however, re-arrested in 1965 and executed the following year.

Many members of the Muslim Brotherhood recognise that Quṭb's experience of incarceration and torture drove him to adopt extremist views – views which are now rejected by the leadership of the movement.[30] Unfortunately, however, we cannot relegate them to the lumber room of history. The didactic and homiletic style of *Fī Ẓilāl al-Qur'ān* ensures that it continues to have a wide circulation and extensive influence.[31] Moreover, Quṭb's portrayal of Christians and Jews as implacable enemies of Islam undoubtedly still appeals to some Muslims who think of Christianity and Judaism as politico-religious entities. It should not be difficult to see why this is. I write these words in August 1998, almost exactly thirty-two years after Quṭb's execution. On no less than thirty-two occasions since then, the USA – the most powerful "Christian" nation on earth – has vetoed the decisions of the United Nations Security Council in order to protect Israeli interests. Moreover, Washington has continued to insist on maintaining harsh sanctions against Iraq, despite already having caused the death of over half a million innocent people in that country. Bombs planted by terrorists have recently exploded in United States embassies in Kenya and Tanzania. Washington alleges that they were planted by members of Osama Bin Laden's "International Front for Islamic Holy War against Jews and Crusaders." Instead of taking its case to the United Nations, however, the USA – whose Defence Secretary, William Cohen, has a decidedly Jewish name – has flouted international law yet again, by launching punitive attacks on sites in the Sudan and Afghanistan. In such circumstances, it is more urgent than ever to insist that not all Jews are Zionists; that many Jews and Christians both inside and outside the USA are appalled by America's foreign policy; that the number of Muslims who are Islamists is comparatively small; that the number who swallow Quṭb's rhetoric in its entirety is even smaller; and finally, that even Quṭb in his most radical phase would have condemned as totally un-Islamic the planting of bombs which killed and maimed non-combatants.

NOTES

1 An earlier draft of this paper was delivered at the conference on "Islamic Perspectives of Christianity" at Glasgow University in May 1997. I am grateful for the lively discussion which ensued, and I have endeavoured to develop a number of points in the light of various comments that were made on that occassion.

2 There is a useful introduction to Quṭb and his thought in Ibrahim M. Abu-Rabi', *Intellectual Origins of Islamic Resurgence in the Modern Arabic World* (Albany: SUNY Press, 1996) pp. 92–219.

3 Sayyid Quṭb, *Fī Ẓilāl al-Qur'ān*, 30 parts in 6 volumes (Cairo: Dār al-Shurūq, 1992). Quṭb's comments on part 30 (*sūras* 79–114) have been translated into English as Sayyid Quṭb *In the Shade of the Qur'ān*

Volume 30 (New Delhi: Taj, 1990) since this paper was written, the Islamic Foundation (Leicester) has announced its intention of publishing a translation of the whole commentary.

4 See further Olivier Carré, *Mystique et politique: lecture révolutionnaire du Coran par Sayyid Qutb Frère musulman radical* (Paris: Cerf, 1984), pp. 27–30.

5 For a complete list of the Qur'ānic passages which refer to Jesus, see Neal Robinson, *Christ in Islam and Christianity: The Representation of Jesus in the Qur'ān and the Classical Muslim Commentaries* (Basinstoke & Albany: MacMillan & SUNY Press, 1991), pp. 4–7.

6 For a brief survey, *ibid.*, pp. 15–22.

7 Cp. Qur'ān 5: 72f which condemns as unbelievers those who say that God is the Messiah or that God is the third of three.

8 Sayyid Quṭb, *Fī Ẓilāl al-Qur'ān*, volume 3, pp. 1619–1650.

9 Qur'ān, 2: 256.

10 Quṭb, op. cit., p. 1628.

11 *Ibid*, pp. 1628f.

12 Qur'ān, 5: 72.

13 Qur'ān, 5: 73.

14 Cp. Qur'ān, 2: 80.

15 Cp. Qur'ān, 5: 18.

16 Quṭb, op. cit., p. 1633.

17 Qur'ān, 2: 256.

18 The unfinished commentary begun by Muḥammad Abduh (d. 1905) and continued after his death by Riḍā. The edition I have used is Muḥammad Rashīd Riḍā, *Tafsīr al-Qur'ān al-Karīm al-Shahīr bi-Tafsīr al-Manār* (Beirut: Dār al-Ma'rifa, n.d.) 12 volumes.

19 *Ibid*. Volume 6 pp. 88–95. In a footnote on p. 88, Riḍā recommends the reader desirous of further information to consult a book entitled *al-Aqā'id al-Wathaniya fī al-Diyānāt al-Naṣrāniya* together with the English books mentioned in it. According to J. Jomier, *Le Commentaire Coranique du Manār: Tendances Modernes de l'Exégèse Coranique en Égypte* (Paris: Maisonneuve, 1954) p. 310, the author of this work was the Syrian scholar Muḥammad Ṭāhir al-Tannir al-Bayrūtī, and he summarised more than forty English works.

20 Contrast 5: 69, which is positive, with 5: 72f and 5: 82 which are negative.

21 R. Bell, *A Commentary on the Qur'ān* (Manchester: Manchester University Press, 1991) vol. 1, p. 163.

22 See the magisterial study by Jane Dammen McAuliffe, *Qur'ānic Christians: An Analysis of Classical and Modern Exegesis* (Cambridge: CUP, 1991). McAuliffe deliberately limits her research to the positive statements about Christians. She does not, therefore, discuss 9: 29–35.

23 See S. M. Stern, "Abd al-Jabbār's Account of how Christ's Religion was Falsified by the Adoption of Roman Customs," *Journal of Theological Studies*, N. S., vol. XIX, part 1, April 1968, pp. 28–185.

24 See J. M. Gaudel and R. Caspar, "Textes de la Tradition Musulmane Concernant le Taḥrīf (falsification) des Écritures," *Islamochristiana* VI (1980), pp. 61–104. On this issue there has long been a spectrum of

opinion. At one extreme there are those like Quṭb who regard Christian Scriptures as worthless. At the other, there are those who hold that it is only Christian interpretation of them that is in error.

25 For further details see Neal Robinson, op. cit., pp. 97–100.

26 See M. H. Kamali, *Principles of Islamic Jurisprudence* (Cambridge: Islamic Texts Society, 1991), pp. 283–96.

27 Qur'ān, 3: 153, 5: 50, 33: 33 and 48: 26.

28 'Alī 'Abd al-Rāziq, *al-Islām wa uṣūl al-ḥukm* (Cairo, 1925) translated into French as Ali Abderraziq, *L'islam et les fondements de pouvoir* (Paris: la Découverte/CEDEJ, 1994).

29 Sayyid Quṭb, *Mārakat al-Islām wa al-Rasmāliyya* (Beirut: Dār al-Shurūq, 1975 (fourth printing)) pp. 67–8. Cited by Yvonne Y. Haddad in John E. Esposito (ed.), *Voices of Resurgent Islam* (Oxford: OUP, 1983), p. 71.

30 See Ibrahim M. Abu-Rabi' op. cit., p. 209.

31 Yvonne Y. Haddad in Esposito, op. cit., p. 68.

8

Muslim Perceptions of Christianity and the West

Kate Zebiri

It is axiomatic that interfaith relations, or mutual perceptions of different religious groups, cannot be seen in isolation from their political and social context. This is perhaps especially true when looking at Muslim perceptions of Christianity, in which the association of Christianity with the West is a crucial element. Because of this association, and in the context of a recent history of Western dominance, Muslim views of Christianity are often highly politicised.

Following a preliminary section on the ways in which the identification of Christianity with the West is rationalised, this article is divided into sections which reflect various strands of discourse, all of which have to do with the degree of Christianity's involvement in state and society. The link between Western imperialism and Protestant missions is one of the main reasons for the association of Christianity with the West. Missions are regarded as part and parcel of the imperialist venture, with little or no reference to differing motives or aims of missionaries on the one hand and imperialists on the other. However, Christianity's involvement in power is seen as going beyond the missionary movement and extending to mainstream international politics, as observed in the third section. The relationship between Christianity and Western civilisation is another facet of this discourse, and this is often expounded in such a way that the positive aspects of the latter are dissociated from Christianity, which is generally regarded as irrational and therefore inimical to scientific investigation. Finally, Muslim analyses of the relationship between Christianity and secularism provide a somewhat different view of Christianity to that which emerges in the earlier sections; here Christianity is often seen as weak, or even moribund, rather than powerful and threatening.

This discourse is not confined to any one Muslim context or geographical area, but can be found both in the Muslim world and in the West. A variety of sources have been used, including the writings of leading international Muslim figures such as Yūsuf al-Qaraḍāwī as well as those of lesser-known individuals living in the non-Muslim West or non-Arab-speaking areas of the Muslim world such as Pakistan and Malaysia.

I. CHRISTIANITY AS AN INHERENTLY WESTERN PHENOMENON

Most Muslim writings on Christianity, regardless of the geographical location of the author, portray it as a more or less exclusively Western phenomenon, and feel that "the Christianity of today is inseparable from the culture of the West."[1] This association is often implicitly treated as an accident of history, but some writers essentialise the polarity between Christianity\West and Islam\East and attempt to rationalise it in various ways.

Maryam Jameelah, an American Jewish convert who resides in Pakistan, traces the view of Christianity as Western (and of the West as intrinsically inhospitable to Islam) back to the earliest period of Christianity. She writes that "Christianity and Western civilization have been inseparable from each other ever since the time of St. Paul," the latter having transplanted Christianity from Semitic to Graeco-Roman soil. While the Christians of Western Asia and North Africa were quick to embrace Islam, Europe by contrast evinced "hostility and resistance to the spread of Islam," and since then "the interests of Islam and Western civilization have always conflicted with each other."[2]

Isma'il al-Faruqi (d. 1986), a scholar of religions of Palestinian origin who spent most of his academic career in the United States, has a more explicitly racial explanation, both for the non-acceptance of Islam and for the successful spread of Pauline Christianity in the West. In his book *On Arabism: 'Urubah and Religion*,[3] he refers to first-century (CE) Western man's obtuseness, "contempt for everything cultured," "spiritual flat-footedness," and "brutalized" character, since he had not previously received any ethical teachings at all (p. 72). Furthermore, in an image which seems more appropriate for the twentieth century than the first, al-Faruqi remarks that Western man was "accustomed to pursue existence only at the cost of neighbour and nature," and speculates that if only Paul had travelled eastward his distorted teachings would have fallen on arid soil, and would have come up against the "*largeur de coeur*" of the Arab spirit (p. 73). He elaborates on this thesis with a linguistic argument: while the "Arab attitude of mind" is accustomed to poetic and metaphorical language, and as such would have no problem even with John's Gospel, the Westerner's literalism led him to misunderstand the teachings of the Gospels (p. 85). With regard to the New Testament description of Jesus as the "son of God," al-Faruqi comments that "only a crude, naive, and, most important of all, a non-Arab mind could take it literally" (p. 87). He draws a distinction, particularly for the early period, between "Arab Christianity," which was "rationalistic, tolerant, affirmative, optimistic, purely monotheistic and universalistic," and "Western Christianity" which was simply "the opposite" (p. 108).

Jameelah also gives a racial explanation for Christianity's alleged failure to spread beyond Western countries, suggesting that "Christianity cannot appeal to the African or the Asian because it has always been identified in his mind (and rightly so) as the white man's religion. Christianity, the notion of the superiority of the white race and its inseparability from the aims of European imperialism are irrefutable when taken in the context of history."[4] She rejects any suggestion that Christianity is not a Western religion, since "it is rather late in the day to proclaim Christianity as a religion of Asia and Africa or attempt to disentangle it from the development of Western civilization,"[5] and quotes a Muslim source which claims that outside of Europe and the New World, "the number of Christians is negligible."[6]

References to Christianity outside the West are often for specific purposes. Jameelah, for example, cites Ethiopia as an example of a backward Christian country in order to counter claims that Islam is responsible for the "present-day decadence of Muslims."[7] Abdalhaqq Bewley, an English convert to Islam and a member of the Darqawi Sufi order in Britain, de-emphasises the association of Christianity with the West in the context of the possibility of Islam gaining ground in Western countries, arguing that "there is no logical reason to propose that Christianity is any more European than Islam since both have their origins in exactly the same part of the world."[8]

Muslims living in Muslim countries with Christian minorities not surprisingly sometimes refer to these indigenous, non-Western Christians. In Islamist sources, they may be seen as a potential fifth column; however, others in the Islamic movement may wish to allay Christian fears of Islamisation by emphasising national unity and political pluralism.[9] Such scholars may draw a distinction between Eastern and Western Christians; the influential Egyptian religious scholar Muḥammad al-Ghazālī (d. 1996), for example, expressed the opinion that "Arab nationalism (*qawmiyyah*) would liberate the Eastern Church from the contaminating influence of Western leadership."[10]

II. WESTERN IMPERIALISM AND CHRISTIAN MISSIONS

The close relationship between Western imperialism and Christian missions in the minds of most Muslims is a crucial factor for the perception of Christianity as a Western phenomenon. Since missionaries are seen as the foremost representatives of Christianity, to discredit them is to discredit the religion in general, especially if no reference is made to Christian ideals which some missionaries may have failed to live up to. In this discourse, missionaries are not generally credited with any honourable motives, and are seen in terms which are diametrically opposed to the invariably idealistic self-definition of missionaries themselves.

A highly influential book by the Lebanese scholars 'Umar Farrūkh and Muṣṭafā Khālidī, entitled *Al-Tabshīr wa'l-Isti'mār fi'l-Bilād al-'Arabiyyah* (*Missions and Imperialism in Arab Lands*) was first published in 1953 and has now run into several editions.[11] It bears the subtitle: "an exposition of the efforts of missionaries, which aimed to subjugate the East to Western imperialism," showing that missionaries are regarded not just as having taken advantage of Western political dominance in order to spread their message, but as having deliberately paved the way for it. In fact it is claimed that missionary activity is more harmful to Muslim countries than imperialism, since the latter only entered those countries under the cloak of missions (p. 6). According to the authors, only a very small proportion of missionaries are genuinely religiously motivated – for the vast majority, religion has nothing to do with their aims, as evidenced by the atheistic and materialistic character of the Western countries from which they come (p. 34). Farrūkh and Khālidī assert, among other things, that missionaries attempt to stir up divisions and unrest in Arab and Muslim countries, so that their own nations can assert political and economic control over them (pp. 22–3).

Christian missionary activity is frequently characterised in Muslim discourse in the same terms as colonialism: as oppressive, exploitative, unscrupulous as to methodology, ruthless, arrogant, immoral, and destructive of indigenous cultures. The assertion made by the British

Muslim intellectual Ziauddin Sardar that in the name of mission "Christians have carried out, and continue to carry out, programmes of brutal extermination of members of 'pagan' faiths as well as adherents of traditional world views" is not exceptional.[12]

Jameelah provides specific details of alleged atrocities; she says of Christian missionaries that

> their sinister hands were behind the murder of Ahmadu Bello and Abu Bakr Tawafa Belawa in Nigeria which put an end to Islamic rule in that country ... The same hands were behind the overthrow of Muslim rule in Zanzibar and the wholesale massacre and expulsion of the Arabs there. They gave whole-hearted support to the Emperor Haile Selassie's brutal attempt to exterminate the entire Muslim population of Ethiopia.[13]

Jameelah's description of the methods used by missionaries is typical:

> Equipped with huge funds, they are using every means, including persuasion, temptation and compulsion, to convert ignorant people in non-Christian areas. Libraries, seminar halls, schools, clubs, colleges, orphanages, hospitals and social welfare centres are extensively utilized by them to serve as missionary platforms.[14]

The close relationship between missions and imperialism is not just regarded as a moment of history which is now past; the imperialist age has given way to neo-imperialism, Western dominance is still an ever-present reality, and Christian missions are still vigorous in many parts of the world. Although actual Western political hegemony may have declined, missionaries are charged with being agents of secularisation (a wholly pejorative term) and with continuing to serve the interests of Western governments. Jameelah comments that "the missionary is so hypocritical and intellectually dishonest that he applauds the defeat of Christian temporal power and ... its strange marriage with secularism and imperialism."[15] Another aspect of missionaries' hypocrisy is, in her view, revealed by the irreligiosity which prevails in the West; she expresses a common sentiment when she says that "if the Christian missionaries were sincere, they would find more than enough work to do at home."[16] Sardar asserts that "most Christian missionaries exhibit the major characteristics of liberal secularism – imperialistic tendencies, dehumanization, domination and meaninglessness."[17]

One aspect of the continuing power-nexus between Western political interests and Christian missions is the phenomenon of Christian Zionism. Jameelah says of missionaries that

> they applaud every illicit territorial gain of the Zionists in retrieving the Arab world for Western civilization and destroying the Muslim character of Palestine. They make no efforts to restrain their glee over the colonization of Palestine by European Jews and the expulsion of the Arabs, including even the Christian Arabs![18]

Farrūkh and Khālidī also speak of the co-operation between missions, colonialism and Zionism. They describe Protestant missionary efforts going back to the early nineteenth century which aimed among other things to establish a nucleus of Jews believing in Jesus as the Messiah in Jerusalem. In their view the aim was not purely religious, but also political, arising from a desire on the part of Anglicans to establish a political influence there, which also provided the motivation for establishing an Anglican Bishopric of Jerusalem.[19] Farrūkh and Khālidī refer only in brief to the fact that some Christians see the establishment of the modern-day State of Israel as a fulfilment of Old Testament prophecies. However, they lay considerable emphasis on the material relating to the Jews contained in the documents arising from the Second Vatican Council (1962–5), and the subsequent improvement of relations between the Jews and the Vatican. These documents inaugurate a change of attitude to the Jews, stressing the continuity between ancient Israel and the Christian Church and the special place of the Jews in God's plan, and refuting the idea that Jews are collectively responsible for the death of Christ.[20] Farrūkh and Khālidī end their book by reproducing a Vatican document calling on Catholics to recognise the religious meaning of the State of Israel for Jews, and to acknowledge their special link with that land.[21]

Safar al-Ḥawālī, a Saudi Islamic scholar and preacher, provides a more recent source which shows a rather more detailed knowledge of Christian Zionism.[22] In his book of published lectures entitled *Al-Quds bayna al-Wa'd al-Ḥaqq ... wa'l-Wa'd al-Muftaraq*,[23] he relies heavily on an American work, *Prophecy and Politics: The Secret Alliance between Israel and the U.S. Christian Right*, by Grace Halsell.[24] His second main source of information is a book by an Egyptian scholar, Dr. Yūsuf al-Ḥasan, entitled *Al-Bu'd al-Dīnī fi'l-Siyāsat al-Amrīkiyyah* (*The Religious Dimension of American Politics*).[25] In contrast to many contemporary Muslim authors who emphasise the prevalence of irreligion and secularism in the West, al-Ḥawālī draws attention to the religious revival in America (pp. 47ff). He describes the way in which biblical prophecies are applied to current events by popular preachers and in popular works such as Hal

Lindsay's *The Late Great Planet Earth*. He also observes that the fact that the modern State of Israel is generally seen as central to the fulfilment of these prophecies sometimes results in a call for unconditional political support for Israel. The strength of Christian Zionism within American fundamentalist Christianity is in fact seen as an important factor in America's support for Israel. Describing the pro-Israeli stances of several prominent evangelists such as Jerry Falwell, Pat Robertson, and George Otis (pp. 55ff.), al-Ḥawālī emphasises and at times exaggerates the political influence of these preachers and their connections with people in high places.[26] Presidents Nixon, Carter, Reagan and Bush in particular are seen as having been sympathetic to Christian fundamentalists. Al-Ḥawālī wryly observes that Christian fundamentalists and Islamists like himself have something in common: they both oppose the Israeli-Palestinian peace process because they believe it to be contrary to God's will and His promise (pp. 68–9).

The morals of missionaries are sometimes impugned; al-Ghazālī implies that missionaries have been instrumental in the spread of Aids in his reported reply to a friend who suggests that the missionaries' success in converting pagans to Christianity might be a good thing: "You don't know the evils which afflict missionary institutions, and the moral disintegration which is rife in them!! Don't you read in the papers about how Aids has spread in Africa to the point that it's become a plague threatening its very existence?."[27] The overriding characteristic attributed to missionaries is, however, that of dishonesty. Above all they stand accused of having used deceptive and devious methods, and of having ulterior motives for the educational, medical or welfare services they offer. The alleged dishonesty may extend to wholly cynical acts on the part of missionaries; one example of this is the allegation that they give sick people coloured water to drink in the name of Muḥammad, then ask them to drink an apparently similar liquid, which in fact contains medicine, in the name of Jesus.[28] One Muslim scholar relates a conversation between a Muslim who did not reveal his Islamic allegiance and a Christian missionary, who allegedly confessed that missionaries paid people to spread the false rumour that missions had failed in Africa, in order to assuage Muslim fears and forestall any preventative action, and also to attract financial support from rich Christians.[29]

The growing desire of missionaries to distance themselves from Western culture in recent decades has found expression in concepts such as indigenisation, enculturation, and contextualisation. Where

Muslims show an awareness of such recent developments, they are seen in wholly negative terms and taken as further evidence of the deviousness of Christian missionaries, no doubt in part because for Muslims, religious rites and forms of worship, and even many cultural elements, are far more specific, and may therefore be considered unchangeable. The Malaysian scholar Munawar Ahmad Anees describes contextualisation, which has given rise to phenomena such as "Jesus mosques," as a "crypto-Muslim strategy." He goes on to explain that for the Muslim, "it appears to confirm the suspicions that these people want to win them over by hook or by crook ... those who can favour abandoning their own religious rituals can teach them nothing about truth and integrity."[30]

The perception of missionary activity in primarily political terms is illustrated by the use in Arabic of the pejorative word "*tanṣīr*" (Christianisation), as in the title of a recent work by al-Ghazālī: *Ṣīḥat Tandhīr min Du'āt al-Tanṣīr* (*A Cry of Warning against the Propagators of Christianisation*). This usage may be partly inspired by the parallel concept of Islamisation, which is generally considered to be a legitimate part of *da'wah* (Islamic missionary activity), in the sense that setting up Islamic institutions (e.g. in education, law, and government) creates an ethos which is conducive to conversion; this is in fact what happened in the early centuries of Islamic rule in non-Muslim areas.

Not only is the power relationship between Christian missions and the West invoked, but missionaries are also seen as involved in, if not the initiators of, orientalism, in the sense of a biased and hostile Western study of Islam. This is both because many of the early orientalists were in fact missionaries or supporters of missions, and because missions and orientalism are seen sharing a common aim, i.e. the destruction of Islam. Farrūkh and Khālidī comment that one of the aims of missionaries is to put an end to non-Christian religions, in order to enslave their followers; however, this is seen as a purely political rather than religious phenomenon (p. 45). They also observe that some missionaries familiarise themselves with branches of Arabic and Islamic learning in order to make detrimental comparisons with Western sciences, and convince Muslims of the inferiority of their own heritage (p. 24). They speak of a movement which is more dangerous than missions to the Islamic *ummah* and the Arab people, namely "a group of people in Europe and America who have put their pens at the service of missionaries, and have set about impugning the Arabs and Islam and distorting their image" (p. 22).

Mahmoud Ayoub, a modernist Lebanese Shi'ite Muslim who teaches in the Department of Religion of Temple University in the United States, describes the writings of three prominent scholar-missionaries, namely Samuel Zwemer, Temple Gairdner and Hendrik Kraemer, and finds them to be characterised by an "attitude of insensitive superiority."[31] One writer describes how missionaries are trained not just in defending Christianity but also in attacking and distorting indigenous religions,[32] and others mention missionary or Christian attacks on Islam as their main motivation for writing refutations of Christianity.[33]

The view that the association between missions and orientalism is still strong is apparent in some of the Muslim critique of recent Christian-authored books on Islam. Kenneth Cragg, a well-known Islamicist and former missionary, is described by one Muslim writer, and subsequently by several others, as attempting "not conversion but 'subversion'."[34] The same writer sees him as a direct successor to the nineteenth-century missionaries, who came "to teach the colonized people how to view themselves, for just as they found the 'natives' unfit to govern themselves, so too they found them unfit to entertain any *general* notions about their own cultural or religious values" (his italics).[35] Another Muslim scholar sees Cragg's relatively more sympathetic treatment of Islam, as compared to his predecessors, as "evidence rather of changed tactics rather than of changed objectives."[36] Similarly a Muslim reviewer says of the Islamicist and Anglican clergyman William Montgomery Watt that his "recent writings ... show that his much-acclaimed courtesy and sympathy were part of a studied effort, more in the nature of a tactical compromise than any renunciation of the ultimate strategic aims of the Christian approach to Islam."[37]

The strength of Muslim feeling against Christian missions is evidenced by the fact that even modernist or liberal Muslims sometimes call for severe restrictions or even a moratorium on missionary activity in Muslim lands.[38] The reasons for the objections to Christian missions, however, are not necessarily entirely political; one should also bear in mind the strong stigma against conversion away from Islam. Classical Islamic law laid down the death penalty for apostasy, which was considered tantamount to treason. Even disregarding legal consequences, conversion from Islam to another religion is often considered unthinkable if not impossible;[39] and where it occurs it is felt to be a betrayal of family, tribe, and nation, and a defection to the West. This is to be understood in the light of the fact that religious identity is differently constructed and perceived in Muslim societies than in the more secular West, where individual choice is now strongly emphasised.

The Muslim discourse on missionaries shares much with both the liberal and Marxist critiques – the latter insofar as missionaries are seen as agents of imperialism or as identified with other Western vested interests. The liberal critique applies insofar as they are seen as engaging in the illiberal activity of expending efforts in order to persuade others to think like them (Muslims tend to present a more *laissez-faire* or organic vision of *da'wah*). Another dimension to this is that Christianity is sometimes portrayed as being more exclusivist than Islam. Hasan Askari, who is himself an unusual figure in that he is a Muslim who advocates a pluralist vision of religions, sees Christians who seek to convert Muslims from a unitarian to a trinitarian view of God, specifically "Evangelical and Missionary Christians," as thereby sacrificing their own rights as minorities should they happen to live in a Muslim country. He argues that those who don't believe in democracy (on the basis that their views are "exclusive and judgemental") should not be allowed to enjoy its benefits.[40] Sardar sees imperialism as intrinsic to Christianity, in that "the claim that the route to salvation lies only in the recognition of the divinity of Jesus has led to a cultural and personal arrogance and imperialism that has done untold damage to non-Christian societies."[41] However, the Muslims who advance this type of criticism often have more in common with missionaries than they do with liberals or Marxists, believing as they do in the need for a transcendent point of reference, and rejecting a thoroughgoing secular humanism. Furthermore, they usually believe in the legitimacy and desirability of propagating one's religion, i.e. *da'wah*.

III. CHRISTIANITY AND POWER IN THE CONTEMPORARY PERIOD

For the Muslim looking at Christian history, there is no shortage of examples of unholy alliances between temporal authorities and religion, the Crusades being the prime example. What may surprise some is that this is seen as being equally true of the present age. The case of Christian Zionism has already been mentioned; more generally, there is a marked tendency to see international relations in primarily religious terms.

'Abd al-Halīm Maḥmūd held the position of Shaykh al-Azhar, i.e. the head of the most prestigious Sunni religious university, from 1973 until his death in 1978. In his book, *Urubbā wa'l-Islām* (*Europe and*

Islam), written in the post- or neo-imperialist era, he supports the view attributed to a professor of sociology at the Sorbonne that the Roman Emperor Constantine chose to adopt Christianity because it was the most fanatical (*muta'aṣṣib*) religion available, and was therefore the most suited for persecuting dissenters and achieving his ultimate goal of unifying the Empire (pp. 34–5). Coming to the present, Maḥmūd states that after the imperialists left, some countries with Muslim populations of over 95% were left with a "fanatical Christian ruler." He juxtaposes this with the allegation that Muslim communities in Christian countries do not enjoy natural rights of citizenship, do not enter the army or participate in higher education, and live in a lowly condition (p. 196). In neither case is any specific country mentioned. Maḥmūd speaks of a "Western, American, Communist, Zionist plot ... to weaken Muslims from the inside." Christian missions are involved in this plot in that they aim to reduce Muslims quantitatively (by conversion), as opposed to qualitatively. An example of this is that 350,000 African children (again, no specific countries are mentioned) were gathered together "by Satanic means, and brought up as fanatical Christians, and educated as engineers, doctors and economists." These were then placed in positions of leadership when the imperialists left, and were able to produce "generations and generations brought up as fanatical Christians, to take over, in succession, the reigns of government" (p. 194).

Christianity and Christians are often characterised as power-seeking and politically oriented, not just in the age of popes and kings but also in the present age. Al-Ghazālī addresses this topic in several of his works. In *Kifāḥ Dīn* (*A Religious Struggle*), he maintains that Christians are asking Muslims to separate state and religion despite the fact that they themselves wish to use governments to extend their own influence and to hold on to power in order to be able to oppress Muslims (pp. 37–8). He speaks at length of past examples of intolerance and oppression carried out in the name of Christianity (pp. 32ff.) and in this respect does not see any discontinuity between past and present. He sees it as a general rule that "Christianity – and in this it is like any group of people [*sic*] – always called for religious freedom when it felt oppressed, but denied the freedom of others when it was victorious" (p. 32). He speaks of the present as a time when "dozens of Christian states are launching continual attacks on Islam" (p. 37). Since the book was originally published some thirty or forty years ago, this is presumably a reference to Western colonialism, but no changes are made for later editions, which go into the nineties.

In *Ẓalām min al-Gharb* (*Oppression from the West*),[42] al-Ghazālī evokes a past in which religion was, for the West, the overriding factor in foreign policy. Thus he asserts that from the early nineteenth century, "Christian countries clubbed together to liberate Christian peoples from Muslim rule, merely because they were Christians ruled by Muslims" (p. 119), citing as examples the Greeks', Bulgarians' and Romanians' liberation from the Ottomans. He speaks of a "blind religious fanaticism, working for the subjugation of Muslims by Christians and the liberation of Christians from Muslims," concluding that "the Christian world – i.e. the stronger world – cannot forget its religion, or free itself from religious fanaticism" (pp. 120–1). This represents the perception of things thirty years ago, when the book was first published, rather than in the present day, when Western society is more commonly seen as secular, even atheist; al-Ghazālī himself has in a more recent publication referred to the irreligiosity of the West.[43]

IV. CHRISTIANITY AND WESTERN CIVILISATION[44]

Despite the close identification of Christianity with the West, it is usually denied by Muslims that the achievements of Western civilisation are in any way attributable to Christianity. The highly influential Egyptian modernist scholar and reformer Muḥammad 'Abduh (d. 1905) argued that modern civilisation has nothing to Christianity since the latter urges asceticism and detachment from the world, while the former is overwhelmingly materialistic.[45] Jameelah accounts for the achievements of Western civilisation as follows: "Only the resurgence of the paganism, atheism and secular humanism of ancient Greece and Rome during the 'Renaissance', stimulated by the intellectual activity of the Muslim scientists and philosophers and the *violent rebellion against the Church*, brought about the social, economic and scientific revolution which has brought the West to its present world domination" (her italics).[46]

Ahmad Azhar, who was educated in a Christian school in Pakistan and has worked in London for the Pakistan High Commission, is openly admiring of the achievements of Western civilisation, which he describes as "undoubtedly humane";[47] further, "the Christian world today is admittedly resplendent, the Muslim world – if you please – rotten."[48] However, this admiration is to be seen in conjunction with references to the West's civilisational debt to Islam; there is a general awareness among Muslims that this has been insufficiently acknowledged in the West. Azhar emphasises Christian backwardness at the time of Muslims' greatest enlightenment: "The Muslim Civilization taught these dark-age Christian Europeans all the arts and sciences forbidden at the height of Christianity; it taught them how to wash and how to spend; how to read and write and how to behave; indeed how to live."[49] He argues that in ascending the "pedestal of knowledge" from which the Muslims have fallen, Europeans have in fact "given up true Christianity – and adopted the spirit of Islam";[50] the Westerner adopted "the spirit of the Islamic progress, but with the label 'Christian'. The adversary had converted himself to Islam in all but *name*" (his italics).[51] However, he does draw an ethical distinction, in that the drive for knowledge in the West is motivated by greed rather than a genuine love of learning, while in the case of the Islamic civilisation "Muslims thought only of knowledge."[52]

One important aspect of civilisational achievement is that of scientific discovery. Christianity's inimicality to science, both historically and intrinsically, is a common theme. 'Abduh writes that miracles are an essential principle and foundation of faith in Christianity, even though they contravene natural laws, and feels that this acts as a disincentive to scientific research. Furthermore, he cites as one of the essential principles of Christianity that the Bible "contains all that humans need to know," thus deterring Christians from seeking knowledge elsewhere.[53] Muslims often refer to the historical conflicts between the Catholic Church and scientists, notably Galileo, and infer from this an inveterate Christian hostility to science. Adeleke Ajijola, a Nigerian lawyer who was educated in missionary schools in Nigeria, claims that "in no instance did the Christian Church encourage the pursuit of knowledge,"[54] and maintains that Christianity "has proved an irreconcilable enemy of human advancement. It crushed science as long as it had the powers to do so and it would do the same today if the modern world allowed it."[55]

One reason for the tendency to see Christianity and Western civilisation, or Christianity and science, as inimical to each other is the conviction that Christian belief is inherently irrational. 'Abduh states that Christians make a virtue out of believing that which is unreasonable, seeing faith as a gift which has nothing to do with reason and can neither be validated nor invalidated by it.[56] Professor Jalaluddin Ahmed, a Pakistani scholar, states that its central doctrines constitute an "unintelligible dogma" which is "implacably hostile to reason."[57] Ajijola similarly claims that Christian doctrine "paralyzes the intellect" since "it is based on mysteries and miracles";[58] this is in contrast to Islam whose creed is "so simple and rational that its fundamentals cannot be easily attacked," and which appeals to "reason and conscience."[59]

Clearly many areas of potential or alleged contradiction between religion and science would apply equally to Islam and Christianity; in the light of this several writers attempt to explain why scientific discoveries are more problematic for Christianity than for Islam. Ahmed seeks to demonstrate that "scientific thinking in Europe could only have been possible through cutting adrift from the tradition and control of orthodox Christianity."[60] He claims that it was "the special character of Christian Revelation which compelled scientists to eschew all references to the Supernatural," whereas "as long as the Muslims were pioneers of science, such an attitude was not possible."[61] The doctrine of Incarnation, for example, "has succeeded only in confusing the realms of the Supernatural and the Natural," which has in turn led to a division between "Revealed Religion" and "Natural Religion."[62] The idea of original sin "makes life on earth meaningless,"[63] causes a man to "abdicate all responsibility" and to cease believing that progress is possible in history, and therefore Christianity had to be repudiated in order for any progress to be possible.[64] Azhar maintains that in contrast to this the Islamic belief that man is born pure "produces the self confidence that leads ... to the spirit of inquiry and the conquest of Nature."[65] With reference to the Creation story, Ahmed refers to "the retreat of Christian orthodoxy before science," but does not say why the creationist-evolutionist debate should have different implications for Islam.[66] The shift away from a geocentric universe, however, is felt to be more problematic for a religion "where God himself becomes man and comes at a particular time in history."[67]

A minority of writers acknowledge a positive role for Christianity in the discoveries and achievements of modern Western civilisation. One such is Ahmed Shafaat, a lecturer in Maths and Business Statistics in Canada. He believes that the teaching of love in Christianity made it possible for Europe to build on the achievements of the Islamic civilisation by creating "a spirit of constructiveness which found expression in the use of science and technology for improving the lot of man." This technology came to be seen as "an instrument for realizing the Kingdom of God," and the Church therefore gave its support to such developments.[68] However, he maintains that this was only possible after the Bible came to be considered less authoritative than before. For the greater part of Christian history, a different situation obtained, since "various parts of the Christian scriptures often conflict so violently with one another that a spirit of learning, which at the very least would demand consistency in contents, would be fatal for faith." Furthermore Christian doctrines are not rooted in actual experience, whereas "it is precisely such experience on which the spirit of learning is based."[69] By contrast, the Islamic teaching of the Oneness of God is seen as providing "an urge to unify and integrate observations and experiences," an urge which is "probably the most important single impulse behind scientific developments."[70]

Sardar and his Muslim co-author, Merryl Wyn-Davies, have a rather more nuanced and informed view of Western history than most of the above-quoted writers. They see the Reformation as a turning point in the West, and as belying any simple opposition between religion and science. In their view, "Protestantism gave a positive value, indeed a duty, to the devout believer to study the other book of God, nature, and thus gave an impetus to science."[71] They go on to mention Newton and Descartes as scientists who were motivated by their faith, and conclude that "without the Reformation the scientific spirit would have meant far less than it does in the modern world."[72]

Similarly, only occasionally is the decline of Christianity seen as detrimental to Western society; Bewley states that this decline represented a shift in emphasis from the Creator to the created, but goes on to argue that this decline is irreversible and only Islam can fill the resulting vacuum.[73] An exception to the general rule in this respect is to be found in the writings of one particular group of Muslims, namely those Sufis who follow the "perennial philosophy," including René Guénon, Frithjof Schuon, and Seyyed Hossein Nasr. These express regret at the way in which the West has moved away from its religious roots, a regret which corresponds to their belief that spiritual value is to be found in religions other than Islam.

V. CHRISTIANITY AND SECULARISM

Christianity is often seen as containing the seeds of secularism in its very origins, with verses from the New Testament such as "Render unto Caesar that which is Caesar's, and render unto God that which is God's" (Mt. 22:21), and "My kingdom is not of this world" (Jn. 18:36), frequently being quoted in support of this. This links up with the view of Islam as superseding Christianity and supplying what was lacking, i.e. the political element, representing as it does the final and complete form of religion.

However, this does not preclude tracing the historical stages of secularisation in the West, or as seeing secularism as a result of certain flaws in Christianity in its historically evolved form, a form which is often seen as a distortion of the original, authentic message of Jesus. The flaws in question are most commonly regarded as being asceticism and monasticism, bringing a this-worldly reaction; the clergy\laity divide, bringing an anti-clerical reaction; the intolerance which culminated in the religious wars, leading to a disillusionment with the political role of religion; and intellectual suppression (or the inherent irrationality of Christianity), leading to a reaction of liberalism.[74]

The Reformation is often seen as a stage on the path to secularisation in certain respects. Jameelah feels that it promoted a destructive individualism. The emphasis on the Scriptures rather than the Church, for example, gave the individual "license to interpret the Bible exactly as he wished, choosing and discarding according to whim, convenience and circumstance."[75] Furthermore she sees the idea of the priesthood of all believers as having led to permissiveness and freedom to do as one pleases.[76] Bewley agrees with this view, seeing Luther as "positing the supremacy of the individual over divine revelation," and thus opening the door to "situational ethics whereby anything at all can be right or wrong according to the situation."[77]

Sardar and Wyn-Davies see the Reformation as crucial to the development of Western secularism in a somewhat less pejorative way. The emphasis on individual access to scripture is seen by them as "ushering in the concept of a mass society," while the new emphasis on individual conscience led eventually (and despite the initial imposition of Reformed Christianity by various temporal authorities) to the toleration of different religious beliefs in the same state: "the Reformation was a search for a new orthodoxy that contained within it the seeds of fragmentation, the impossibility of there being a uniform orthodoxy once a coercive authority had been dethroned."[78] The nature of the secularism to which Christianity gave birth, is, however, far from benign in Sardar and Wyn-Davies' view, since it has now become a "proselytizing creed" which seeks to compel all others to subscribe to its basically irreligious worldview.[79]

Perhaps the most common explanation for the prevalence of secularism in the West is that Christianity has lost the battle for hearts and minds and is a spent force, even in its former stronghold, i.e. Europe. 'Abd al-Qadir as-Sufi, an English convert and head of the Darqawi Sufi order, makes some sweeping statements on the demise of

Christianity in the Introduction to ‘Ata ur-Rahim’s widely distributed *Jesus, Prophet of Islam*. He writes that “today Christianity as a body of metaphysics is frankly non-existent … Christianity is over. The myth has finally exploded … At the end of the day, Christianity was, simply, Europe. And Europe is finished.” In his view, the Church’s spiritual bankruptcy is such that it is “grasping at every hint of spirituality outside it and trying to annexe it (e.g. Christian Zen and Jung’s suggested Christian yoga).” In short, present-day Christianity is “a religion which at the popular level celebrates its two central rites by tying gifts to a fir tree and rolling eggs down the hill, and at the intellectual level no longer exists at all” (pp. 3–6).

‘Ata ur-Rahim himself refers to “the total sickness of Christianity today” due the fact that it “lacks a science of social behaviour,” and as a consequence “the churches of the world are emptying – the mosques of Islam are filling up” (p. 205). Ajijola takes up the theme of Christianity having nothing to offer for the guidance of society, pointing out that Christianity “never had and never will have a programme for the welfare of mankind”; he adds that it “offers no solution to the material side of life … to industrial relations, family life, nor does it advocate any economic doctrine. Christianity has no social philosophy.” This is because it views the Law as a curse, therefore any definite programme “will be part of the Law and hence a curse.”[80]

Some feel that Christianity is irrelevant to the needs of modern-day humanity. Ajijola for example believes that a religion such as Christianity which depends on “magic and miracles” will “lose its hold over the living world and will become a dead weight of obsolete rites. Its rituals and ceremonies and even its prayers will not be better than a repetition of meaningless incantations and such a religion in modern times is bound to meet with decay and death.”[81] Furthermore “Christianity is irreconcilable with modern ideas of democracy and equality of man,” and its doctrines “cannot expect any reasonable allegiance from the advanced nations of the world as it is a religion of primitive people.” It therefore “ceases to exist in the land of culture and advancement … That is why education is alienating the human mind from the Church.”[82] On an intellectual level, Christian belief “no longer satisfies the modern mind … The God man of Christianity has become incredible to civilized man.”[83] Bewley feels that Christianity had a certain efficacy in the medieval world, but that the Christian tradition has now suffered “irreparable damage,” having capitulated to Godless ideologies; it “has proved itself powerless to stem the flood of moral decline and there is now no way that the moral authority of Christianity can be restored in such a way as to enable it to become an effective force in the re-establishment of a balanced, safe, human society."[84] He feels that only Islam can cope with the demands of the modern world, for "the other spiritual traditions are only archaeological fragments, incomplete or altered teachings, intended for other peoples and former times."[85] Maurice Bucaille, a French neurosurgeon and a Muslim convert, maintains that "Judaism and Christianity make no secret of their inability to cope with the tide of materialism and invasion of the West by atheism. Both of them are completely taken off guard."[86]

One aspect of the perceived weakness of Christianity in the face of modernity is the rise of higher criticism, and the subsequent development of liberal Christian theology. Jameelah comments: "What a reduced and emasculated faith the Christian modernists preach which can scarcely appeal to anybody, much less the non-European peoples,"[87] but at the same time expresses the view that traditional Christianity "cannot ... survive the scientific and historical criticism."[88] She sees recent intellectual developments as an attempt "to rationalise Christianity by weeding out all that is objectionable to the modern scientific view, which, though it may temporarily succeed in deceiving people, actually ends in the virtual negation of Christian verities."[89] According to Muhammad Ansari, a graduate of the Aligarh university in India, the "drastic recasting and reforming of Christianity ... is a proof by itself that Christianity is false," and "once the historical and textual criticism of the Bible is accepted, the whole case for Christianity collapses automatically."[90]

Yūsuf al-Qaraḍāwī is an Islamic scholar of international standing based in Qatar. His many publications have been widely circulated throughout the Muslim world, and he is also a high-profile media figure, especially in Arab-speaking countries. In his book *Al-Islām wa'l-'Almāniyyah Wajhan li-Wajh* (*Islam and Secularism Face to Face*),[91] he expounds the reasons why secularism has taken hold in the Christian West but has, in his view, failed to do so in Muslim lands.

Al-Qaraḍāwī argues that in Islam there is no divide between religion and non-religion, between "men of religion" and "men of science," or between religious and temporal authority. In Islam, religion is mingled with the whole of life "just as the soul mingles with the body"; secularism is therefore a Western product which did not grow in Muslim soil, and so doesn't accord with Muslims' beliefs and intellectual assumptions (pp. 51–2). The reason that secularism cannot succeed in Muslim countries is, quite simply, that it is contrary to the nature of Islam, a foreign body which it resists with all its might. The struggle between Islam and secularism in Muslim countries is thus a struggle between the self and its enemy. Turkey is cited as an example of a country where the people were "fleeced of their values and heritage like a sheep"; however, Ataturk was unable to suppress the peoples' love of Islam, which has therefore reasserted itself in various forms in recent times (pp. 60–2).

Al-Qaraḍāwī refers to the alleged scriptural mandate in Christianity for distinguishing between temporal and worldly authority (Mt. 22:21), and extrapolates from this a Western Christian theology which is diametrically opposed to the Islamic view: Western thought does not know the God of Islam, "Who encompasses all things." The god of Western thought is therefore "a different god, like the god of Aristotle, who knows nothing except his own essence"; furthermore he is a "poor god," a monarch who doesn't rule (pp. 53–4).

Al-Qaraḍāwī acknowledges that secularism is not necessarily atheistic, and in fact believes that it can coexist quite happily with Christianity. Thus the Christian can accept secularism, since he can still go to church on Sunday and celebrate Christmas and other religious rites, "and Christianity itself doesn't demand any more of him than that"; unlike Islam, "Christianity didn't come as a whole system for living" (pp. 72–3). Al-Qaraḍāwī believes that Christianity is not only not opposed to secularism, but is even conducive to it in that it "has no detailed legislation for the affairs of life," confining itself to spiritual and ethical matters, in contrast to Islam which is both creed and law (*'aqīdah wa-sharī'ah*). He lays considerable emphasis on the comprehensiveness of Islam, which has "laid down principles of life from the cradle to the grave," and whose jurisprudence (*fiqh*) covers everything from eating and drinking to state-building and international relations (p. 54). He argues that "if a Christian is ruled by man-made law, that doesn't bother him in the slightest, because it's not invalidating a law which his religion has imposed on him. He therefore doesn't feel any contradiction between his faith and the reality he lives, as a Muslim would" (p. 55). The Muslim, on the other hand, has a Shari'a and is guilty of unbelief (*kufr*), even apostasy, if he accepts secularism, and must therefore suffer the consequences, including separation from his wife and children.[92]

A slightly more unusual argument employed by al-Qaraḍāwī is that Christianity is not in fact robbed of temporal power by secularism since it has its own independent power-base, namely the papacy. If the state is separated from religion, religion thus still has "its armies of monks, nuns, and missionaries" which are independent of the state. Islam, by contrast, has neither papacy nor priesthood nor clergy, thus it would be destroyed by secularism, and reduced to a government department which has far less influence than the papacy. Secularism could therefore not take hold in Muslim countries unless the people wished to renounce their faith and deny their history (pp. 55–6).

Another argument adduced by al-Qaraḍāwī is the historically-based one that the history of the Church is one of oppression and intolerance, therefore in the eyes of the Christian West, secularism is regarded as preferable to a return to the intolerance of the past. However, like other Muslims, al-Qaraḍāwī also feels that to a greater or lesser extent, Christianity has been involved in far more recent atrocities. He quotes a Western author to the effect that millions of innocent people have been "killed, taken by force ... dispossessed, exiled or enslaved, and they met this fate at the hands of Christians, who came from the loins of Christian families who for centuries had belonged to the Roman Catholic or the Western Protestant Churches."[93] This in turn is adduced as evidence of Christianity's inability to control humans' baser proclivities, and its failure to create more than a thin veneer of morality and civilisation (p. 58).

CONCLUDING REMARKS

Perhaps the most striking element in this literature is that it continues to promulgate an East-West divide which is still often expressed in terms of a Muslim-Christian divide. It is not difficult to detect an "occidentalism" which falls into many of the same traps as did orientalism in the past; but one should perhaps draw a distinction between this and orientalism in that it is not accompanied by political domination. Many of the sources referred to are popular rather than academic, so one would not necessarily expect the authors to uphold academic standards in terms of accuracy and balance; yet some of the authors do have considerable academic standing in the Middle East.

Muslim critique of Christianity in its Western forms is partially dependent on Western critiques of the same, as witnessed by the frequent citations of Western authors in this literature. However, it would be interesting to speculate how far Muslim discourse on Christianity and the West is dependent on an anterior Western discourse on Islam and the East. The view of Christianity which is reflected in some of this discourse, as aggressive, power-mongering, intolerant and fanatical, incompatible with democracy, backward, irrational and primitive, is very similar to an image of Islam which has been and still is promoted in some Western sources. The racialist theories of Jameelah and al-Faruqi inversely mirror those promoted by nineteenth-century European scholars such as Ernst Renan which asserted the superiority of Aryan or Western civilisation over Semitic. Askari's comment that those Christians who are so exclusivist as to belie democratic ideals should not be allowed to enjoy the benefits of democracy may or may not be a conscious echo of an argument which is frequently used against Islamists seeking power through democratic means in Muslim countries.

Interestingly, as regards the ideas expressed there seem to be no clear lines of demarcation between those living in the West and those living in Muslim countries, between converts and born Muslims, Arab and South Asian, Sufi and non-Sufi, the non-specialist and the academically qualified. Jameelah, a convert, and 'Abd al-Qadir, a Sufi, were among those who produced the most outspoken polemic. It is also striking that there is no necessary dilution of polemic in the works of some of the most eminent, respected and high-profile religious scholars in Muslim countries, including a former Shaykh al-Azhar. One could therefore speak of a universal and pervasive Muslim discourse on Christianity and the West. Inevitably there are occasions when local factors come into play, but on the whole this is surprisingly rare. Living in the West does not necessarily preclude generalisations about Westerners, and living in a Muslim country with a significant Christian minority doesn't usually detract from the overwhelming impression conveyed by most works that Christianity is a Western phenomenon.

However, the discourse is neither homogeneous nor necessarily self-consistent. Christianity is at times portrayed as strong and threatening, at others as weak and moribund. While some draw attention to Islam's superiority over Christianity by stating that it is unthinkable or impossible for a Muslim to convert to Christianity, as where al-Ghazālī compares a Muslim reverting from Islam to Christianity to a University student reverting to primary education,[94] many are nevertheless highly concerned about the possible subversive impact of missionary activities on Muslims.

An ideal view of Islam often forms the backdrop for criticisms of Christianity and the West. Not infrequently, as in the writings of al-Qaraḍāwī, Islamic ideals are juxtaposed with Christian or Western historical realities, to the detriment of the latter. This is partly because

Islam remains an untried and therefore untarnished ideal, not just for those who live in non-Muslim societies but also for those who live in a Muslim society, but feel that their aspiration to establish a truly Islamic state is opposed or blocked by Western or Westernised forces.

What emerges from the foregoing is the consistency with which Christianity is seen in almost purely political terms,[95] and the fact that it is often difficult to disentangle anti-Christian polemic from anti-Western polemic. Where a distinction is drawn between Christianity and the West, the latter may even be considered the lesser of the two evils. One Muslim writer suggests that "it is not Christianity that has civilized Europe but Europe ... that has civilized Christianity,"[96] while another holds that "the West made no progress as long as it was in the grip of Christianity."[97] As a general rule, however, popular Muslim criticisms of the West, although at times extreme and given to conspiracy theories, are rather better-informed than their criticisms of Christianity and its relation to the West. Although in some cases writers have gained access to accurate information, on the whole caricatures of Christianity as either oppressive and tyrannical or powerless and ineffective tend to prevail.

NOTES

1 M. 'Ata ur-Rahim, *Jesus, Prophet of Islam* (Elmhurst, New York: Tahrike Tarsil Qur'an, 1991), p. 205.
2 M. Jameelah, *Islam Versus Ahl al-Kitab: Past and Present* (Delhi: Taj Company, 1989), pp. 351–2.
3 Amsterdam: Djambatan, 1962.
4 *Islam Versus Ahl al-Kitab*, pp. 362–3.
5 *Ibid.*, p. 363.
6 *Ibid.*, p. 394.
7 *Ibid.*, p. 316.
8 A. Bewley, *The Key to the Future* (London: Ta-Ha Publishers, 1992), p. 38.
9 See for examples Y. Haddad, "Islamist Depictions of Christianity in the Twentieth Century: the pluralism debate and the depiction of the other," in *Islam and Christian-Muslim Relations*, 7, 1996, esp. pp. 85ff.
10 *Kifāḥ Dīn*, fifth edition (Cairo: Maktabat Wahbah, 1991), first published some three decades earlier, p. 9.
11 The edition referred to here is the fourth (Beirut: Al-Maktabat al-'Asriyyah, 1970). See M. Ayoub, "Roots of Muslim-Christian Conflict," in *Muslim World*, 79, 1989, pp. 35–7, for an exposition of this work.
12 Z. Sardar, "The Ethical Connection: Christian-Muslim Relations in the Postmodern Age," in *Islam and Christian-Muslim Relations*, 2, 1991, p. 58.
13 *Islam Versus Ahl al-Kitab*, p. 262.

14 *Ibid.*, pp. 381–2.
15 *Ibid.*, p. 317.
16 *Ibid.*, p. 203.
17 "The Ethical Connection," p. 61.
18 *Islam Versus Ahl al-Kitab*, p. 262.
19 *Al-Tabshīr wa'l-Isti'mār*, p. 262.
20 *Ibid.*, pp. 264–5.
21 *Ibid.*, p. 266.
22 See M. Fandy, "Safar al-Hawali: Saudi Islamist or Saudi nationalist?," in *Islam and Christian-Muslim Relations*, 9, 1998, pp. 15–18, for a description of this aspect of al-Ḥawālī's thought.
23 Cairo: Maktabat al-Sunnah, 1994.
24 Chicago: Lawrence Hill Books, 1986.
25 Beirut: Markaz Dirāsāt al-Waḥdat al-'Arabiyyah, 1990, based on the author's doctoral thesis. In contrast to the aforementioned two works, which aim to foster dialogue and to change attitudes by peaceful means, al-Ḥawālī's aim is to galvanise his listeners\readers to undertake a military *jihād* against the State of Israel, insisting that to fail to engage in it is apostasy (p. 74).
26 For example, al-Ḥawālī (p. 61) quotes Halsell as saying that a lesser-known evangelist, Mike Evans, is a friend of George Bush, whereas in fact Halsell (p. 187) describes the attempts of a certain pastor to create the *impression* that Evans was close to Bush, in order to enhance the latter's status and credibility.
27 M. al-Ghazālī, *Ṣīḥat Tandhīr min Du'āt al-Tanṣīr* (Algiers: Dār al-Intifāḍah li'l-Naṣr wa'l-Tawzī', 1992), p. 125.
28 Jameelah, *Islam versus Ahl al-Kitab*, p. 385.
29 'Abd al-Ḥalīm Maḥmūd, *Urubbā wa'l-Islām* (Cairo: Dār al-Ma'ārif, 1979), pp. 195–6.
30 M. Anees, "The Dialogue of History," in M. Anees, S. Abedin & Z. Sardar (eds.), *Christian-Muslim Relations: Yesterday, Today, Tomorrow* (London: Grey Seal, 1991), pp. 29 and 31.
31 "Roots of Muslim-Christian Conflict," p. 39. In Christian missionary circles Gairdner, to whom Ayoub directly applies this quote, is known as an unusually sympathetic observer of Islam; see, e.g., L. Vander Werff, *Christian Mission to Muslims: The Record. Anglican and Reformed Approaches in India and the Near East, 1800–1938* (Pasadena: William Carey Library, 1977).
32 'Abd al-Ḥalīm Maḥmūd, *Urubbā wa'l-Islām*, pp. 41–2.
33 E.g. A. Ajijola, *Myth of the Cross* (Chicago: Kazi Publications, 1979), p. 1; A. Azhar, *Christianity in History* (Lahore: Sh. Muhammad Ashraf, 1991), p. 25.
34 J. Qureshi, '"Alongsidedness – In Good Faith?": An Essay on Kenneth Cragg," in A. Hussain, R. Olson & J. Qureshi (eds.), *Orientalism, Islam, and Islamists* (Vermont: Amana Books, 1984), p. 203.
35 *Ibid.*, p. 204.
36 A. L. Tibawi, review of *The Dome of the Rock*, in *Islamic Quarterly*, 12, 1968, p. 120.
37 P. Manzoor, review of *Islam and Christianity Today* in *Muslim World Book Review*, 6, 1, 1985, p. 7.

38 See, e.g., Hasan Askari, "Christian Mission to Islam: A Muslim Response," in *Journal of the Institute of Muslim Minority Affairs*, 7, 1986, p. 329.
39 German convert Murad Hofmann states that "it is a well-known fact that Muslims cannot be converted to Christianity"; see his *Islam: The Alternative* (Reading: Garnet, 1993), p. 44.
40 "Christian Mission to Islam," p. 329.
41 "The Ethical Connection," p. 58.
42 Maṭba'at Dār al-Ta'līf, 1965 (second rev. ed.).
43 *Ṣīḥat Tandhīr min Du'āt al-Tanṣīr*, p. 125.
44 This theme is treated in greater detail in K. Zebiri, *Muslims and Christians Face to Face* (Oxford: Oneworld, 1997), esp, pp. 71–8.
45 *Al-'Amāl al-Kāmilah li'l-Imām Muḥammad 'Abduh* (Beirut: Al-Mu'assassat al-'Arabiyyah li'l-Dirāsāt wa'l-Nashr, 1972–3), vol. 3, pp. 204–5.
46 *Islam Versus Ahl al-Kitab*, p. 317.
47 *Christianity in History*, p. 5.
48 *Ibid*., p. 28.
49 *Ibid*., p. 28.
50 *Ibid*., p. 171.
51 *Ibid*., p. 166.
52 *Ibid*., p. 181.
53 *Al-A'māl al-Kāmilah*, pp. 260 and 263.
54 *Myth of the Cross*, p. 80.
55 *Ibid*., p. 127.
56 *Al-A'māl al-Kāmilah*, p. 262.
57 J. Ahmed, *Christianity: Its Appeal, Reaction and Failure*, third edition (Karachi International Islamic Publishers, 1994), p. 54.
58 *Myth of the Cross*, p. 128.
59 *Ibid*., pp. 144 and 180.
60 *Christianity*, p. 40.
61 *Ibid*., pp. 78–9.
62 *Ibid*., p. 53.
63 *Ibid*., p. 151.
64 *Ibid*., pp. 51–2.
65 *Christianity in History*, pp. 170–1.
66 *Christianity*, p. 75.
67 *Ibid*., p. 73.
68 A. Shafaat, *Islam, Christianity and the State of Israel as Fulfillment of Old Testament Prophecy* (Indianapolis: American Trust Publications, 1989), pp. 60–1.
69 *Ibid*., p. 60.
70 *Ibid*., p. 58.
71 Z. Sardar and M. Wyn-Davies, *Distorted Imagination: Lessons from the Rushdie Affair* (London: Grey Seal, 1990), p. 19.
72 *Ibid*., p. 20.
73 *The Key to the Future*, pp. 35 and 44.
74 See for example the analyses offered in Ahmed, *Christianity*, and Azhar, *Christianity in History*.
75 *Islam Versus Ahl al-Kitab*, p. 332.

76 *Ibid.*, p. 201.
77 *The Key to the Future*, p. 7.
78 *Distorted Imagination*, pp. 19–22.
79 *Ibid.*, p. 31.
80 *Myth of the Cross*, pp. 127–8.
81 *Ibid.*, p. 191.
82 *Ibid.*, pp. 126–7.
83 *Ibid.*, p. 193.
84 *The Key to the Future*, p. 44.
85 *Ibid.*, p. 35.
86 M. Bucaille, *The Bible, the Qur'an and Science: The Holy Scriptures Examined in the Light of Modern Knowledge*, trans. A. Pannell & M. Bucaille (Indianapolis: American Trust Publications, 1978), p. 117.
87 *Islam Versus Ahl al-Kitab*, p. 340.
88 *Ibid.*, p. 337.
89 *Ibid.*, p. 345.
90 M. Ansari, *Islam and Christianity in the Modern World*, fourth edition (Karachi: World Federation of Islamic Mission, 1965), p. 141.
91 Second edition (Algiers: Maktabat Riḥāb, 1989). The book bears the subtitle: "an academic reply to Dr. Fu'ad Zakariyyah [an Egyptian secularist] and secularists in general."
92 Pp. 73–4. Al-Qaraḍāwī doesn't explicitly refer to the death penalty, but states that the apostate should be given an opportunity to repent (a precondition for the execution of the death penalty in classical jurisprudence), and that "all the rulings of the apostate will be applied to him in this life and after death."
93 Pp. 57–8. Specific nations mentioned here are the Germans, Spanish, Italians, Polish, Romanians, Hungarians, French, Serbs, Croats, and Russians.
94 *Ṣīḥat Tandhīr min Du'āt al-Tanṣīr*, p. 113.
95 This holds true even when some of the above-mentioned Muslim writers deal with Christian doctrine, since the doctrine itself is seen as the end-result of political manoeuvrings.
96 A. Qadri, *Dimensions of Christianity* (Islamabad: Da'wah Academy, 1989), p. 40.
97 Ajijola, *Myth of the Cross*, p. 127.

9

Depictions of "Christianity" within British Islamic Institutions

Philip Lewis

To speak of British Islamic institutions is misleading if it is assumed that it is possible to isolate Muslims in Britain from their co-religionists across the world. Most of the Muslim institutions in Britain have continuing links with the wider *ummah*, especially South Asia, Saudi Arabia and Egypt. Inevitably, where such organisations are staffed by personnel from these countries, perceptions of Christianity owe as much, if not more, to their country of origin, than to the situation in Britain. One critical issue, which this chapter will seek to illuminate, is the extent to which the experience and questions of Muslims born and educated in Britain, is finding a voice in Islamic institutions.

Before addressing the range of attitudes to Christianity to be found in Islamic institutions, it is worth recalling how relatively recent significant Muslim settlement in Britain is. Muslims in Britain have grown from about 23,000 in 1951 to 1 million in 1991 – a figure likely to double within twenty years – of whom 75% have their origins in South Asia, the majority from Pakistan.[1] In addition, over a third of a million were born in the Middle East and North Africa. Estimates for converts range between 5,000 and 50,000. In all, there is in Britain an array of Muslim communities, bearers of different nationalities, languages, regional identities and migration histories, embodying an equally diverse set of cultural practices and economic locations. Arab élites in London, bearers of what has been dubbed a "Beirut on Thames" syndrome, often have little in common with large South Asian communities in East London, Birmingham or Bradford.[2]

For Muslim communities considered reflection on Christianity has to compete with far more pressing demands. These range from developing appropriate institutions which can relate to the state, addressing Islamophobia, worrying about the emergence of a Muslim underclass in inner cities, developing an Islamic jurisprudence appropriate for minority status, networking groups of professionals within the legal and educational system, to organising Islamic aid to help Muslim groups across the world, suffering from oppression and natural disasters. In such a situation, the frank supersessionism written into the Islamic tradition vis-à-vis Christianity, leaves little need or energy for "curiosity" about the "otherness of the other."[3]

To anticipate my argument I suggest that broadly there are four responses to Christianity generated from within self-consciously Islamic institutions and organisations.[4] For most Islamic *madāris* (seminaries) in Britain, Christianity is simply invisible, part of non-Muslim society often painted in lurid colours as irredeemably corrupt. Institutions committed to *da'wa* (invitation to Islam) often draw on and develop a rich anti-Christian polemical tradition. Radical Muslim groups have developed a rejectionist stance of all things western/christian, for which the term "occidentalism" has been coined.[5] Finally, a disparate group of organisations is beginning to respond to and create forums for those Muslim professionals and academics – some active in inter-faith movements – who want to co-operate with Christians on a range of pressing social issues. Such pragmatic engagement is beginning to generate a more informed and Islamically serious encounter with Christianity in its particularity and "otherness."

In what follows, I seek to make sense of these developments within their institutional contexts, as well as speculating on the possibilities for a more open engagement with "lived Christianity" in Britain today, in contrast to an imagined Christianity, unrecognisable to Christians. I have, where possible quoted directly from Muslim sources, to provide something of the texture and argumentation of such Muslim perspectives on Christianity.

I. CHRISTIANITY INVISIBLE: THE WORLD OF BRITISH *MADĀRIS*

The mosque and its personnel continue to be the main agent of transmission of Islam to British Muslims. Muslim communities have invested hugely in these institutions of which there are more than 600, about one in six of which are purpose built.[6] Most reflect the diverse schools of Islamic thought of South Asia, especially the Deobandi and

Barelwi traditions. The Deobandis have been most successful in establishing a network of Islamic "seminaries" in this country. Bury in Lancashire was their first in 1975 and then Dewsbury in 1982. The latter is the centre of an Islamic revivalist movement. There are now a dozen *madāris* across the country which have patterned themselves on Bury.

The Deobandi tradition is rooted historically in one Islamic response to the trauma of colonialism in India after the failure of the "mutiny": an attempt to construct a self-sufficient Muslim world, minimise interaction with non-Muslims and to provide Muslims with alternative sources of knowledge, sociability and identity. In India they deliberately held aloof from the colonial milieu, shunned English and the inclusion of western subjects in their curriculum. This rejectionist stance towards non-Islamic knowledge is evident in the words of their greatest scholar as rector of Deoband, Ashraf Ali Thanawi (d. 1943), for whom "to like and appreciate the customs of the infidels" is a grave sin.[7]

In England it has not been possible to avoid English entirely: in their seminaries youngsters in their privates school from 13–16 years old have to conform to the dictates of English law. Thus four subjects are offered at GCSE level: English language, general science, maths and Urdu.[8] They provide a closed process of socialisation within total institutions which organise all aspects of life – study, leisure and sleeping – and where all activities are carried out in the company of people from the same institution and regulated from above. There are no televisions and radios and newspapers are excluded as a distraction. Music is considered *ḥarām* and often preached against. Paradise and Hell frame the horizon within which life is conducted.

I attended a meeting for "professionals" in September 1996 at the Dewsbury centre. This comprised some 1,200 people who came from all over Britain in a twenty-four hour meeting. On the walls of the prayer halls were signs for the different groups from Yorkshire, Lancashire, Scotland, London, the Midlands and Wales to gather and place their bedrolls. In the address I attended, the speaker worried about "rebellious" women and youth, along with "westernism, materialism and egotism." Muslims were urged to assume their responsibilities and duties to their neighbours and friends. They were to banish any feelings of inferiority since they had the superior *dīn* (religion). The speaker admitted that to wear a beard was to be scorned and assailed with slogans such as fundamentalist, extremist and militant. However, he insisted that Muslims could not "be assimilated or absorbed."

Imāms who are content to stay within such a world have little understanding of, or curiosity about the role of Christianity in contemporary society. Indeed, there is no study of such in their curriculum. The challenge of religious pluralism and allowing for the genuine "otherness" of the other simply does not enter their intellectual horizons. Nor, in reality does Islamic history, philosophy or the great names in Islamic civilisation – whether Avicenna, Al-Ghazālī or Ibn Khaldun. Christianity is simply an undifferentiated part of "westernism, materialism and egotism." An apologist for the movement in Britain can declare that "a major aim of *tablīgh* (preaching) is to rescue the *ummah* from the culture and civilisation of the Jews, Christians and (other) enemies of Islam and to create such hatred for their ways as human beings have for urine ... and excreta."[9] Fortunately, such intemperate language features more in non-English publications than English.

Some *imāms* trained within the Deobandi tradition are seeking ways of connecting with young British Muslims and their street culture. In Bradford a group of young Bury-trained *'ulamā'* in 1998 wrote a series of pamphlets in English for young Muslim adults. The picture that emerges from these pamphlets offers an unvarnished, if selective, picture of life at street level among many local Muslims: drug taking, "lavish wedding parties" whereby "the *sunnah* of the prophet ... are replaced with ridiculous Hindu and other *kāfir* (infidel/unbeliever) traditions"; neglect and abuse of wives, indifference to Islamic education of children, an increase in divorce, playing loud music from "obscene films" even when passing mosques where worshippers are at prayer. In seeking to counter such un-Islamic behaviour the *imāms* realise that it is no longer enough simply to rehearse what the Qur'ān and *sunnah* have to say on this or that issue. Reasons have to be given. Thus, in a pamphlet criticising gambling they cite material produced by Gamblers Anonymous.

What is significant, for the purpose of the present topic, is that while the *imāms* include a pamphlet critical of "the False Prophet of the Qadiyan," the founder of a nineteenth century Indian religious movement, the *Aḥmadiyya*, whose self-definition as Muslim has been fiercely contested, there is absolutely nothing about Christianity. The "People of the Book" are invisible, subsumed beneath the category of *kufr*, unbelief.

So far I have dwelt on the world of the Deobandi "seminaries." The Barelwis are less well organised but are beginning to develop a few *madāris* in Britain. Dr Musharaf Hussain was the driving force behind one such initiative in Nottingham. Dr Hussain acquired elementary religious education from a Bradford *'ālim*, then earned a Ph.D in medical biochemistry from Birmingham University. After some years as a research scholar at Nottingham University he spent a year in a traditional "seminary" in Pakistan and rounded off his Islamic formation by gaining a B. A. in Islamic Studies from the most famous traditional centre of Islamic scholarship in the Muslim world, al-Azhar in Cairo.

Dr Hussain found al-Azhar education was much broader than that of a traditional Pakistani *madrasa*. It was much more ready to consider and learn from a wider band of Islamic scholarship, including classical Islamic philosophy and Shī'-ite works. Yet, he still found his al-Azhar teachers largely insulated from the intellectual world of modern society. He felt a radical new start was required if British *'ulamā'* were to have any chance of relating to the intellectual and cultural world of Muslims educated in higher education in Britain. In the event, he left the seminary because the weight of traditionalism frustrated change.[10]

Dr Hussain now runs a mosque in Nottingham and produces a magazine in English – *The Invitation* – mainly for young Muslim adults. His desire to bridge the gap between western and Islamic intellectual and cultural traditions was partly motivated by a desire to enable Muslims to feel more at ease in British society. He worries that most Muslims were still reticent about calling themselves British Muslims, preferring to regard themselves as Pakistanis or Bengali Muslims living in Britain. A recent article in his magazine entitled "Unity and Tolerance as a Defence against the Evils of the West" provides a sober insight into the anxieties of some young Muslims. The author, Aamer Naeem, cautions against appropriating western definitions of Islam and asks a rhetorical question:

> How do you feel at the mention of the removal of hands for theft, or the stoning to death of adulterers? By the standards of the West these are barbaric, but remember these are laws ... sanctioned by Allah ... As a Muslim born in this country I often found myself [questioning] the wisdom behind such laws ... but I now know Muslims must not question the Shariah ... A slave does not question his Master ... [such is tantamount to] disbelief.[11]

It is clear that Dr Hussain's priority is to instil a sense of confidence in British Muslims. Thus the magazine will carry stories by converts to Islam from Christianity but little about contemporary Christianity in Britain. *The Invitation* evinces none of the visceral dislike of

Christianity evident in some Deobandi publications. Still, during a recent conversation, Dr Hussain smiled at my question whether an understanding of Christianity was on the agenda. He politely reminded me of the Islamic supersession of Christianity.

Another distinguished Barelwi scholar working in England, Sheikh Mohammad Raza, has written a devastating analysis of the sectarianism and intolerance characteristic of traditional South Asian Islam, exacerbated by Saudi influence, exported to Britain. Here "mosques have been turned into medieval sectarian fortresses."[12] Most *imāms* are unable to connect with the world of Muslim youth and women.

Sheikh Raza's study contains a few asides about Christianity:

> The mosques ... [function] like the Christian churches – providing a place for prayer and some other rituals such as funerals, marriages, etc. British society is ... secularist. While the churches have their congregations they are neither full nor have any impact on the political structure of British society. Religion is a personal matter ... Secularism in so far as it denies the existence of God ... is in direct opposition to Islam.[13]

When I asked what Urdu word he had in mind when he used "secular" he replied *lādīnī* (irreligious) – this also explains why the term *kufr* (infidel) is used in his book to describe Britain. He admitted that he did not understand the role of Christianity in British society and, after nearly a decade of involvement with an inter-faith movement, he saw the need for Muslims to begin to develop such an empirical understanding of Christianity's self-understanding and continuing influence in British society.

While Sheikh Raza, through his exposure to Christians active in inter-faith forums, could acknowledge that he did not understand contemporary Christianity, many *'ulamā'*, when asked by Muslims about Christianity often have recourse to the so-called "Gospel of Barnabas" or refer them to the myriad pamphlets and videos of Ahmad Deedat. Both belong to an older anti-Christian-polemical tradition. No account of Muslim perceptions of Christianity in Britain today can afford to neglect either since they continue to shape and colour Muslim attitudes and militate against any honest encounter with Christianity.

II. ANTI-CHRISTIAN POLEMIC ALIVE AND WELL

A couple of years ago in Bradford posters were put up inviting Muslims and non-Muslims to a lecture in the city's central library. The posters advertising the meeting included the words in large bold letters: "Banned – The Gospel of Barnabas," subtitled "The True Teaching of Prophet Jesus." Accompanying the invitation was background information which included the following:

> St Barnabas was a disciple of Prophet Jesus ... the most faithful of all [his] disciples ... [who] spent the latter part of his life with his master. He was a devout monotheist and believed in God. Barnabas recorded a true account of the life and teachings as his master Jesus wished ... in 478 AD, when the remains of Barnabas were discovered, the original gospel was found on his chest. It must be said with profound anger and regret that the Christian world has banned the Gospel of St Barnabas in the Church since the Council of Nicea met to denounce the Gospel in 325 AD. The gospel is still banned today because it contains the teachings of Prophet Jesus ... which are compatible with Islamic teachings. Today very few people are aware of [its] existence ...
>
> The most objectionable things which Christendom find detestable in the Gospel of Barnabas are: references which refer to the coming of the Final Prophet of God the Prophet Muhammad ... the Salvation unto Mankind, references which destroy the idea of the Trinity promoting the Oneness of God, and the true events which occurred at the so-called "Crucifixion" of Jesus ... which did not occur as God had planned to save His Prophet from this doom. Below we have a verse from the Gospel of Barnabas ... to prove that the Messiah awaited by Jews, Christians and others is none other than the Prophet Muhammad.

The lecture elaborated on such themes with the speaker exhibiting righteous indignation that the Church could perpetrate such a deception, intended simply to prevent Christians from knowing the truth. The lecturer, part of an international Sufi circle, was the son of the city's best educated *imām*. His father subsequently told me that he too had a copy, his in Arabic rather than in English.

The fact that a late medieval forgery without textual pre-history can be passed off as the authentic gospel is a somewhat desolating insight into contemporary Muslim attitudes to Christianity. The contents of this pseudo-gospel only came to the attention of the Muslim world after it was translated from Italian in 1907 by two Christian scholars, Laura and Lonsdale Ragg. Their translation was prefaced by a lengthy critical introduction which drew attention to anachronistic historical details and its eccentric topography. Its author, supposedly an intimate of Christ, was "apparently of the opinion that one can sail by boat to Nazareth, and his narrative suggests such a voyage from Nazareth to

Jerusalem. Evidently he possesses no first-hand knowledge of Palestine."[14] There was also a mistaken reference to the year of the Jubilees "recurring every hundred years," a projection back into New Testament times of the first such recorded Jubilee of 1300 instituted by Pope Boniface VIII. Recent scholarship locates its origin within a series of Morisco forgeries of supposedly early Christian texts in Granada in the 16th century.[15]

This pseudo-gospel was almost immediately translated into Arabic in 1908 by the Egyptian scholar Rashid Rida who serialised it in his journal *Al-Manār.* Two Urdu editions were published in India in 1916 and there have since been Persian and Indonesian editions. In 1973 a pirated edition of the English translation was published in Pakistan. I acquired my paperback edition, newly reprinted in 1990, from a local Muslim bookshop in Bradford which had imported it from Pakistan. Other copies are to be found on the shelves of the city's libraries. Needless to say these editions lack the critical introduction. This one work has left its impress on a generation of anti-Christian polemical literature, nowhere more than in Pakistan.[16] Notwithstanding the fact that a few Muslim scholars have also rejected it as a forgery it continues to circulate widely.

Ahmad Deedat (b. 1919), a South African of Gujarati background, belongs to a tradition of public religious controversy which reached an earlier climax in a famous debate in 1854 held at Agra, North India, between Revd. Carl Pfander and Maulana Rahmat Allah Kairanawi. An historian who has documented these debates locates the responsibility at the door of Pfander:

> The catalyst in the transformation [of the *'ulamā'*] from passive observance to active remonstration, was the campaign launched by Carl Pfander in 1841, to engage ashrāf [North Indian élite tracing their ancestry back to the Prophet] Muslims in religious interchange ... [through the distribution of] tracts in Arabic, Persian and Urdu, accompanied by new translations of the Bible in those languages.[17]

Maulana Kairanawi's account of the debate, *Iẓhār al-Ḥaqq*, Demonstration of the Truth – was to be an inspiration for Deedat who tells us that:

> It was in 1939 when I was working as a shop assistant at Adams Mission near a Christian seminary by that name, producing preachers and priests, that I and my fellow Muslim workers were the target of young aspiring men of the cloth ... The discovery of the book – "IZHARUL

> HAQ" – was the turning point in my life. After a short while I was able to invite the trainee missionaries of Adams Mission College and cause them to perspire under the collar until they developed a respect for Islam and its Holy Prophet.[18]

Unfortunately, respect is not what he generates. The titles of some of his pamphlets indicate his vituperative style: "50,000 errors in the Bible," "Crucifixion?," "The God that Never Was," "Resurrection or Resuscitation," "His Holiness plays hide and seek with Muslims." Deedat also produces videos of "debates" with American evangelists such as Jimmy Swaggart. His booklets are crude but clever compilations of allegedly damning evidence to prove that the bible is incoherent, full of mistakes and contains sexually reprehensible material, unworthy of any serious publication.

Deedat draws indiscriminately from whatever material is at hand, whether the writings of the Jehovah's Witnesses, the Seventh Day Adventists or the American evangelist Billy Graham. The stuff of elementary bible study, such as distinct genealogies for Jesus and differences between various biblical translations, are used to endorse an Islamic reading of scripture. Deedat points out that the bible speaks in the first person for God or Jesus, as well as in the third person. The latter he equates with history. Deedat then triumphantly declares that Muslims carefully distinguish between these three types – God's speech (the *Qur'ān*), Prophetic discourse (the *ḥadīth*) and the works of Muslim historians. For Deedat the conclusion is clear: "the 'Holy Bible' contains a motley type of literature, which [includes] the sordid and obscene – all under the same cover – [with the] Christian ... forced to concede equal spiritual import and authority to all."[19]

To confine oneself to an analysis of his pamphlets would be incomplete. Mr. Deedat is a consummate performer. His last tour of Britain in 1995 was devoted to a contemptuous and dismissive interpretation of "The Threshold of Hope" written by the present Pope. I quote from the report of one such meeting written by an R. E. Adviser for a local education authority, which provides an excellent insight into his performance:

> Deedat invited the audience to join him in mockery of the papacy and of an elementary and literal reading of the Bible and central Christian beliefs. He scolded them because they remained ignorant of Papal trickery: behind the smooth talk of dialogue there was a dangerous attempt to undermine and attack Islam ... Deedat uses humour and

> scurrilous innuendo to make sure his audience see Christianity, the Pope, the Catholic church and the Bible as unworthy of respect. His approach is populist. He invites his audience to join him in an infantile and sneering assault on central tenets of the Christian faith. He quotes strong and occasionally obscene language (e.g. a recent Christian drama about the crucifixion) without fully appraising the audience of the context from which he quotes, to pour scorn on Christianity. The person of the Pope emerges from this treatment as, at best a self-deceived clown, at worst a consummate and skilful deceiver ... bent on attacking Islam under the guise of false calls to a dialogue.
>
> He presented a woefully inadequate, inaccurate and distorted caricature of Christianity ... unworthy of both Muslim scholarship and attitudes. He ... held up this distorted image for general mockery and abuse. The audience responded with a mixture of outright glee and rather self-conscious tittering like naughty children caught mocking something they had been taught to respect. This was an opportunity ... to sneer at what the prevailing culture (still based on Christianity in Muslim eyes) forbids them to do. Here was the deepest and most cherished beliefs of Christians being held up for public mockery and it was OK to join in wasn't it? Very few could resist the temptation ... [or were aware] that they were being manipulated ... [personal correspondence].

It would be gratifying to suppose that Mr Deedat was a maverick without influence in the community, a throwback to a discredited era of polemic. This would be a mistake. He was the recipient in 1986 of the King Feisal Award, a prestigious and lucrative prize given by Saudi Arabia for his services to Islam, and his organisation Islamic Propagation Centre International (IPCI) has a major centre in Birmingham. Until his recent illness, he regularly travelled to the USA, Europe and into the Middle East: his books are available in English and have been translated into Arabic and even circulate in the Lebanon.[20] His meetings are free and he has packed the Albert Hall in 1985 and the National Exhibition Centre in Birmingham in 1988. His more popular pamphlets have innumerable print runs of 50,000.

As I write this, the IPCI roadshow is touring the country playing to packed Muslim audiences in the three largest centres of Muslim population in the country – London, Birmingham, Bradford – as well as Newcastle upon Tyne, Walsall and Leicester. In London and Birmingham the meetings are held in the most prestigious mosques, the Islamic Cultural Centre and Central Mosque respectively. Among the speakers is an Indian, Dr Zakir Naik, often introduced as "Deedat plus"! Needless to say at these meetings Ahmad Deedat's pamphlets are being recycled to a new young British Muslim constituency. Because his meetings are held in English most who attend are young British-born and educated Muslims between 18–40. In Bradford the meeting was co-sponsored by one of the most successful young Muslim businessman in the city. Thus a new generation is exposed to his malicious disinformation.

The reasons for the popularity of such polemicists and their literature are varied: the trauma colonialism wrought on Muslim peoples whose religious self-understandings as "the best of all communities" led them to suppose that Islam should prevail over all religious and ideological alternatives; the wounded pride of living in a post-colonial world within the continuing hegemony of western culture; the painful realisation that for many Muslims voluntary exile or political asylum in the West provides greater security and religious freedom than many Muslim-majority countries; the dislocation wrought by migration, exacerbated by racism and Islamophobia; the scandal and horror of ethnic cleansing of Bosnian Muslims in the heart of Europe. In a world in which history seems to have gone all wrong "some dignity at least can be preserved by the claim to moral and religious superiority."[21]

While an earlier generation of Christians must assume some responsibility for such anti-Christian polemic, it is sobering to be reminded that such works even "fall short of medieval Muslim scholarship, which sometimes demonstrated a detailed knowledge of the contrasting beliefs and practices of different Christian sects."[22] More disturbing is the influence of Saudi Arabia in lending lustre and economic support to a polemicist who contributes nothing to serious Islamic engagement with non-religious traditions.[23]

Such expressions of Saudi influence over Islamic institutions in Britain give cause for concern. Not least, because "Saudi Arabia is the most theocratic state in the contemporary Sunni Muslim world. By definition, a non-Muslim cannot be a Saudi citizen. The idea of religious pluralism has neither meaning nor support in many segments of the population, and religious norms and practices are encouraged, promoted and even enforced by the state."[24] Further, its uncompromising *Wahhābī* ideology considers "*kufr* (unbelief) ... an attribute of ... otherness *tout court* [with *kufr*] not confined to non-Islamic monotheism, but describes non-Wahhabite co-religionists as well."[25]

In Britain the Saudis have strong links with the South Asian *Ahl-i Ḥadīth* tradition. In July 1998 their central mosque in Birmingham advertised a two week course open to all on *Qur'ān* and *Ḥadīth*. A Catholic priest with long experience in the Muslim world attended the entire course as part of his responsibility to build bridges with peoples of other faith. It was attended by about one hundred local young Muslims between 20 and 30 years old. The lectures were delivered by five Sheikhs from the Islamic Department of Medina University and were translated into English:

> [The Sheikhs] had absolutely no doubt in their minds about the superiority of Islam over all other religions. This is the final revelation of God. It is now the duty of all Muslims in the Western world to preach Islam to the unbelievers. God has ordained that there be Muslims in the western world to preach God's word ... There was a lot of anti-Christian, anti-Jewish, anti-Western sentiments expressed. The west is morally bankrupt, Christianity has failed and now it is up to Islam to rescue the west from this chaos. All non-Muslims were disdainfully referred to as *kafirs*, unbelievers ... [personal correspondence].

III. MUSLIM COMMON SENSE ABOUT CHRISTIANITY UNCHALLENGED

If much Pakistani and Saudi religious influence in Britain is not such as to encourage any serious religious interest in Christianity we now turn to consider the activities of a distinguished Egyptian religious scholar, the late Dr Syed Darsh (1930–97). Many educated British Muslims had begun to look to him to develop a new *fiqh* (Islamic jurisprudence) which could connect with the complex social reality of contemporary British society. Before we reflect on Dr Darsh's role in Britain, it is worth just spelling out some of the dilemmas which confront Muslims in Britain as a minority.

Firstly, while Islamic jurisprudence had discussed the predicament of the Muslim under a non-Muslim government, what was envisaged was the situation of new converts, temporary visitors and traders or those Muslims residing in areas conquered by non-Muslims. For the new phenomenon, "minority communities formed by voluntary migration from Muslim lands to predominantly Christian countries ... there is no precedent in Islamic history or jurisprudence."[26] In short, "Muslim theology offers, up to the present, no systematic formulations of the status of being in a minority."[27]

Secondly, within Islamic history, with the exception of the recent trauma of colonialism, Muslims took power and dominance for granted. "In the arsenal of group attitudes they knew either how to command or how to obey. They had, through most of their history, rarely learnt *to live with others in equality and fraternity.*"[28] Thirdly, and related to these two points, is the question of who can offer appropriate and relevant religious guidance to Muslims in Britain, a new and bewildering environment whose public life, culture and institutions owe little or nothing to Islam. The *'ulamā'*, the custodians of traditional Islam, are confronted by new institutions of public education which have undercut their monopoly of religious learning. Muslim students can now learn about Islam in school and university from teachers who – if Muslims themselves – are the product of tertiary education rather than the traditional *madrasa*. Moreover, modernists and Islamists alike, have created their own separate institutions of Islamic study. This can generate a pick'n mix approach to Islam.[29]

Dr Syed Darsh had begun to address some of these issues. Trained at al-Azhar and lecturer in their faculty of theology, he came to Britain in 1971 and spent nine years as *imām* of the prestigious Islamic Cultural Centre. Subsequently, he was involved as a freelance columnist and broadcaster, while discharging a diversity of responsibilities within the burgeoning Muslim communities, including chairman of the Sharī'ah council in London.

He spent the five years before his death writing an "agony uncle" column for the innovative Muslim magazine *Q-News* during which time he answered over 500 questions. While many of the Deobandi and Barelwi *'ulamā'* were content to remain within the safety of a familiar social and cultural world, Dr Darsh exposed himself to the questions from across the community, not least from the best educated British Muslims, including converts. The variety of roles he fulfilled in Britain, in addition to a wide network of contacts across the Muslim world, gave him an unrivalled vantage point from which to engage with British Muslims. In the words of the editor of *Q-News*, he was someone who "understood the pain, traumas and real challenges involved in the process of constructing a Muslim community in Britain."[30]

Leafing through the back numbers of *Q-News* the following questions were posed: What was the Islamic attitude to "gay" Muslims? Whether workers could go on strike? Was it licit to watch footballers prancing around in shorts during international football tournaments? Can live bait be used in fishing? Should prostitution be decriminalised? Was it right to do jury service in a non-Islamic judicial system? What of involvement in British party politics? Was it right to send children to state schools with their un-Islamic ethos?

A representative selection of Dr Darsh's *fatāwa* have been collected and organised thematically in a recent book. I want largely to focus on this collection of questions and his answers since it provides plenty of material, direct and indirect, for his views about Christianity and is the form in which his views will continue to be accessible and influential.

> Q: Could you please comment on the suggestion that marriage to Jews and Christians should be ruled out as both the Jews and Christians of the 1990's differ markedly to their forbears as the "people of the book" ... around at the time of the Prophet?
>
> A. There is no difference between the Jews and Christians of today with their ancestors of the past, and certainly of those that lived in the days of the Prophet ... Most of the major Christian ... sects that exist today were in existence 1,400 years ago (sic) ... [and they continue to be] mistakenly defined by a belief that the Prophet Jesus ... was the son of God and a part of a "Holy Trinity" ... The Qur'ān also makes references to the fact that the Prophet Jesus was not killed and did not die on the cross ... [Dr Darsh sought to discourage Muslim men from marrying women from People of the Book when in a minority situation]. When I was working at the Islamic Cultural Centre in Regent's Park, I tried to get brides-to-be to sign affidavits ... promising they will not interfere in the Islamic upbringing of children ... [such] paper proved worthless [in British courts]. If you go back to Islamic history, the majority of inter-faith couples that lived during and after the time of the Prophet ... did so in Muslim lands in the security of Muslim institutions, schools, colleges, courts, and within the context of a flourishing Islamic culture. The mother was free to practise her own faith, while the father took responsibility of raising the children in Islam. At no stage, was there any danger of the children reverting to Christianity or Judaism. Sadly such security does not exist here in the West ...[31]
>
> Q: What are the obligations to Muslims living in any *kāfir* non-Muslim country? Are we supposed to comply with the law of the land even if this law conflicts with the Sharī'ah?
>
> A. Before I go any further in answering this question, I would like to say I totally disagree with Muslims ... who while ... enjoying the

benefits of living in the West, have the gall to turn around and refer to non-Muslim inhabitants as *kāfir* [unbeliever]. Not only is such a term inaccurate, it is also indecent, rude and totally wrong ... [outside academic theological discourse] the correct Qur'ānic phrase is "People of the Book" ... disagree where you have to, but do it with civility, not rancour.

On the second question: I will begin by pointing out that Muslims enjoy innumerable freedoms in many western non-Muslim countries. Freedom to speak, think, to associate with whom they like. Freedoms which people in many Muslim countries only dream about ... in Britain ... the authorities do not prevent us from performing basic religious obligations. We pray, we fast, we hold Islamic meetings without the threat of being followed, abducted or detained. And at another level we are not forced to drink, womanise, or to enter into contracts that are against the Islamic point of view. Where our world-view differs from the law of the land, the safest course of action is to opt out as a conscientious objector – again, an opportunity to choose which is almost non-existent in most Muslim lands.[32]

Q: Will the good non-Muslims go to *Jannah*, Paradise? I would like to know whether there is a place in jannah for kind-hearted, sincere and genuinely honest non-Muslims – particularly those who are involved in selfless acts of humanitarianism towards Muslims. Sometimes I find it quite difficult to reconcile their not being Muslim when all around me, I see Muslim brothers and sisters constantly at each other's throats, exhibiting totally un-Islamic behaviour.

A: If we look into the Qur'ān, *sūra* 3: 85 ... it is very clear that God says: "**And as for anyone who desires a religion other than Islam (submission to Allah), it will not be accepted from him – and in the Hereafter he will be among the losers.**" As far as the *Aḥādīth* are concerned, it is authentically reported ... that the Prophet ... said: "By Him in Whose hands is the life of Muḥammad, whoever among the community of the Jews or the Christians hears about me, but does not affirm his belief in that which I have been sent, and dies in this state of disbelief, shall only be one of the denizens of Hellfire." So there is an obstacle in the path of jannah for those who are good-natured, well-mannered, warm-hearted people who do a lot of good to others – but who at the same time do not believe in Allah, and in His last Messenger and in the Final Day. As justice is one of God's attributes, He will compensate them for their kindness, but only in this life. He will bestow them with good health, peaceful existence, and many blessings on this earth – but that does not amount to safety in the life to come.[33]

Q: Why is apostasy punishable by death in Islamic law? I have heard that some scholars, notably Rashid Rida, have dissented from this view. Isn't this penalty a bit harsh bearing in mind that Islam allows freedom of worship and the Qur'ān itself declares that there is no compulsion in religion?

A: … In *sūra* 2: 217, Allah says, "**And whomsoever apostasies from amongst you and passes away as unbelievers, their good actions are lost in this life and the life to come, and they will be among those who dwell in hellfire.**" An authentic *ḥadīth* records the Prophet … as saying, "Whosoever changes his religion, kill him." In another report he said: "It is not allowed to shed the blood of a person except in three circumstances: disbelieving after believing, committing adultery and killing anyone without reason." The act of apostasy comprises two essential conditions: turning one's back on Islam and behaving in a hostile manner against the Islamic way of life. The punishment of apostasy is death … The gravity of the punishment reflects the gravity of the crime and also its nature. Islam is more than an individual faith that can be kept in isolation. *It is a faith, a social order and a legal system. In this sense, it is different to other religions, particularly Christianity, which has always separated personal belief from public life – in keeping with the statement of Jesus to render unto God and Caesar their respective dues.* Anyone committing apostasy is firstly going against Islam, secondly he is rebelling against Islamic society and thirdly, he is repudiating the *sharī'ah.* Publicly going against the social order and the legal system is considered to be an act of treason. Treason against the state in many countries … is still punishable by death. The idea that freedom to publicly turn away from Islam is a human right is propagated by those who are usually intent on subverting the Islamic way of life … When [Egyptian] scholars like Sheikh Muhammad al-Rida and Mahmud Shaltut, who was the rector of Al-Azhar, were talking about freedom of religion, they were concerned with private apostasy – something which remains confined to the heart of the individual.[34]

Dr Darsh was a significant and informed voice in the construction of a Muslim community in Britain. His status as an al-Azhar teacher of *kalām* (theology) gave weight to his forthright and unapologetic teaching about Islamic views of Christianity. What is evident from Dr

Darsh's column is that his frank espousal of Islamic supersession of Christianity does not preclude constructive personal and professional relationships with Christians.

However, his lack of understanding of western Christianity reinforces common sense views, widely held by Muslims, namely the existence of some rigid separation between religion and politics with Christianity content to remain in the private domain, indifferent to public life. Clearly Christian reflection on the relationship between church and state is different from Islamic reflection on the relationship of religion and politics, although if one takes the rich tradition of Sufism into account suspicion and even avoidance of too close a relationship with the centres of political power can be found there. What is surprising is that Dr Darsh lived in Britain in the 1980s at a time when the Church of England was frequently an outspoken critic of Mrs Thatcher's government.[35] Yet the whole conflict between the "established church" and the government simply passed him by. Certainly it did not lead him to question the supposed apolitical nature of Christianity.

IV. BRITISH MUSLIMS BETWEEN DIALOGUE AND DIATRIBE

Fortunately, this is not the end of the story. There are an increasing number of British Muslims who want to relate to wider society and are ready to work with Christians on a range of issues. I have documented elsewhere this pragmatic engagement with wider society in one British city within five contexts: local politics, race relations, education, business and inter-faith relations.[36] What is encouraging is the willingness of some Islamic institutions both to encourage this engagement and to enable it to develop into a principled religious encounter.

I shall focus here on the work of the Islamic Foundation in Leicester. The Foundation was the initiative of Khurshid Ahmad, a leader of Pakistan's Islamist movement, Jamā'at-i Islamī. The Islamic Foundation was registered in 1968 and became a religious and educational charity in 1971. Its work has concentrated on two main areas: educating the growing Muslim population in the West, particularly in Britain, and removing disinformation about Islam in the West. In 1978 it established an Inter-Faith unit.

The unit is now headed by Dr Ataullah Siddiqui, whose recently published monograph, Christian-Muslim Dialogue in the Twentieth

Century, from which I have already cited, was based on his Ph. D completed at the Centre for the Study of Islam and Christian-Muslim Relations in Birmingham, itself a collaborative venture between Christians and Muslims. As well as being active in Christian-Muslim relations, Dr Siddiqui co-edits with the Foundation's director, Dr Ahsan, a new journal, *Encounters, Journal of Inter-Cultural Perspectives* which is proving a valuable conduit for contemporary Muslim reflection and debate on inter-civilisational and inter-faith issues. Recent editions include contributions from distinguished Muslim scholars such as Tunisian Muhammad Talbi, Emeritus Professor of History in the University of Tunis and the Lebanese Shīʿ-ite scholar, Mahmoud Ayoub, Professor of Islamic Studies at Temple University in the USA, as well as Rachid al-Ghannouchi, the Tunisian Islamist leader.

In the light of the existence of a pervasive and dismissive anti-Christian polemic it comes as a relief to read the following words from an article in *Encounters* by Professor Talbi:

> Western society cannot be reduced, as we used to think, to the twinkling and glittering facades of the public bars and dancing halls. More than ever before it appears to me that the true "followers of the Book" ... are really pious, seeking salvation, and striving sincerely in the way of God, moved by values of charity and love of their neighbours. They pray. In these conditions, how, without pain and questioning, to dedicate them to hell.[37]

Such material represents a striking departure from both the polemical and apologetic approaches we have so far met. The Foundation is also able to make available information about debates elsewhere in Europe. In a recent article Dr Siddiqui wrote of an instructive development in France, whereby the Union of Muslim Organisations had brought together a group of *'ulamā'* with first-hand experience of the problems and issues of living as a minority in Europe. The consultation concluded that Muslims living in a non-Muslim majority country could no longer automatically be classified as living in the *Dār al-Ḥarb*, the House of War. The painful reality was that many Muslims had fled thither from *Dār al-Islām*, the House of Islam, because of persecution by dictatorial regimes. Such non-Muslim nations to which they had fled were better classified as *Dār al-'Ahd*, the Abode of Treaties,

> This entails Muslims living in harmony and co-operation with people around them ... The difference [in terminology] changes [their] whole

> perception ... *Dar al-Harb* suggests temporality, otherness and a sense of compulsion. *Dar al-'Ahd* suggests participation, belonging, and responsibility.[38]

Dr Siddiqui is fully aware that an Islamically grounded encounter with western Christianity poses myriad challenges: Who is to represent British Muslims with Churches and public bodies? Where are the national forums for Muslims to debate difficult and contentious issues? Many British Muslims have not yet formulated the important questions, let alone begun to address them. One urgent task is the need to re-think the meaning of the word "secular":

> 'Secular' with a capital 's' is routinely construed by Muslims as meaning a society without a belief in God, lacking a revelation, materialist and without a concept of an afterlife and, therefore, without any notion of divine accountability. There is a need to make space for 'secular' with a small 's': a society which respects religious diversity, where the different religions are free to influence public life, and where there is security for religious communities.[39]

What is encouraging is the beginning of a dialogue with evangelical Christians on the public role of Christianity and Islam in Britain. A conference in October 1998 jointly convened by Christians and Muslims is to take place at the Islamic Foundation with workshops on law, media, education, faith and civil society, the family, sexuality and gender. This is clearly a welcome initiative – it is envisaged that these workshops will continue to meet after the conference.

One welcome addition to the staff of the Inter-faith Unit at the Foundation is an L.S.E. graduate, Mr Sohail Nakhooda. Mr Nakhooda spent two years in Rome with the Dominicans studying Catholic theology before studying Protestant theology at Nottingham, where he is now working on a Ph. D comparing Biblical and Qur'ānic hermeneutics. Here, then, a Muslim institute is laying the foundation for a religiously serious and academically rigorous encounter with the Christian tradition.

Before I leave the Islamic Foundation it is worth rehearsing two reasons Dr Siddiqui advanced for Muslim involvement in interfaith dialogue with Christians and others in a Muslim publication which accompanied the national "Islam Awareness Week" in September 1997:

> Firstly, Christianity is ... one of the defining forces of Western culture and civilisation. Notwithstanding its denominational variations and

> historical developments, the concept of God, prophethood, sin and salvation are overwhelmingly provided by Christianity in Western society. Christianity in fact has provided a soul for Europe. Ethics and morals in the West have a strong connection with the Judaeo-Christian traditions on the one hand, and with Greco-Roman civilisation on the other. Therefore, Muslims who want to engage in *da'wah* have to grasp the understanding of the Judaeo-Christian perspectives on God, revelation, prophets, sin and salvation ... Secondly, there is a common thread that links so many faiths to God. Those who believe in God, despite the fact that their confessional identity is different, are under an obligation to join hands ... to face mutually perceived threats, such as ecology, social and moral issues, value of education, use and abuse of the doctrine of human rights, exploitation of women, child labour etc ... In other words, the areas which the Qur'ān describes as *mar'uf* (good) and *mankar* (bad) are the very areas of our engagement in dialogue.[40]

The useful publication *British Muslims Monthly Survey* (BMMS), produced by the Centre for the Study of Islam and Christian Muslim Relations in Birmingham, now includes an inter-faith section which indicates that an increasing number of Muslims are moving from diatribe to shared dialogue, especially at a civic level. We may suppose that they will provide a growing pool of British Muslims on which organisations such as the Islamic Foundation will increasingly be able to draw.

As always there exists an opposite pole, radical groups on the fringes of Muslim politics – *Hizb at-Tahrir* (HUT), the Party of Liberation – whose coinage is political diatribes against the West and whose simplistic appeals to return to the sources of the *Qur'ān* and *sunnah* often discount fifteen hundred years of history and disciplined reflection. The leadership, dynamics and rhetoric of such radical groups had been vividly and sympathetically drawn in a recent novel, *The Black Album*, by Hanif Kureishi.

Movements such as HUT with roots in the Middle East, have been fishing in the London campuses among Arab students and professionals since the early 1980s. However, from the late 1980s they began working in schools and universities across the country deliberately targeting the highly educated youth from factory-worker families of South Asian backgrounds.

> Compared with their parents and many other organizations within British Islam, the party appears not only intellectually sophisticated, but also radical and highly political. This combination has enabled it to

> exploit the growing cultural chasm between youth and their tradition-bound elders, and to tap into their feelings of alienation as they struggle to find a new identity against the background of their elders traditional preoccupations with subcontinental politics and social, norms.[41]

Such groups are frank about a civilisational conflict between Islam and the West. A typical contribution ends with the peroration:

> O Muslims! Do not let the *kuffar* take the initiative on our issues, and do not be fooled by them, thinking that they are "helping" the Muslims, as Allah ... clearly warns us of their poisonous schemes and warns us not to trust the *Kuffar* for they are allies, friends and protectors only of one another. Allah says, "O you who believe! Do not take your *'awliyah* (friends, allies, protectors) from the Jews and the Christians, they are *'awliyah* to each other" [*sūra* 5: 51].[42]

A meeting of HUT at Leicester University on 20 November 1997 distributed a leaflet, "The Inter-Faith Dialogue Campaign," a response to the creation of the three [Abrahamic] faiths forum in January 1997. The pamphlet presents this as part of a nefarious scheme by Christians and Jews to suggest some commonalities exist across the three faiths. "More specifically, it is hoped that the Muslims come to believe that Islam, like Judaism and Christianity, only deals with "spiritual matters." In this way 'Trialogue' aims to break Muslims away from referring to their [articles of belief] in political matters ... "[43] Here Christianity is presented as part of this civilisational conflict between the West and Islam. Unfortunately, such groups are good copy for the media and feed Islamophobia, which, in turn, creates the very alienation which makes such groups attractive to some students.

V. A CONTRIBUTION FROM MUSLIM ACADEMICS

In this chapter I have deliberately focused primarily on individuals reflecting on Christianity from within Islamic institutions. Such institutions remain influential in shaping Muslim attitudes towards Christianity, both negative and positive. There are, however, a small but increasing number of Muslim academics active in British universities, who also write about Christianity. I shall conclude by referring to two of them, one a specialist on race and ethnicity studies, the other a lecturer in Islamic Studies.

I have chosen Dr Modood because, while not a scholar of Islam, he has made a signal contribution to race and ethnic relations in this country by insisting on the importance of religious identity as a vital component of personal and communal self-understanding. This is particularly evident in *Ethnic Minorities in Britain, Diversity and Disadvantage*, an excellent volume he recently co-edited for the Policy Studies Institute, PSI, in London.

However, here I wish to draw attention to his writings on the established church. In an important article in the *Political Quarterly* - "Establishment, Multiculturalism and British Citizenship" – he challenged the ploy of those who, while antagonistic to any religion, urged dis-establishment on the basis of formal equality for all religions, without of course, canvassing the views of religious minorities themselves! Modood himself gave cautious support for the established church as offering a slight counterweight to a secular hegemony.

In a later book of essays which he edited – *Church, State and Religious Minorities* – the other Muslim contributor, Daoud Rosser-Owen, enlarged on Modood's position. He broadly agreed with the Chief Rabbi's position which was summarised thus:

- in the religious context of massive but incomplete secularisation, the fate of all religions, minority and majority, hang together.
- moreover, diversity requires that there be an over-arching public culture;
- if this public culture is to have a religious dimension, it will be that of the premier religion, which for historical reasons is the Church of England, consequently all minorities ought to support it as a national institution.[44]

To this Daoud Rosser-Owen added that the Muslim position was that politicians exercise authority as a temporary trust from God to whom they will be accountable on the Day of Judgement. The existence and role of the established churches in the United Kingdom goes some way to acknowledging this fact and is thus to be supported on this basis, albeit not uncritically. The book also included a perceptive contribution by Professor Bhikhu Parekh who challenged what he considered the untenable and long-held beliefs that only a secular state can be liberal and democratic.

Abdal Hakim Murad is an example of an English convert to Islam who has studied both at Cambridge (Arabic) and at Al-Azhar and is active in translating key Islamic texts into English. He is thus in an ideal position to interpret mainstream Islam to a British audience. At present he lectures in Islamic Studies at a prestigious British university. Murad's work is extensive and appears on the internet. I want to draw attention to three of his recent articles, "The Trinity: a Muslim Perspective," "Islamic Spirituality, the Forgotten Revolution" and "British and Muslim," the first was initially delivered to a group of Christians and the third was presented at a conference of British converts.

Murad's lecture on the Trinity is a model of courteous and religiously serious reflection by a Muslim thinker. He remarks that while

> medieval Islam knew much more about Christian doctrine than the doctors of the Church about Islam ... most of them never quite "got" the point about the Trinity. Their analysis can usually be faulted on grounds not of unsophistication, but of insufficient familiarity with the complexities of Scholastic or Eastern trinitarian thinking. Often they merely tilt at windmills.[45]

His own treatment pays tribute to the writings of the distinguished Jewish scholar, Professor Geza Vermes. Not surprisingly Murad's comments about the Trinity echo a now familiar line of criticism, namely that trinitarian speculation represents a desemiticised and hellenized reading of a semitic Jesus. Nevertheless, the Christian reading his article will clearly understand the Muslim perplexity and grounds for Islamic disquiet at such developments. Murad's willingness to engage with Christians directly in discussion of their central beliefs represents a welcome development in British Islamic reflection on Christianity.

The non-Muslim can also learn much from Murad's two other articles which together represent a robust defence of Islamic spirituality – Sufism – a perceptive analysis of the reasons for its eclipse amongst many contemporary young Muslim activists and an imaginative attempt to retrieve and repossess elements of English religiosity serviceable for the construction of an Anglo-Muslim identity. For our purposes his comments on the obscurantism and intolerance of *Wahhābī* Islam are pertinent and worrying. Murad insists that Saudi oil wealth is systematically being used to drown out the voices of mainstream Islam. "Many, even most Islamic publishing houses in Cairo and Beirut are now subsidised by Wahhabi organisations which prevent them from publishing traditional works on Sufism, and remove passages in other works unacceptable to Wahhabi doctrine."[46]

Such influence is not confined to Egypt and Lebanon. A recent study documenting the relationship between the West and the Arab élite noted Saudi Arabia's financial control of the extensive London Arabic-language newspapers and magazines. This includes some forty or fifty daily and weekly publications, more than the number published in Cairo, Beirut or the whole of Saudi Arabia, and includes the television station MBC and the BBC's World Television Arabic Service. "Because the Saudis want to use Beirut-on-Thames to monopolise Islamic teachings and advance their version of Islam, they have banned [the independent Islamic magazine] *Al-'Alam* and this publication also receives no advertising."[47]

Our review of attitudes to Christianity current within a selection of influential Islamic institutions and organisations in Britain has indicated a complex but changing situation. Ill-informed and dismissive caricatures still largely predominate, the legacy of a long history of mutual incomprehension, conflict and colonialism. However, what is also clear is that in certain quarters there are signs of the emergence of a constructive and religiously serious engagement. If British Muslims are allowed to develop their own agenda, without petrol dollars keeping a previous generation's polemic artificially alive, Britain could move into the new millennium with the foundation laid for an encounter which has few parallels in western history – a dialogue conducted by a Muslim minority not enjoying political power in a language other than Arabic. Because such a meeting would be conducted in English it could have a much wider impact, not least in Muslim majority areas.

NOTES

1 S. Vertovec and C. Peach, *Islam in Europe, the Politics of Religion and Community* (London: Macmillan, 1997), pp. 18–19).
2 See S. K. Aburish, *A Brutal Friendship: The West and the Arab Elite* (London: Indigo edition, 1998).
3 A. Siddiqui, *Christian-Muslim Dialogue in the Twentieth Century* (London: Macmillan, 1997), p. 196.
4 In this chapter because of the limits of space I have confined my attention to the majority Sunni communities. Such Shī'-ite organisations as the Al-Khoei Foundation in London produce an excellent journal devoted to dialogue.
5 A. Ahmed, *Postmodernism and Islam: Predicament and Promise* (London: Routledge, 1992), p. 177.
6 These figures were taken from an article by Mr Sher Azam the ex-President of Bradford Council for Mosques, in a newspaper promoting "Islam Awareness Week," 23–9 September, 1996. Mr Azam is a leading member of various national Muslim bodies including the recently formed

Muslim Council of Britain (MCB). Numbers for mosques are notoriously unreliable but this figure at least provides the order of magnitude assumed by a national body such as the MCB.

7 M. Saroha, *Heavenly Ornaments: Being an English Translation of Maulana Ashraf Ali Thanawi's Bahishti Zewar* (Lahore: 1981), p. 23.

8 Bury also offers 'A' level courses in Arabic, Urdu and Islamic Studies. The autumn 1998 term sees the first cohort of five students from Bury accepted to study on the BA course in applied theological studies offered by Westhill College of Higher Education in Birmingham. This innovative scheme majors on Islam and is largely taught by Muslim scholars. It is probably the first time a group of graduates from a traditional *madrasa* has sought to bridge the divide between their world and that of western study. The immediate incentive is largely economic – too many graduated from such Islamic institutions cannot find jobs outside the mosque.

9 Y. S. Sikand, "The Origins and Growth of the Tablighi Jamaat in Britain" (*Islam and Christian-Muslim Relations,* 9, 1998), p. 189.

10 See P. J. Lewis, "British Muslims and the Search for Religious Guidance," in J. Hinnels and W. Menski, *From Generation to Generation: Religious Reconstruction in the South Asian Diaspora* (London: Macmillan, 2000).

11 *The Invitation* (October/November 1997), p. 30.

12 M. S. Raza, *Islam in Britain, Past, Present and The Future* (Leicester: Volcano Press, 1991), p. 35.

13 *Ibid.*, pp. 55, 105.

14 Lonsdale and Laura Ragg, *The Gospel of Barnabas, edited and translated from the Italian MS in the Imperial Library at Vienna* (Oxford: Clarendon Press, 1907), p. 37.

15 See J. Slomp, "The 'Gospel of Barnabas' in Recent Research" (*Islamochristiana* 23, 1997) 81–109.

16 See H. Goddard, "Modern Pakistani and Indian Muslim Perspectives of Christianity" (*Islam and Christian-Muslim Relations*, 5, 1994) 165–88.

17 A. A. Powell, *Muslims and Missionaries in Pre-Mutiny India* (London: Curzon Press, 1993), p. 264.

18 A. Deedat, *Is the Bible God's Word?* (Birmingham: IPCI, 1987), p. 62.

19 *Ibid.*, p. 6.

20 See G. Butt, *The Arabs, Myth and Reality* (London: I. B. Tauris, 1997), p. 291.

21 K. Zebiri, *Muslim and Christians Face to Face* (Oxford: Oneworld, 1997), p. 45.

22 *Ibid.*, p. 87.

23 In the letter columns of the Muslim magazine *Q-News* under the heading "Wahhabi Arrogance" a writer fro London recently drew attention to a pamphlet about Christianity sponsored by the Islamic Cultural Centre in London. The writer asked rhetorically, "What are the implications for inter-religious harmony in Britain when the most visible representative institution of British Muslims supports extreme and vituperative pamphleteering against another religion. Who, in fact sponsors the Islamic Cultural Centre? None other than the Saudi Embassy . . . which is committed to spreading the Wahhabi creed. The Saudis are sponsoring insults and abuse to the religion of the English crown . . .!" October 1998,

p. 4. The fact that such a letter was published in a Muslim magazine suggests that some British Muslims are worried about the implications of such a policy.

24 J. Nevo, "Religion and National Identity in Saudi Arabia" (*Middle Eastern Studies* 34:3, 1998), p. 35.

25 A. AL-Azmeh, *Islams and Modernities* (London: Verso, 1993), p. 105

26 B. Lewis (ed.), *Muslims in Europe* (London: Pinter Publishers), p. 16.

27 Z. Badawi, *Islam in Britain* (London: Taha Publishers), p. 27.

28 S. Z. Abedin, "Minority Crises: Majority Options," in H. Mutalib and T. Hashmi (eds.), *Islam, Muslims and the Modern State* (London: Macmillan, 1994), p. 36.

29 See G. Blunt, "Decision-Making Concerns in British Islamic Environments" (*Islam and Christian-Muslim Relations* 9:1, 1998) 103–13.

30 *Q-News,* October 1997, p. 14.

31 *Ibid.*, 17–24 June, 1994, p. 5.

32 S. M. Darsh, *Questions and Answers about Islam* (London: Taha Publishers, 1997), pp. 154–5.

33 *Ibid.*, pp. 199–200.

34 Q-News, 28June–4July, 1996, p. 5. Dr. Darsh's position on apostacy has a respectable lineage but is increasingly being challenged. A good recent treatment can be found in Muhammad Hashim Kamali's *Freedom of Expression in Islam* (Cambridge: Islamic Texts Society, 1997). The Sudanese Islamist leader Hasan Abdullah al-Turabi has also challenged the traditional teachings in a robustly argued article in the magazine *The Diplomat*, June 1996, pp. 38–9.

35 See H. Clark, *The Church Under Thatcher* (London: SPCK, 1993).

36 See P. J. Lewis, "Arenas of Ethnic Negotiation: Co-operation and Conflict in Bradford," in T. Modood and P. Werbner (eds.), *The Politics of Multiculturalism in the New Europe* (London: Zed Books, 1997), pp. 126–46.

37 H. Goddard, "Christianity from the Muslim Perspective: Varieties and Changes," in J. Waardenburg (ed.) *Islam and Christianity, Mutual Perceptions since the Mid-20th Century* (Leuven: Peters, 1998), p. 248.

38 A. Siddiqui, "Muslims in the Contemporary World: Dialogue in Perspective," *World Faiths Encounter* (20 July 1998), pp. 26–7.

39 I owe these remarks to a recent conversation at the Islamic Foundation with Dr Siddiqui. I wish to put on record my gratitude to him for his help in researching this chapter and his generosity in giving me copies of his articles, some of which have not yet been published.

40 *Islam Awareness Week* (September 1997).

41 S. Taji-Farouki, *A Fundamental Quest: Hizb al-Tahrir and the Search for the Islamic Caliphate* (London: Grey Seal), p. 178.

42 *Khilafah Magazine* (5:2, September 1995). There is clearly a hermeneutical task facing Muslim scholars in the West to decide which verses in the Qur'ān are to be considered normative and in what circumstances when relating to Christians. HUT's selection is intelligible given their ideology. But so are those selected by eirenc scholars such as Professor Akbar. In his recent study accompanying a major BBC television series – Living Islam: From Samarkand to Stornaway (London: BBC Books, 1993) – it is

intimated that *sūra* 5: 82 shapes Muslim perspectives on Christianity, namely: "You will find the most affectionate among them towards those who believe are those who say, 'we are Christians'" (*ibid.*, p. 31). He is silent on *sūra* 5: 51.

43 A. Siddiqui, "Issues in Co-existence and Dialogue, Muslims and Christians in Britain," (unpublished paper, 1997), p. 14.

44 Daoud Rosser-Owen, "A Muslim Perspective" in T. Modood (ed.), *Church, State and Religious Minorities* (London: Policy Studies Institute, 1997), p. 82.

45 A. H. Murad, "The Trinity: A Muslim Perspective," 1997, p. 1. http://ds.dial.pipex.com/masud/ISLAM/ahm/british.htm

46 *Ibid.*, "Islamic Spirituality: The Forgotten Revolution," 1998, p. 9. See E. Sirriyeh, *Sufis and anti-Sufis: The Defence, Rethinking and Rejection of Sufism in the Modern World* (London: Curzon, 1999) for a useful historical survey of this ongoing struggle across the Muslim world.

47 S. K. Aburish, *A Brutal Friendship*, p. 361.

10

Christian-Muslim Relations in Nigeria and Malaysia

Hugh Goddard

At first sight the topic of this chapter may appear to be rather different from the other chapters of this book. They focus on Muslim perceptions of Christianity, in different historical periods and in different regions of the world, whereas this paper, by contrast, focuses on the rather different matter of the relationships between the Christian and Muslim communities in two important regions of the world. Part of the reason for this difference is that neither Nigeria nor Malaysia has produced very much distinctive or original Muslim thinking about Christianity, most of the literature about Christianity which is found there being derivative from other material produced elsewhere.[1] But a more important reason is that in these two contexts, for a number of reasons which will be made clear later, an even more urgent issue than the way in which Muslims perceive Christianity (or how Christians perceive Islam) is the practical matter of the day-to-day relationships between the communities.

METHODOLOGY

The observations and conclusions in this chapter are based upon visits to each country which were undertaken during Sabbatical leave from my university in 1993.[2] I was able to spend roughly five weeks in each country, as follows: in Nigeria I flew out to Lagos, the traditional capital of Nigeria, in the southern, more Christian, part of the country, and from there I travelled north to Ibadan, the seat of the oldest university in the country, and on northwards, firstly to Jos, in the Middle Belt (which is mixed religiously), and then finally to Zaria, Sokoto and Kano in the traditionally more Islamic north of the country. In each of these places I tried to visit firstly universities and secondly Christian and Muslim institutions and leaders in order to gain insights into both the academic study of religion in Nigeria and the perspectives of religious communities on Christian-Muslim Relations and their political implications. I was able to make some particularly useful contacts in Ibadan, but attempts to develop contacts in northern universities were somewhat hampered by strikes during the second half of my visit.

In Malaysia I flew out to and returned from Kuala Lumpur, which served as my main base throughout my visit, but from there I travelled both north, to Ipoh and Penang, and south, to Malacca and Singapore, in Peninsula (West) Malaysia, and I was also able to spend ten days in East Malaysia, in Sabah, learning about the rather different religious situation there. Again my approach was to visit universities and religious institutions, both Christian and Muslim, and I am grateful to many colleagues and friends in both the academic and the religious communities for their time and help in gaining some understanding of the complexity of Christian-Muslim Relations in each country.[3]

RATIONALE

The reason for selecting these two countries for investigation with respect to Christian-Muslim Relations was essentially that in both of these regions Islam and Christianity have become established relatively recently, in other words they have not been present since the earliest phases of their expansion. Both Christianity and Islam, obviously, had their roots in the Middle East, but with the expansion of Islam in the seventh century CE the heartland of the Christian church initially moved westwards and northwards to Europe, and then from there to all continents, including West Africa and South-East Asia, in the modern period. Islam, by contrast, moved northwards from Arabia to incorporate firstly the southern and eastern shores of the Mediterranean Sea and Iran, and secondly South-Eastern Europe, Central Asia and the Indian Sub-Continent, and then from this central region it worked out later to the "further Islamic world" – West Africa and South-East Asia.[4]

In West Africa and South-East Asia, then, the student discovers regions where Islam and Christianity met at similar stages of their expansion. In West Africa Islam spread through trade, across the Sahara Desert, working down from the north; Christianity also spread as a result of trade, but sea-trade in this case, first in the hands of the

Portuguese and later in the hands of the British and the French, so that it was established first on the coast and then worked inland from there. In South-East Asia too the two faiths spread in the wake of trade, with Islam this time arriving by sea from the West, from India, and Christianity arriving by sea from both West and East, through the agency of the Portuguese and the Dutch from the West, across the Indian Ocean, and the Portuguese and the Spanish from the East, across the Pacific Ocean. So today in both West Africa and South-East Asia Christians and Muslims meet, in the context of their total histories, as relatively recent arrivals. Within these regions Nigeria and Malaysia were selected simply on the basis of both being to a large extent English-speaking.

THE SITUATION IN NIGERIA

Nigeria is in many ways the giant of Africa – according to some figures one in five Africans is Nigerian and one in three Black Africans (i.e. discounting the Arabs of the north of Africa) is Nigerian. It is not the largest African country in terms of area – which is the Sudan – but it is by far the largest in terms of population, which is currently estimated at about 120 million and growing fast, to the extent that, according to some estimates, in around 25 years time Nigeria will be the fourth most populous nation in the world, after China, India and Indonesia, and in front of the current third and fourth most populous nations in the table, the USA and Russia.

The nation was created in the early years of the twentieth century, by the British, and the name Nigeria was coined by the correspondent of the Times in the country at the time, based upon the name of the major river of the country, the Niger, but in such a way as to distinguish it from the French colony of Niger, further upstream.

In terms of the make-up of the population Nigeria is a staggeringly diverse country, with some 250 ethnic/language groups within its borders. (It is for this reason that English is still the official language, as in India). Three groups are particularly significant, the Yoruba in the south-west, the Ibo (or Igbo) in the south-east, and the Hausa in the north and north-west. These three, however, even put together, make up only some 50% of the population.

Religiously, the situation is also complex. Basically, as already suggested, Islam is the dominant religion in the north, having worked its way across the Sahara, while Christianity is the dominant religion in the south having spread up from the coast in some kind of association with British colonial influence, which was established first on the coast. More particularly, this means that the Hausa are overwhelmingly, but not entirely, Muslim; the Ibo are overwhelmingly, but not entirely Christian, with Roman Catholic influence particularly strong; and the Yoruba, most interestingly, are roughly 50/50 – i.e. half Christian and half Muslim.

The other ethnic/language groups – which make up the other half of the population – are also split between two faiths, with those in the north tending to be Muslim and those in the south tending to be Christian. So the population of Nigeria as a whole is roughly half Christian and half Muslim. But the statistics, of course, are highly unreliable, and the fairly even balance between the two main religious communities is, as might be expected, the cause of some tensions and problems. A good illustration of this can be seen in a BBC television programme which was shown while I was in Nigeria in 1993. The final programme of the series entitled "Living Islam," presented by Akbar Ahmad, then the Muhammad Iqbal Fellow in the University of Cambridge, included interviews with a number of religious leaders, both Christian and Muslim, from the city of Kano, concerning the riots which had taken place there between the two communities during the previous five years. During one interview with a Christian priest, in response to the question "How would you react if Muslims launched a *Jihad* (Holy War) against Christians?" the reply was that there was a well-established Christian response to such a move, namely a Crusade. Relationships between the two communities in some parts of the country are thus rather tense.

What we have therefore, in this situation of a population which is roughly half Christian and half Muslim, is essentially competition for not only religious but also political influence. If the Christians can get to 51% of the population, then they will be able to set up a Christian state – and the above mentioned extract from the television programme gives a little flavour of what exactly a Christian state might going to mean. And if the Muslims can get to 51% of the population, then they will argue that they will be entitled to set up an Islamic state, with its legal system based on the Sharīʿa (Islamic Law). Neither, of course, has very much enthusiasm for the vision of the other. The Christians see the Muslim quest for an Islamic state as meaning that the Muslims will be unhappy unless the state is actively discriminating in their favour – against, that is the Christians. And the Muslims interpret the Christian search for, if not a Christian then at least a secular state, as meaning that the Christians want a godless state

– so there is a lot of education to be done concerning the difference between secularism as an ideology and the secular (in the sense of religiously neutral) state.

This competition also has some interesting effects within both major religious communities, but perhaps particularly within the Christian community. In economics competition is meant to keep things like inflation down, but in religion, in Nigeria at least, it seems to result in rapid inflation, or escalation, of the claims that are made by different Christian groups. Posters seen in different Nigerian cities, advertising Christian meetings, are powerful evidence of this. One claimed to offer attenders at the meeting "Healing, Salvation, Success, Prosperity and Dominion" while another offered "Unforgettable Encounter, Unprecedented Answers to Prayers, Fruitfulness and Spiritual Progress, Restoration and Renewal, Personal Revival and Divine Visitation" (no less). And the names of the organisations concerned are also telling – "Holy Ghost Thunderbolt" and "God-will-do-it Ministries" to name but two.[5]

Denominationalism seems to have run amok in Nigeria, so that according to some estimates, a new Christian denomination is created every day, but what denomination usually means is simply a man (or woman), a friend, a hall or building of some kind, a loudspeaker system (essential) and somebody willing or gullible enough to pay for the hire or use of the hall. And in this state of denominational anarchy the claims which are made by different groups or individual evangelists become even more dramatic. To give another example, ecclesiastical titles also seem to become victims of inflation, so that the Head of the Methodist Church in one part of Nigeria calls himself Patriarch.[6] The Muslims have something of the same problem of different individuals and organisations establishing themselves on the basis of their own programmes, but the problem is not as great.

This competition between the two major religious communities for influence also has some other results, particularly in the field of ecumenism. To gain influence, Christians clearly have to co-operate, and so as well as the well-established but not particularly active Christian Council of Nigeria, which had its roots in the world-wide move towards trying to establish local united Christian (or at least Protestant) churches in the years after World War II, there is now also the Christian Association of Nigeria, which attempts to speak for the whole Christian community in dealing with the government. The criteria for membership of these two bodies are strikingly different: to be accepted as a member of the former, things like theology, acceptance of creeds, and the concept of authority are important, whereas to join the latter all that matters is that a person calls him or her self a Christian. This point was made powerfully by an Anglican Bishop in the south of the country, who, when asked who could join the Christian Association of Nigeria, replied: "Anyone," and then after a moment's thought added "provided that they call themselves a Christian." Such are the results of the determination to get to that magical figure of 51% as soon as possible.[7]

So for the future the relationship between the Christian and Muslim communities in Nigeria is likely to be tense. In many towns and cities, especially in the north, there have been riots in recent years, with in some cases thousands meeting their end. The causes of these riots have as often as not been economic, political and social, but the readiness with which some religious leaders have publicly interpreted them as essentially religious conflicts and also the extreme insensitivity towards the feelings and opinions of the other community which has sometimes been evident in both major communities, as seen, for example, in the visit of the South African evangelist Reinhard Bonnke to Kano, do not inspire much confidence for the future.[8]

All this unfolds in the midst of an economic crises that is dire by any standards. When oil was discovered in considerable quantities in Nigeria in the 1970s, it seemed like good fortune; oil quickly became the country's largest export, earning up to 90% of its foreign exchange. When the price of oil plummeted, however, Nigeria found itself earning a mere 20% of what it had been earning, and in a situation of such dire economic necessity tension between communities, including, perhaps especially, religious ones, is likely to increase.

While I was in Nigeria some observers were hopeful that the general election, planned for June 1993, would ease some of the tensions, since, they argued, if people could argue about politics (which they were not able to do under the military government) then they would be less likely to argue about religion, but although the election took place the military government declared the result, a victory for the Yoruba Muslim Chief Moshood Abiola, invalid, and the transfer of power from the military to civilian rule only took place in May 1999.[9]

The situation is perhaps most hopeful among the Yoruba, who are, as mentioned earlier, roughly half Christian and half Muslim, so that among them it is not uncommon to find families in which some members are Christian and some Muslim. The Anglican Bishop of

Ibadan, for example, told me that his uncle, a Muslim, came to his consecration and enjoyed the occasion very much. Here, then, family loyalties and identity seem to outweigh religious loyalty and identity, both Christian and Muslim. But even here one of the most disconcerting of recent years has been the growth of groups sponsoring a much more militant and antagonistic approach to other communities – and this is true of both Christians and Muslims, some of whom are falling under the influence of confrontational groups, usually from North America and Iran respectively.

An example of this may be found on the campus of the University of Ibadan where there are two Christian chaplaincies, one Anglican and one Roman Catholic, near the new mosque of the Muslim community. Opposite the Roman Catholic Chaplaincy is a concrete cross, and between the cross and the mosque is a large concrete screen, intended to prevent, or at least minimise, the possibility of members of one community seeing the place of worship and religious symbols of the other. In many respects, this seems to symbolise very effectively the attitudes of some members of both Christian and Muslim communities to the other. I was not able to ascertain, however, which community was responsible for the building of the screen: Muslims assured me that the Christians had built it because they were jealous of the new mosque and did not wish to look at it, while Christians assured me that the Muslims had built it because they did not wish to see the sign of the cross.

This incident indicates a less positive model of Christian-Muslim Relations. But in both communities there are some who view these developments with considerable alarm and try to develop a more positive model of Christian-Muslim interaction, for example through PROCMURA, the Programme for Christian-Muslim Relations in Africa. Which group gains influence will be interesting to see, and depends, I suspect, on developments outside Nigeria anyway.[10]

THE SITUATION IN MALAYSIA

Malaysia is a country which in many ways could not be more different from Nigeria. Firstly it is much smaller, with a population of around 20 million. Secondly it is much more homogenous than Nigeria, though as we shall see that does not preclude the existence of considerable variety. And thirdly, until the global economic crisis of 1998, it has been a spectacular economic success. This economic success is also of interest in the Asian context, as of the "East Asian Tigers," the countries whose rates of economic growth have exceeded those of any other country over the last decade or so (Taiwan, South Korea, Singapore, Hong Kong, Thailand and Malaysia), Malaysia is the only one which has a Muslim majority population, and this raises some interesting questions in connection with the debate about the contribution of "Asian values" to the region's economic success.

As hinted already, however, Malaysia, despite being more homogenous than Nigeria, does contain considerable diversity. In particular the ethnic mix of the population contains three main groups. Firstly there are the Malays, the original inhabitants of the country, and indeed of the rest of what was once called the Malay Archipelago (i.e. including Indonesia); this group makes up the bare majority of the population as a whole and so is usually stated to be 51% of the population.[11] Secondly, there is a substantial Chinese population, usually reckoned at about 35% of the population; the Chinese are the traders and entrepreneurs of East Asia, rather like the Germans in some parts of eastern Europe, and the majority of them arrived in what is now Malaysia in the 19th or 20th centuries, either to develop industries such as the tin industry, or to take part in trading and other business activity. Thirdly there is then a substantial Indian minority, usually put at about 10% of the population, which was brought in by the British colonial administrators in the 19th century to perform various tasks such as working on the rubber plantations, running the railways and assisting in the civil service and the educational and legal professions. The remaining 5% of the population belong to what are sometimes called tribal groups, living in the more inaccessible regions of the country.

Religiously this works out as follows: all Malays are Muslims, so that it is technically not possible to be Malay without being Muslim, although it is possible to be Muslim without being Malay, by, say being a Chinese or Indian Muslim.[12] Islam is thus the largest religious community in Malaysia, and is indeed described in the Constitution as being the state religion. The majority of the Chinese are believers in what is usually called traditional Chinese religion, a kind of synthesis of ancient Chinese custom, Confucianism, Taoism and Buddhism, and the majority of Indians are Hindu, but in both of these ethnic groups other religions are also represented. Thus some Indians are Sikh, some Chinese and Indians are Muslims, and in both there is a significant Christian presence.

At this point an important geographical point needs to be made: the modern state of Malaysia consists of two distinct territorial areas, which are separated by over 1,000 miles of ocean. Partly because of this the two halves of the state are rather different. West Malaysia, which is far more populous and prosperous, is sometimes referred to as Peninsula Malaysia, and is made up of what used to be called the Malay Federated States, which were assembled into a federation by the British at the end of the 19th century. East Malaysia, far less developed or sophisticated, is made up of two states, Sarawak and Sabah, each of which has its own distinctive history. Sarawak was given by the British government in the 19th century to an adventurer or trader called Charles Brooke, and administered as a kind of personal fief by him and his descendants. Sabah, by contrast, was run by a British trading company, the North Borneo Company. When Britain in the 1960s withdrew from colonial responsibilities all of these units were linked together to form the new state of Malaysia. Why?

The main reason for the link was concern on the part of the British government over the ethnic balance within the independent nation. The first idea was to give independence to the Federated Malay States, including Singapore. Since Singapore, though, was overwhelmingly Chinese in population, this would have resulted in the Malays, the original inhabitants of the area, being a minority in the new state. The idea of including Sarawak and Sabah in the new state was therefore to ensure that the Chinese would remain in a minority. Singapore soon withdrew from Malaysia anyway, which solved this problem, but the linking of what are now known as West and East Malaysia had some interesting consequences religiously.

In West Malaysia Christians are a tiny minority of the population, perhaps 3% only. But in Sabah Christians and Muslims are roughly equal in number, perhaps 25% each, and in Sarawak Christians make up the largest religious group, consisting of perhaps one third of the population. (The remaining population belongs to different tribal groups in the interior, apart from small Chinese and Indian communities). In Malaysia as a whole, therefore, the Christian population is perhaps 8%.

This has some interesting consequences politically. In West Malaysia, despite the large non-Malay presence, the whole tradition has been that it is the Malays who are politically dominant – thus the king, the Prime Minister and the chief ministers of each of the states have all traditionally been Muslims. In East Malaysia, however, the Chief Minister of Sabah when I visited the state in 1993, was a Roman Catholic Christian, Datuk Joseph Pairin Kittingan, who was sworn in as Chief Minister of Sabah in 1986. The party which he led, the United Sabah Party, was always careful to present itself as representing the whole population of Sabah, and not simply the Christian elements within it, but the Chief Minister's religious identity did seem to cause some tension between the central and state governments, though other factors, both political and economic, were also responsible for this.

Whatever the cause of these tensions, it is undeniable that the government of Sabah prior to 1993 had followed policies significantly different from those of the central government in matters of religion, particularly by giving state financial help to both Christian and Muslim groups, whereas the federal government gave support only to Muslim activities. Thus in Sabah state money was made available not only for the construction of a state mosque, which is a common pattern throughout Malaysia, but also – uniquely – for the construction of the Roman Catholic Cathedral, the Anglican Cathedral, and many other churches too. The situation in East Malaysia as regards Christian-Muslim Relations was therefore significantly different from that in West Malaysia.

One other religious development of note was taking place in Malaysia at the time of my visit, namely a debate about Islamisation. This, of course, is a debate which is by no means unique to Malaysia, as many Islamic societies, from the Sudan to Iran and Pakistan, have all proclaimed their intention of pursuing policies based on the pursuit of Islamisation, but some features of the debate in Malaysia are particularly interesting.

Generally in a Malaysian context the approach to Islamisation has been a gentle and moderate one, stressing the importance of gradually raising the profile of Islam in different aspects of public life, including education. Manifestations of this approach include the establishment of a number of high-powered political and cultural think-tanks devoted to the study and promotion of Islam, for example ISTAC (The International Institute of Islamic Thought and Civilization) established in 1987, and IKIM (The Institute of Islamic Understanding, Malaysia) established in 1992. The intention behind the establishment of these institutes seems to be twofold: firstly, by stressing the great achievements of Islamic Civilisation in its medieval heyday, the intention is to stress the relevance of Islam as a progressive force, rather than the backward-looking force it is sometimes understood to be. By stressing the tolerance and cultural glories of medieval Spain, for example, it is hoped that modern Malaysia can progress rapidly in the scientific and economic areas without having to sacrifice anything of its Islamic identity.[13]

The stress on Islam is also intended to counteract the trend whereby in all other developing societies so far, at least, material progress has led to moral and ethical decline. Islamisation is meant as a kind of inoculation against this process. It was interesting to find Malay Muslim academics, with Ph.Ds from Western universities on subjects such as Islamic ethics, in positions where they advise the Prime Minister on ethics in the school curriculum, and host weekly television programmes designed in part to highlight the importance of traditional Muslim ethics.[14]

But the whole policy of Islamisation has other effects too: firstly, even if the central government's pronouncements and policies have generally been moderate and applied carefully, this has not prevented the emergence of Islamic groups whose views have been more extreme, such as the group known as al-Arqam, founded as long ago as 1968, but whose activities the government sought to restrict in 1994, or the coming to power in the north-eastern state of Kelantan, in 1990, of PAS (The Islamic Party of Malaysia) which caused considerable controversy in the field of law when it decreed that Islamic law was to be made applicable to all citizens, regardless of religion. This meant that, contrary to the main tradition of classical Islamic law, the Islamic prohibition of alcohol was to be applied even to the Chinese community, for whom, at the time of the Chinese New Year the consumption of alcohol is practically a religious obligation. The state government, by its zeal for Islamisation thus succeeded only in embarrassing the federal government.[15]

Secondly the policy of Islamisation has had some unfortunate consequences with respect to the position of the Christian minority in Malaysia, since part of the intention of the policy seems to have been to raise the level of confidence in Islam among Muslims and thus to heighten their sense of a distinctive Muslim identity. One illustration will have to suffice: the government has seen fit to intervene in the rather sensitive matter of Bible translation by the Christians. In particular it has prohibited the use of Bible translations where the word which in English translations occurs as "God" appears in the Malay versions as "Allah," which is, of course, the word used in the Qur'ān.[16] This, interestingly, is exactly the opposite course to that adopted by the neighbouring Muslim country Indonesia, which has prohibited the use of Bibles in which the word for "God" is represented by anything other than "Allah." Theology, Bible translation, and government policy concerning the identity of citizens thus seem to have become thoroughly intertwined, with some interesting questions as to the priority of the three emerging.

There have been several different Christian responses to these challenges. Firstly, efforts have been made to establish groups which can speak for the Christian community as a whole in commenting on matters of public life: thus in addition to the Council of Churches in Malaysia, which was established in the 1940s to create links between the mainline Protestant churches, in 1986 the Christian Federation of Malaysia was set up, and this group represents some 95% of Malaysian Christians, including Roman Catholics and Evangelical Christians as well as the churches involved in the Council of Churches.[17] Secondly, given the religious diversity in Malaysia as a whole, in 1983 the Malaysian Consultative Council of Buddhism, Christianity, Hinduism and Sikhism was established, in order to represent the interests of all the non-Muslim communities in the country where they coincide, as they do on such matters as proposals to apply Islamic Law to all Malaysian citizens rather than to Muslims only.

On a more theological level, it is possible to discern widely differing evaluations of Islamisation and of Islam in general among the Christians in Malaysia. In particular, there seem to be widely differing attitudes among Chinese and Indian Christians on these questions, with Chinese Christians generally being far more negative about Islam in general and fearful of Islamisation in particular, and Indian Christians being generally more positive about Islam, and more relaxed about Islamisation. This was true among Anglicans and among Jesuits to name just two.[18]

What are the possible reasons for the difference? Three explanations may be offered. One is the different theological opinions of the different groups, some being more "exclusivist" and some being more "inclusivist." This works for Anglicans, as of the Anglican missionary societies it was the more catholic USPG which worked among Indian Anglicans and the more evangelical CMS which worked among Chinese Anglicans, but clearly it does not work for the Jesuits. Two other factors therefore suggest themselves. Perhaps religious developments in China and India, with which overseas Chinese and Indian Christians certainly keep in touch, are responsible: China, after all, has seen harsh repression of the church since the Revolution in 1949, and perhaps this makes all Chinese Christians particularly sensitive to any whiff of religious harassment. India, by contrast, is a secular state, and with one or two recent exceptions there has generally been a shared emphasis on religious co-operation. The third reason for the different attitudes towards Islam among Indian and Chinese Christians is the Malaysian situation itself, and the fact of the government's policy of expanding the proportion of the economy which is run by Malays. The group which has suffered most from this policy is the Chinese, since prior to the implementation of this policy, it had an overwhelming predominance in business. It is probably this reason, namely the economic disadvantage experienced by the Chinese (including Christian Chinese) at the hands of the (Muslim) Malays which is the most important in explaining their different attitudes towards Islam, and this raises interesting general questions about the social context of theology.

CONCLUSION

Two points perhaps above all emerge from the experience of visiting these two countries and observing something of the contemporary realities of Christian-Muslim Relations within them.

Firstly, different as they are, the experience of both Nigeria and Malaysia points to the truth of the statement that for the foreseeable future in matter religious one of the most important questions on a global level is going to be the relationship between Christianity and Islam. Is it going to be a question of competition and confrontation, or is it going to be rather a relationship of co-operation and mutual exploration? The recent Nigerian experience of riots between Christians and Muslims may not be particularly encouraging on this question, but there are more positive models available there and it will be interesting to see which perspective wins out.[19]

Secondly, and this is a fundamental question of an ethical nature for both communities: what does love for one's neighbour mean today in a plural society? Does it mean "love your neighbour provided that he/she is a member of your own religious community (or at least not the other community)?" – or does it mean – "love your neighbour even if, maybe especially if, he/she is a member of another/the other community?" And how does all this work out with respect to questions of citizenship – is citizenship to be linked in some way to religious allegiance, and is the alternative of separating the two from each other a secular idea which will prove unacceptable to Muslims in particular? These perhaps are the questions which have only just begun to be addressed, both in Nigeria and Malaysia. But as recent events in South-Eastern Europe have shown, they are questions which need further reflection in every continent.[20]

NOTES

1 See, for example, from Nigeria, A. D. Ajijola, *The Myth of the Cross* (Lahore: Islamic Publications, 1975). This is a fairly traditional Muslim account of Christianity, stressing the historical corruption of the Christian message over the course of the centuries, beginning with St. Paul. The author was a barrister in several of the northern states of Nigeria, and it is interesting that his book was printed in Pakistan and distributed in Nigeria from there. In South-East Asia, there may not be very much original thinking about Christianity emanating from Malaysia, but the situation is rather different in Indonesia: see, for example, W. C. Hofsteede "Muslim Initiatives for Harmonious Relations in Indonesia" in *Studies in Inter-religious Dialogue* 2 (1992), pp. 123–35, K. Steenbrink, "The Study of Comparative Religion by Indonesian Muslims" in *Numen* 37 (1990), pp. 141–167, and idem. "Indonesian Politics and a Muslim Theology of Religions 1965–1990" in *Islam and Christian-Muslim Relations* 4 (1993), pp. 223–46.

2 The financial support of the British Academy in making these visits possible is gratefully acknowledged.

3 In Malaysia I was able to meet in particular a researcher in whose footsteps I discovered myself to be following, and to whose researches I would like to acknowledge my debt: see G. Basri, *A Comparative Study on Religious Tolerance in Post-independence Malaysia and Nigeria, with Special Reference to Christian-Muslim Relations*, unpublished Ph.D. thesis, University of Aberdeen, 1988. Dr. Basri's research provides a far greater degree of detail than my own, since as well as being a Malaysian citizen he was able to spend ten weeks in Nigeria, during the course of which he was able to visit all of the (then) twenty states in the country. Elements of Dr. Basri's research have subsequently been published as *Nigeria and the Shari'ah: Aspirations and Apprehensions* (Leicester: Islamic Foundation, 1994), and *Christian Mission and Islamic Da'wah in Malaysia* (Kuala Lumpur: Nurin Enterprise, 1990), but in some instances the emphasis in the published versions is slightly different from the material in the original thesis.

4 Convenient summaries of this process for the two communities may be found in H. Chadwick and G. R. Evans (eds.), *Atlas of the Christian Church* (London: Macmillan, 1987), especially pp. 146–61 for Christian expansion into Africa and Asia; and F. Robinson, *Atlas of the Islamic World Since 1500* (Oxford: Phaidon, 1982), especially pp. 88–100 for the expansion of Islam into South-East Asia and into sub-Saharan Africa.

5 Newer religious groups have also begun to establish a presence. To give just one example, posters for the movement associated with the Maharishi Yogi boldly proclaimed: "Nigeria: the New Holy Land."

6 The classic study of this phenomenon in the African context is D. Barrett, *Schism and Renewal in Africa: An Analysis of Six Thousand Contemporary Religious Movements* (Nairobi: Oxford University Press, 1968). Barrett is also the source of the suggestion that a new Christian denomination is established every day.

7 Inter-religious competition has some other intriguing consequences. For example, since the *Hajj*, the annual Muslim pilgrimage to Mecca, is a religious obligation, the government has sometimes provided financial assistance for Muslims to participate in it. One consequence of this has been demands from some Christians for government financial support for Christian pilgrimages too, as the following newspaper article, under the headline "Christian pilgrims seek N15 [Naira, the unit of Nigerian currency] to $1 exchange rate," makes clear:

> "Fearing that the precipitous decline in naira value may prevent many christians from performing this year's pilgrimage, the Executive Secretary of Plateau State Christian Pilgrims Welfare Board, Mr. Joseph Gotwa, has suggested a N15 to a dollar concessionary exchange rate for potential pilgrims …
>
> "Although a provisional fare of N50,000 per person has been announced for christian pilgrims, with the announcement of fare for moslem pilgrims, usually below that of the christians, it is expected that the ultimate fare for the christians could be higher.
>
> "The hajj fare is less than that of christian pilgrims, because most moslem pilgrims go direct to Saudi Arabia, whereas christians have to fly to London, before connecting flight to Rome and Tel Aviv.
>
> "They also pay more for accommodation because they have to stay in hotels while moslems have the option of staying in tents if they cannot afford hotels.
>
> "Last year, pilgrims to Rome and Jerusalem paid N26,710 as fare because the Federal Government gave them a special rate of N10 to the dollar when the official rate was N17 to the dollar …
>
> "Gotwa said …: 'If the government accepts to give us N15 to the dollar, special rate, the N50,000 will substantially cover the cost of the trip …', adding that many pilgrims may have to cut off trips to Lourdes, France and Mount Sinai in Egypt, to save cost …" [The Guardian [Nigeria], 13.4.1993].

8 The riots in Kano and in other parts of the north and the middle belt of Nigeria are discussed, together with the intra-Muslim tensions caused by the Maitatsine movement, by Jarlath Walsh in "The Religious Riots in Nigeria," *CSIC Papers* No. 11 (May 1993). For background concerning Bonnke, whose visit contributed to the raising of tensions between Christians and Muslims in Kano in particular, see P. Gifford "'Africa Shall be Saved': An Appraisal of Reinhard Bonnke's Pan-African Crusade" in *Journal of Religion in Africa* 17 (1987), pp. 63–92.

9 Abiola died in prison on 7th July 1998, a month after the death of General Sani Abacha, who had been responsible for putting him in prison when he protested against the annulment of the 1993 elections. See *The Economist* 13.6.1998 and 11.7.1998.

10 A useful survey of the general situation with respect to Christian-Muslim Relations in sub-Saharan Africa is J. Haafkens (the General Adviser to

PROCMURA) "The Direction of Christian-Muslim Relations in sub-Saharan Africa" in Y. Y. Haddad and W. Z. Haddad (eds.), *Christian-Muslim Encounters* (Gainesville: University of Florida Press, 1995), pp. 300–13. For more detail on Nigeria in particular see J. Kenny "Christian-Muslim Relations in Nigeria" in *Islamochristiana* 5 (1979), pp. 171–92, supplemented by the reports from Nigeria in the Notes and Documents section of later volumes of *Islamochristiana*; and for a constructive attempt to discern a way forward for Africa as regards the role of religion in nation-building, focusing on Nigeria and the Sudan in particular, see J. O. Hunwick (ed.), *Religion and National Integration in Africa: Islam, Christianity and Politics in the Sudan and Nigeria* (Evanston: Northwestern: University Press, 1992).

11 It is this rather precarious demographic position which gave rise to the production of the famous book by the Prime Minister of Malaysia, Dr. Mahathir, entitled *The Malay Dilemma* (Singapore: Times Books, 1970).

12 One of the most well-known Muslims of Indian origin in Malaysia is Professor Chandra Muzaffar, a political scientist in the Science University of Malaysia in Penang, who campaigns vigorously on issues of justice both in a Malaysian context and in the international arena. See, for example, his books *Islamic Resurgence in Malaysia* (Pataling Jaya: Penerbit Fajar Bakti, 1987), and *Human Rights and the New World Order* (Penang: Just World Trust, 1993).

13 The architecture of ISTAC in particular is intended to symbolize this quite specifically as the institute's buildings imitate the layout and decoration of the medieval Islamic architecture of Cordoba. See Daud, W.M.N.W., *The Beacon on the Crest of a Hill: A Brief History and Philosophy of the International Institute of Islamic Thought and Civilization* (Kuala Lumpur: International Institute of Islamic Thought and Civilization, 1991). The institute is also located next to a new planetarium, which is intended to focus the attention of visitors on the achievements of medieval Muslim astronomers. The same approach can also be seen in some of the publications of IKIM, such as its record of the speech made by Dr. Mahathir at its opening in 1992, entitled "Towards Reviving the Golden Age of Islam"; see M. Mahathir, *Perspectives on Islam and the Future of Muslims* (Kuala Lumpur: Institute of Islamic Understanding, 1993), pp. 1–6.

14 See M. Mahathir, "Imperatives of a Fully Moral and Ethical Society" in his *Perspectives on Islam and the Future of Muslims*, op. cit., pp. 18–23.

15 See *Asiaweek*, 25.8.1993, p. 25.

16 See O. Schumann, "Christians and Muslims in Search of Common Ground in Malaysia" in *Islam and Christian-Muslim Relations* 2 (1991), pp. 254–55, and M. Northcott "Christian-Muslim Relations in West Malaysia" in *Muslim World* 81 (1991), p. 63.

17 East Malaysia in particular has witnessed some intriguing instances of unwitting ecumenical co-operation: in Sabah I heard of a Roman Catholic congregation which had caused some consternation in London by submitting an application for one of its youth groups to join the Boys' Brigade. The consternation was caused by the fact that in the eyes of its founders and of most of its members, the Boys' Brigade is a Protestant

organisation, but clearly this was not appreciated in Sabah, where it was simply thought of as a worthwhile and useful church youth group.

18 As examples of this difference it is instructive to compare the general approach of the Chinese Jesuit Paul Tan Chee Ing in his article "Muslim-Christian Relations in Peninsula Malaysia" in *Islamochristiana* 19 (1993), pp. 125–51, in which the author speaks of discrimination against non-Muslims and the growth of what he calls Malay "chauvinism," which lead him to rather pessimistic conclusions about the future of relationships between Christians and Muslims, and the approach of the Indian Anglican Sadayandy Batumalai in his various contributions to the volume edited by him under the title *Vision 2020: A Malaysian Christian Response* (Kuala Lumpur: Seminari Theoloji Malaysia, 1992) in which Dr. Batumalai is rather more positive about at least some of the aspirations of Dr. Mahathir's 2020 vision, such as its concern for justice and for its emphasis on ecological concern and the importance of ethical values.

19 This is not to offer support for the thesis of the Harvard political scientist Samuel Huntington, expounded in his book *The Clash of Civilizations and the Remaking of the World Order* (New York: Simon & Schuster, 1996), that the relationship between Islam and the West is likely to become the dominant source of geo-political tension in the future, since as the situations of Nigeria and Malaysia both illustrate there are significant Christian presences far beyond what Huntington describes as "the West," but it is to affirm that throughout the Christian and Muslim communities worldwide there are *some* Christians and *some* Muslims who conceive of the relationship between their communities as being one of competition and confrontation, while there are others in both communities who see their relationship as being one of co-operation and mutual learning.

20 These questions have been explicitly addressed in a Malaysian context in the work of S. Batumalai, particularly his *A Malaysian Theology of Muhibbah [Goodwill]* (Pataling Jaya: Seminari Theoloji Malaysia, 1990). See also, from Nigeria, E. A. Obeng "Good Neighbourliness: The Kingdom of God as a Case in Point" in *Bulletin of Christian-Muslim Relations in Africa* 7 (4) (1989), pp. 2–10.

Index